What Readers Are Saying About *Modular Java*

Craig Walls does an awesome job in this book covering this very important topic. Whether you are developing an enterprise application or an application to run on your cell phone, modularization is something you have to master, and I can't think of a better resource than this book you're holding in your hands.

► **Dr. Venkat Subramaniam**
Jolt award–winning author and founder of Agile Developer, Inc.

Well-written and interesting. I found the "hands-on" style engaging. It feels like you are in an OSGi workshop, trying out all the tools and looking at the results. . . well done, Craig!

► **Frederic Daoud**
Author, *Stripes. . . And Java Web Development Is Fun Again*

Craig does a great job covering the "why" and "how" of writing modular Java web applications with OSGi in this book.

► **Erik Weibust**
Senior architect, Credera

Craig takes what many believe to be a complex subject and strips away the FUD immediately and then goes on to show the power and elegance of OSGi, especially when enabled with Spring for building enterprise-class Java applications. By making OSGi and Spring more accessible to Java developers everywhere, Craig does a great service to his whole industry, and I plan to continue to be part of the wave of developers building modular and flexible applications with these technologies! Perhaps the best proof of this book's value is the fact that it was immediately practical and applicable to me in a real-world project, even before it was fully written! This will be the go-to book for developers looking to take full advantage of these advances in software development.

► **Mike Nash**
President, JGlobal Ltd.

Craig's style is fun and easy to read, while he tackles very technical material. This book demystifies a topic that even experienced developers struggle with. Even if you don't program in Java, this book will improve your design thinking in how to better use components.

► **Derek Lane**
   CTO, Semantra, Inc.

Craig has done it again! As he has in the past with technologies such as the Spring Framework, he has masterfully crafted a book that is clear, concise, and comprehensive. Developers and architects alike will find this to be an invaluable tool as they take Java modularization to the next level.

► **Paul Nelson**
   Software craftsman

Modular Java

Creating Flexible Applications
with OSGi and Spring

Modular Java

Creating Flexible Applications
with OSGi and Spring

Craig Walls

The Pragmatic Bookshelf

Raleigh, North Carolina   Dallas, Texas

Our Pragmatic courses, workshops, and other products can help you and your team create better software and have more fun. For more information, as well as the latest Pragmatic titles, please visit us at

http://www.pragprog.com

ISBN-10: 1-934356-40-9
ISBN-13: 978-1934356-40-1
Printed on acid-free paper.
P1.0 printing, May 2009
Version: 2009-5-26

Contents

Chapter 1

Introduction

Welcome to the world of modular Java!

Building and deploying monolithic applications is a thing of the past. Applications that are composed of several smaller, well-defined modules are a much better way to go. By hiding design and implementation details that are likely to change behind a stable API, each module is easier to maintain, test, and understand. This ultimately affects the overall maintainability and testability of the whole application.

Unfortunately, as of Java 6, Java's built-in facilities for modularity are severely limited. Imperative instructions are modularized into methods, which are then modularized into classes. Classes can be further collected into packages, which offer a weak form of modularization. But that's where Java modularity ends. Java offers no means for modularizing classes or packages of classes into coarse-grained modules.

Where Java falls short, OSGi steps in. OSGi is a framework specification[1] that brings modularity to the Java platform. In this book we're going to see how OSGi can enable development of well-defined, loosely coupled modules that can be assembled into complete applications.

But before we get too carried away, let's get a feel for the type of problem that OSGi solves by listening in on a conversation between two coworkers on their way to lunch.

---

1. You can download the OSGi framework and service compendium specifications from http://www.osgi.org/Specifications/HomePage.

1.1 A New Set of Wheels

Jim: *Hey, is this a new car?*

Brian: *Sure is. Sweet ride, eh?*

Jim: *It's really nice. But didn't you get a new car last week?*

Brian: *Yep. . . it's all part of being a responsible car owner.*

Jim: *What?*

Brian: *You know. . . fresh oil, new air filters, new windshield wiper blades. And I can go only about a week or so on a tank of gas. You know how it is.*

Jim: *Actually, no I don't.*

Brian: *Of course you do! Every car eventually runs low on gas. Time to trade it in for one with a full tank, right?*

Jim: *No. When my car runs low on gas, I go to a gas station and fill it up.*

Brian: *Well, maybe. . . but what are you going to do? Drive the same car around for a few years? At the very least the tires will wear down. What are you going to do then? You can't just buy new tires and swap them in for the old ones.*

Jim: *Well, actually. . .*

(Jim pauses, realizing that he has lost interest in prolonging the conversation.)

Jim: *(after a pause of awkward silence) So, what do you have going on this weekend?*

Brian: *Packing boxes. We're moving to a new house.*

Jim: *Really? You hadn't mentioned that.*

Brian: *Well, it was a recent decision. A lightbulb burned out in our kitchen, and so. . .*

1.2 Modularity

Brian's problem is lack of modularity—or more precisely, his failure to recognize his car's modularity. Cars are not monoliths—they are made up of several distinct and individual components. It's typically more cost-effective to swap out those components when they need to be replaced or upgraded than to swap out the entire car.

If components can be replaced and upgraded in something as rigid as an automobile, then why not something so soft as software?

I know what you're thinking. You're thinking that you already design your applications to be modular. You place your classes and interfaces into packages organized by their function. You design your application into functional layers. You keep coupling low by abstracting that functionality behind interfaces. Perhaps you use a dependency injection framework such as Spring to make it possible to swap out one implementation class for another. And you may have even broken your application into two or more individually built projects.

Those are all great things. But if your application is so modular, then why do you still deploy it as one big monolithic WAR file?

I submit that your applications aren't as modular as you probably think they are.

What Does It Mean to Be Modular?

Put simply, a module is a self-contained component of a much larger system. Beyond that trite definition, however, the two key attributes of a well-designed module are high cohesion and low coupling.

To do one thing and do it well is the essence of cohesion. A module that is highly cohesive is focused on a distinct task and does not contain anything that does not contribute to that focus. As a consequence, cohesive modules tend to be fine-grained, robust, reusable, and more easily understood.

Where cohesion is an internal metric of a module's focus, coupling is an external metric of how a module interacts with other modules. Loosely coupled modules depend on other modules only through stable abstractions, unaware of the implementations that lie beneath. As a result, changes to one module's implementation rarely have any impact on the modules that interact with it.

Applications can benefit from modularity in several ways:

- *Changeability*: If each module in an application is known only through its published interface (and not by its internal implementation), then it's easy to swap out one module with another, as long as they publish the same interface(s). As my friend Mike Nash says, modularity "enables us to change our minds faster."

- *Comprehensibility*: Cohesive modules with well-defined boundaries are much easier to study and understand individually, and ultimately this leads to a greater understanding of the whole application.

- *Parallel development*: Modules can be developed virtually independently of each other, making it possible for development teams to split up tasks along module boundaries.

- *Improved testability*: Although both unit testing and integration testing are good practices, another level of testing can be achieved by testing each module as a cohesive unit.

- *Reuse and flexibility*: Depending on the scope of a module and how well its functionality is abstracted, it's very possible to take a module designed for one application and reuse it in a completely different application. On a larger scale, it's even conceivable that a selection of modules used in one application could be reassembled in another context to produce a different application.

It probably won't come as much of a surprise that modularity is not a new idea. It's a common tactic in the manufacture of all kinds of systems, software or otherwise. In fact, in their 1970 book (see *Designing Systems Programs* [GP70]), Richard Gauthier and Stephen Ponto summarize the benefits of modularity:

> A well-defined segmentation of the project effort ensures system modularity. Each task forms a separate, distinct program module. At implementation time each module and its inputs and outputs are well-defined; there is no confusion in the intended interface with other system modules. At checkout time the integrity of the module is tested independently; there are few scheduling problems in synchronizing the completion of several tasks before checkout can begin. Finally, the system is maintained in modular fashion; system errors and deficiencies can be traced to specific system modules, thus limiting the scope of detailed error searching.

Most programming languages offer some degree of support for modularity. There are even some legacy programming languages such as Modula-2 and MIL that were created with modularity as a core concern.

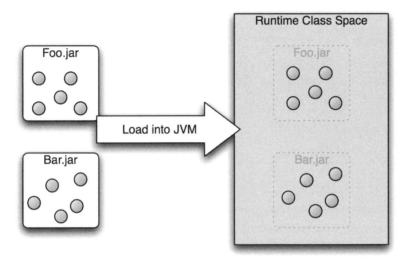

Figure 1.1: THE BOUNDARIES PROVIDED BY JAR FILES ARE ARTIFICIAL AND FADE AWAY AT RUNTIME.

But what about Java? Does Java offer any help in developing modular applications?

Modularity in Java

Java archive (JAR) files are often thought of as the unit of modularity in Java. Unfortunately, however, JAR files give only a thin illusion of modularity.

A typical JAR file is really only a deployment-time convenience, providing a vessel for a given set of classes, interfaces, and other resources. As illustrated in Figure 1.1, once a JAR is placed into the classpath, the JAR boundaries dissolve—along with any notion of modularity. All of the JAR's contents sit in the application's class space alongside the contents of every other JAR file in the classpath. Consequently, every public class in the JAR file is accessible by every other class in the class space.

What's more, aside from embedding a version number in the filename, JAR files offer no practical notion of versioning. It can be difficult to know for certain which version of a given JAR file you're dealing with.

> **Keep an Eye Out for OSGi 4.2**
>
> As I write this, version 4.1 is the latest release of the OSGi spec-
> ification. But version 4.2 is in the works and should be final very
> soon. There's some good stuff in there, such as distributed OSGi,
> a common command shell, and a new declarative service
> model based on Spring Dynamic Modules.

So, although JAR files may give the appearance of supporting modularity, their weak boundaries fail to restrict access to their internal implementation. This leaves them vulnerable to misuse and tight coupling
between JAR files.

What's needed is a way to fortify the boundaries of a JAR file such that
outsiders can see and use only the published API of the library. It just
so happens that is where OSGi steps in.

1.3 Introducing OSGi

OSGi is a component framework specification that brings modularity to
the Java platform. OSGi enables the creation of highly cohesive, loosely
coupled modules that can be composed into larger applications. What's
more, each module can be individually developed, tested, deployed,
updated, and managed with minimal or no impact to the other modules.

Let's take a look at the ingredients that make up the OSGi 4.1 specification and see how they support modular application development in
Java.

The Key Elements of OSGi

From Figure 1.2, on the next page, you can see that OSGi builds upon
the Java platform with a module definition, module life cycle, service
registry, services, and security layers.

At its lowest level, the OSGi specification defines a deployment model
for Java-based modules. The unit of deployment in OSGi is known as a
bundle. Rather than create a completely new deployment mechanism,
OSGi leverages the existing JAR file format for bundles. OSGi bundles
are much like common JAR files, except that their META-INF/MANIFEST.MF

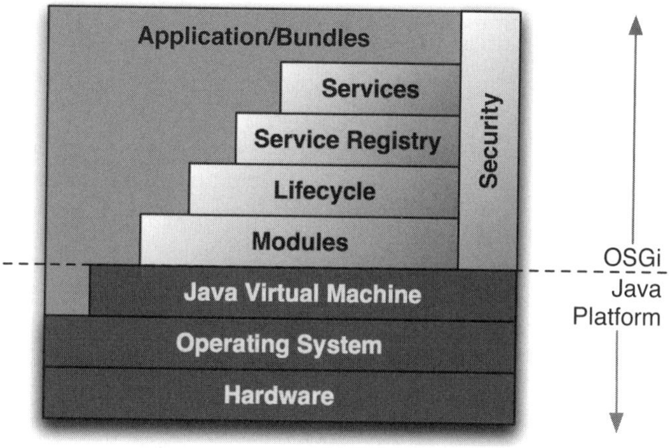

Figure 1.2: THE OSGI FRAMEWORK PROVIDES A LIFE CYCLE FOR MODULES, A SERVICE REGISTRY, AND A COMPENDIUM OF SERVICES FOR BUILDING MODULAR APPLICATIONS.

file contains OSGi-specific metadata, including a definitive name, version, dependencies, and other deployment details.

Once a bundle is installed into an OSGi framework, the OSGi life cycle governs the status of the bundle. A bundle can be installed, started, stopped, and uninstalled from the framework, following the life cycle prescribed by the OSGi specification.

OSGi also provides a service registry, with which bundles may publish and/or consume services. As illustrated by the triad in Figure 1.3, on the following page, OSGi's service registry enables a form of service-oriented architecture (SOA). However, unlike many interpretations of SOA, which rely on web services for communication, OSGi services are published and consumed within the same Java virtual machine. Thus, OSGi is sometimes described as "SOA in a JVM."

Taking advantage of the service registry, the OSGi specification also defines several core services that may be provided in the framework. These include a logging service, an HTTP service, and a configuration service, among others.

Finally, the OSGi specification defines an optional security layer that spans the other layers. This layer ensures that bundles are deployed

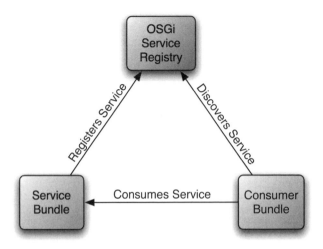

Figure 1.3: OSGi BUNDLES CAN BOTH PUBLISH AND CONSUME SERVICES. AN SOA IN A JVM!

securely by authenticating them with digital signatures or by verifying that bundle updates take place only from the location where the bundle was originally installed. In addition, the security layer may support Java 2–style permissions to control loading and executing bundle classes.

How Does OSGi Address Modularity Concerns?

When we considered Java's built-in support for modularity, we determined that it came up short. Now let's examine the features of OSGi to see how it brings modularity to the Java platform.

Content Hiding

In OSGi, each bundle is loaded into its own class space. Consequently, the contents of a bundle are private unless explicitly exported. This makes it possible for a bundle's internal implementation to evolve without impacting other bundles that depend on its relatively stable public API.

This is in contrast to normal JAR files, whose full contents are spilled out into the application's class space to be seen by every other class.

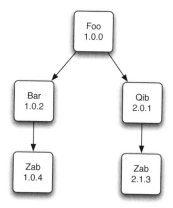

Figure 1.4: MULTIPLE VERSIONS OF A BUNDLE CAN BE INSTALLED INTO OSGI AT THE SAME TIME.

Service Registry

By providing an "SOA in a JVM," OSGi enables modules to publish services and to depend on services published by other bundles. The services are known by their published interfaces, not by the implementation. This means that the coupling is kept low between service publishers and those that consume their services.

Parallel Bundle Versions

Because each bundle is given its own class space, it's possible for two or more versions of a given bundle to reside in the OSGi framework at the same time. Without OSGi, dependency graphs, like those in Figure 1.4, present a dilemma where you must pick which version of Zab to use and hope that it works with both dependent libraries. In OSGi, however, you do not have to choose—both versions can be present at the same time, and each dependent bundle can work with the version of Zab that meets their needs.

Even though it's not likely that your application will directly depend on multiple versions of a library, it may transitively depend on two or more versions through its direct dependencies. OSGi makes it possible for all bundles to depend on the versions of other bundles that serve them best.

Dynamic Modularity

Another consequence of isolating bundles in their own class space is that any given bundle may be installed, stopped, started, updated, or uninstalled independently of other bundles in the framework. Among other things, this makes it possible to swap out a bundle with a newer version of the same bundle while the application continues to run.

Strong-Naming

Unlike traditional JAR files that have no way to definitively identify themselves, OSGi bundles are discretely identified by a name (known as the bundle's *symbolic name*) and version number in the bundle's manifest.

It should be noted that OSGi is not a silver bullet for modularity. Just adopting OSGi into your application architecture will not necessarily make your application more modular. It is still up to you to ensure that the modules you create follow good modular design. OSGi does, however, encourage modular programming practices by making it easy to create well-defined modules and, in some cases, making it more difficult not to do so.

1.4 Road Map

We'll take a progressive approach as we explore OSGi, starting with OSGi fundamentals. In Chapter 2, *Getting Started*, on page 17, we'll kick the tires on OSGi by getting to know two of the most popular OSGi framework implementations, Apache Felix and Eclipse Equinox. We'll also start developing a few simple OSGi bundles and see them in action as we deploy them into the OSGi framework.

Chapter 3, *Dude, Where's My JAR?*, on page 39 will set the stage for the rest of the book by describing *Dude, Where's My JAR?*, the example application that we'll build as we learn OSGi and Spring Dynamic Modules. In this chapter, we'll cover the basic features of the application as well as a high-level design overview of how OSGi will be used to develop it. We'll also get acquainted with an OSGi development kit called Pax Construct.[2]

In Chapter 4, *Working with Bundles*, on page 53, we'll get started on the example application by building one of the bundles that will define the

---

2. http://wiki.ops4j.org/display/ops4j/Pax+Construct

domain objects. In doing so, we'll learn how to share the contents of the bundle with other bundles and how to import contents from bundles that our bundle depends on. We'll also see how to deal with third-party libraries that aren't distributed as OSGi bundles.

Chapter 5, *OSGi Services*, on page 75 will turn things up a notch as we develop two new bundles that publish and consume services. We'll see how OSGi provides a simple framework for an intra-VM service-oriented architecture.

Chapters 1 through 5 lay a foundation that will enable you to start developing OSGi-based components and applications. From that foundation, the next few chapters will layer on Spring Dynamic Modules (also known as Spring-DM). Spring-DM is an extension to OSGi that brings a Spring-style programming model to OSGi, including dependency injection and declarative publication of services.

We will begin our exploration of Spring-DM in Chapter 6, *Spring and OSGi*, on page 107 by looking at how Spring-DM implements another common OSGi pattern known as the *bundle extender pattern* to create and start a Spring application context for each bundle. We'll also see how to publish and consume OSGi services declaratively in the Spring context configuration.

In Chapter 7, *Creating Web Bundles*, on page 127, we'll finally put a face on the example application by building a web front end and deploying it as an OSGi bundle. In this chapter, we'll see how to use Spring-DM's web extender to turn ordinary WAR files into lean, mean (and modular) WAR bundles that can be deployed to either Apache Tomcat or Jetty running within the OSGi framework.

In Chapter 8, *Extending Bundles*, on page 157, we'll look at a special kind of bundle called a *fragment* and see how we can use fragments to extract the look and feel of our application into its own module.

At this point in the book, our example application will be completely functional. But that's just the beginning. In Chapter 9, *OSGi in Production*, on page 171, we'll take steps to prepare the application for its transition from development into production.

Finally, in Chapter 10, *Configuring the Application*, on page 185, we'll wrap up the work to prepare the application for deployment into production by configuring various facets of the distribution.

What's Not in This Book

Just as important as what's in this book, I should make it clear what won't be in this book. Specifically, I will avoid *containerism*—anything that is possible only in a specific OSGi framework implementation. I'll be using Eclipse Equinox in many of the examples, but you should be able to follow along using Felix, Knopflerfish, or any other OSGi implementation you'd like.

Also, even though Eclipse offers a lot of IDE goodness for OSGi development through its plugin development environment (PDE), I'll make sure that what you learn in this book can be applied using whatever IDE you favor. If you're an IntelliJ IDEA or NetBeans user, I won't make you switch IDEs to build OSGi applications.

Finally, the scope of this book will focus on assembling OSGi bundles into web applications. We won't be spending any time digging into OSGi's original purpose of embedded software or discussing other uses of OSGi such as building plugins for Eclipse. And, since the world of OSGi is large and growing larger, we'll avoid diversions that distract us from our core goal of building a modularized Java web application with OSGi.

1.5 Who Is This Book For?

This book is for programmers and application architects already familiar with object-oriented programming. They seek ways to simplify deployment and updates, improve testability, and boost parallel development by breaking their applications into several well-defined modules.

1.6 Acknowledgments

A lot of thought, frustration, hard work, and late nights have gone into the writing of this book. Although very few people aside from myself have lost much sleep over it, there were many whose time, encouragement, and input had tremendous impact on the end result.

First, I'd like to thank the publishers, Dave Thomas and Andy Hunt, for giving this book project a green light. I knew from the beginning that the OSGi story I wanted to tell would be best presented in the Pragmatic style. I'm so glad that they agreed.

I also want to thank Jackie Carter, my editor throughout this effort. She was very effective at asking me the questions that needed to be asked to pull the best thoughts out of my head and put them into words. It has been a pleasure to work with her again, and I hope we'll have more opportunities to work together on future projects.

Thanks to Frederic Daoud, Venkat Subramaniam, Rod Coffin, Paul Barry, Ryan Breidenbach, Erik Weibust, Derek Lane, and Paul Nelson for taking the time to review the book while it was still in progress and provide much needed feedback.

Many thanks to my friends and contacts at SpringSource. I especially want to thank Rod Johnson for the many great conversations over e-mail and in person and to Costin Leau for responding to my many questions and suggestions about Spring-DM.

A shout-out to the Semantra team: Mike Nash, Ryan Breidenbach, Matt Smith, Ben Rady, Ben Poweski, Greg Vaughn, Tom McGraw, Derek Lane, and Paul Holser. Thanks for enduring my OSGi-related ramblings.

Last, but certainly not least, thanks to my beautiful wife, Raymie, and to my two awesome little girls, Maisy and Maddie. Thanks for indulging another book project and for the love and encouragement along the way.

Part I

OSGi Fundamentals

Chapter 2

Getting Started

Now that we've established the benefits of modularity and how OSGi brings modularity to Java, it's time to get down to the business of working with OSGi. In this chapter, we're going to dip our toes into the OSGi waters and see some of the basic stuff that goes into building an OSGi module. This will prepare us for wading a little deeper into the waters of OSGi bundles and services over the next few chapters. Later, once we're acclimated to the fundamentals of OSGi, we'll take a deep dive into Spring-DM starting in Chapter 6, *Spring and OSGi*, on page 107.

First things first, however. Let's start by tinkering with a couple of the most popular OSGi frameworks, Equinox and Felix, to see what makes them tick.

2.1 Getting to Know the OSGi Container

All OSGi-based applications run within an OSGi container (sometimes known as an OSGi *framework*). There are several open source and commercial OSGi containers to choose from, including the following:[1]

- Eclipse Equinox
- Apache Felix (formerly ObjectWeb Oscar)
- Knopflerfish
- Concierge

Each of these containers has its pros and cons, but for the most part you're free to choose the container that you like best and that comes

---

1. For a complete list of OSGi implementations that are certified by the OSGi Alliance as being Release 4 compliant, visit http://www.osgi.org/Markets/Certified.

Joe Asks...

Are Eclipse and Equinox the Same Thing?

It's worth pointing out that the Eclipse IDE and Eclipse Equinox are two different things. And yet, they're very related.

Equinox is an OSGi framework, suitable for deploying OSGi bundles that combine to make up modularized applications.

The Eclipse IDE is a prime example of such an application. Eclipse IDE is an OSGi-based application that is made up of several hundred bundles—or even more than a thousand bundles, depending on what plugins are installed.

You don't have to use the Eclipse IDE to use Equinox. But if you do use the Eclipse IDE, you are certainly using Equinox (whether you realize it or not).

with a license that fits your needs. Equinox and Felix are probably the two most popular OSGi containers available, so let's start by taking each of them for a test drive.

Eclipse Equinox

If you've been programming in Java for any significant length of time, odds are good that you've used Equinox before (even if you didn't know it). The Eclipse IDE is built upon Equinox, taking advantage of the modularity aspects of OSGi to create a development environment that is centered on the notion of plugins, where each plugin is defined as one or more OSGi bundles.

To start kicking the tires on Equinox, let's first download the Equinox runtime.[2] As I'm writing this, the latest stable release is 3.4. After selecting to download version 3.4, you will be presented with several download options, including the full Equinox ZIP file and a stand-alone Equinox Framework JAR file (org.eclipse.osgi_3.4.0.v20080605-1900.jar). For the purposes of this section, you need only the JAR file, but you're welcome to download the full Equinox platform in the ZIP file (which will contain the JAR we need).

---

2. http://download.eclipse.org/eclipse/equinox/

Once you have the JAR, you can start the Equinox container by running the following at the command line:

```
equinox% java -jar org.eclipse.osgi_3.4.0.v20080605-1900.jar
```

After a brief pause, you'll see the command-line prompt. Did Equinox start? Well, yes and no. . . .

Equinox did start. But it had nothing to do and so it immediately shut down. If we want Equinox to stick around for awhile, we'll need to give it something to do. At the very least, let's ask Equinox to present us with its console so that we can interact with the container:

```
equinox% java -jar org.eclipse.osgi_3.4.0.v20080605-1900.jar -console

osgi>
```

A-ha! This time we're greeted with an *osgi>* prompt, indicating that Equinox is alive and well and awaiting our instructions. There are a lot of things we could do here, but let's start by asking Equinox for some help:

```
osgi> help
---Eclipse Runtime commands---
        diag - Displays unsatisfied constraints for the specified bundle(s).
        enableBundle - enable the specified bundle(s)
        disableBundle - disable the specified bundle(s)
        disabledBundles - list disabled bundles in the system
...
osgi>
```

Equinox responds by listing all the commands that it understands. We're not going to try out all these commands now—in fact, I've truncated the list for brevity's sake. But we'll get a chance to use several of them later in the book. For now, let's just get a feel for how Equinox behaves by issuing a very basic command:

```
osgi> ss

Framework is launched.

id      State      Bundle
0       ACTIVE     org.eclipse.osgi_3.4.0.v20080605-1900

osgi>
```

The ss command means *short status* and is probably the one Equinox command that you'll use the most often. It lists all the bundles installed in the OSGi container. In this case, there's only one bundle installed (the Equinox runtime itself). From this list, we know that the Equinox

---

The OSGi Back Door into Eclipse

When you normally start the Eclipse IDE, all of Eclipse's plugins (bundles) are started, and you are presented with the user interface. But under the covers, there's still an Equinox container that makes that happen. And, just like the Equinox container that we're playing with, you can start Eclipse's Equinox container in console mode and interact with it.

Rather than starting Eclipse from an icon, you'll need to start it from the command line so that you can specify the -console parameter. On a Windows machine, find the eclipse.exe executable, and start it with the -console parameter:

```
c:\eclipse> eclipse.exe -console
```

On Mac OS X, find the Eclipse executable (there's probably a symbolic link to Eclipse.app/Contents/MacOS/eclipse in the installation root folder), and execute it like this:

```
$ eclipse -console
```

In either event, the Eclipse IDE should start, and you should be given the Equinox *osgi>* prompt at the command line. Feel free to explore the container using ss. But be careful not to manipulate any of the bundles (such as uninstalling or stopping them) unless you are certain that you know what you are doing.

---

runtime bundle has an ID of 0, is in ACTIVE state, and is described as *org.eclipse.osgi_3.4.0.v20080605-1900.*

As we've already discussed, all OSGi bundles contain a MANIFEST.MF file with special headers. In case you're wondering what headers are defined in a bundle's manifest, you can use the headers command. The headers command takes a single argument—the ID of the bundle that you're interested in. For example, to view Equinox's headers, you'd issue the headers command like this:

```
osgi> headers 0
Bundle headers:
 Bundle-Activator = org.eclipse.osgi.framework.internal.core.SystemBundleActiva
 Bundle-Copyright = Copyright (c) 2003, 2004 IBM Corporation and others.
    All rights reserved. This program and the accompanying materials are
    made available under the terms of the Eclipse Public License v1.0
    which accompanies this distribution, and is available at
    http://www.eclipse.org/legal/epl-v10.html
 Bundle-Description = OSGi System Bundle
```

```
Bundle-DocUrl = http://www.eclipse.org
Bundle-Localization = systembundle
Bundle-ManifestVersion = 2
Bundle-Name = OSGi System Bundle
Bundle-RequiredExecutionEnvironment = J2SE-1.4,OSGi/Minimum-1.1
Bundle-SymbolicName = org.eclipse.osgi; singleton:=true
Bundle-Vendor = Eclipse.org
Bundle-Version = 3.4.0.v20080605-1900
Eclipse-ExtensibleAPI = true
Eclipse-SystemBundle = true
Export-Package =org.eclipse.osgi.event;version="1.0",...
Export-Service = org.osgi.service.packageadmin.PackageAdmin,...
Main-Class = org.eclipse.core.runtime.adaptor.EclipseStarter
Manifest-Version = 1.0

osgi>
```

Upon issuing the command, you'll find a wealth of information about Equinox, including the fact that it was built with Apache Ant 1.7.0, that IBM Corporation holds the copyright, and that it exports several packages, including OSGi Alliance packages (org.osgi.*) that we can import and use in the bundles we'll create.

As we develop and install our own bundles, you'll get to know more about Equinox and commands to interact with it. But for now let's issue one more command before we take a look at Apache Felix:

```
osgi> exit

equinox%
```

Equinox is a very capable OSGi container (and, in fact, it's my personal favorite to work with). But it is licensed under the Eclipse Public License (EPL), which may not be compatible with other licenses (the GNU General Public License, for instance). If license compatibility is a concern, you may want to consider another container such as Apache Felix, which is licensed under the Apache License 2.0. Let's get acquainted with Felix.

Felix

The first thing to do is to download Felix.[3] As I write this, the latest version of Felix is 1.4.1. Download felix-1.4.1.zip or felix-1.4.1.tar.gz, and expand them into a folder on your system.

---

3. http://felix.apache.org/site/downloads.cgi

Next, navigate into the Felix folder, and start Felix by issuing the following on the command line:

```
felix% java -jar bin/felix.jar

Welcome to Felix.
==================

->
```

When we started Equinox, we were immediately greeted with an *osgi>* prompt. Similarly, Felix prompts us with ->. From here we can see a list of Felix commands using the help command:

```
-> help
bundlelevel <level> <id> ... | <id> - set or get bundle start level.
cd [<base-URL>]                     - change or display base URL.
headers [<id> ...]                  - display bundle header properties.
help                                - display impl commands.
install <URL> [<URL> ...]           - install bundle(s).
obr help                            - OSGi bundle repository.
packages [<id> ...]                 - list exported packages.
ps [-l | -s | -u]                   - list installed bundles.
refresh [<id> ...]                  - refresh packages.
resolve [<id> ...]                  - attempt to resolve the specified bundles.
services [-u] [-a] [<id> ...]       - list registered or used services.
shutdown                            - shutdown framework.
start <id> [<id> <URL> ...]         - start bundle(s).
startlevel [<level>]                - get or set framework start level.
stop <id> [<id> ...]                - stop bundle(s).
uninstall <id> [<id> ...]           - uninstall bundle(s).
update <id> [<URL>]                 - update bundle.
version                             - display version of framework.
->
```

The first thing you'll notice is that Felix has a much smaller set of commands than Equinox. Never fear, though. . . you'll find that Felix has a command for most of your basic OSGi needs. For example, to see a list of installed bundles, use the ps command:

```
-> ps
START LEVEL 1
   ID   State         Level  Name
[   0] [Active     ] [    0] System Bundle (1.4.1)
[   1] [Active     ] [    1] Apache Felix Shell Service (1.0.2)
[   2] [Active     ] [    1] Apache Felix Shell TUI (1.0.2)
[   3] [Active     ] [    1] Apache Felix Bundle Repository (1.2.1)
->
```

As you can see, a baseline Felix setup involves four bundles. For the most part, it isn't very important to know what these bundles do. But if you're curious, feel free to use the headers command to see what headers are in each bundle's manifest. For example, to examine the System Bundle headers, do this:

```
-> headers 0

System Bundle (0)
-----------------
Bundle-Description = This bundle is system specific; it
                     implements various system services.
Bundle-SymbolicName = org.apache.felix.framework
Export-Package = org.osgi.framework; version="1.4.0" ...
Export-Service = org.osgi.service.packageadmin.PackageAdmin,
                 org.osgi.service.startlevel.StartLevel,
                 org.osgi.service.url.URLHandlers
Bundle-Version = 1.4.1
Bundle-Name = System Bundle
->
```

The *Bundle-Description* header indicates that this bundle implements various system services. A close look at the *Export-Package* header finds that, among other things, this bundle exports the core OSGi packages (org.osgi.*). A similar inspection of the other bundles reveals that bundle 1 is a simple OSGi command shell service, bundle 2 is a textual user interface for the shell service, and bundle 3 provides a bundle repository service.

Feel free to explore Felix further, if you'd like. When you're done, use the shutdown command to close Felix:

```
-> shutdown
-> felix%
```

There is only so much fun to be had by poking around in a baseline OSGi container. The real fun begins when we install and manipulate our own bundles. So, with no further delay, let's create our own bundle to tinker with: the obligatory *Hello World* bundle.

2.2 Hello, OSGi

There's an unwritten rule that all technical books include a *Hello World* example to gently introduce readers to the subject of the book. Not being one to buck tradition, I feel compelled to stick to that rule and share a *Hello World* example—OSGi-style.

Creating the Bundle

You'll recall that an OSGi bundle is little more than a JAR file with some special entries in its META-INF/MANIFEST.MF file. So, using your favorite IDE or text editor, let's first create a MANIFEST.MF file for our *Hello World* bundle:

hello/src/main/resources/META-INF/MANIFEST.MF

```
Bundle-ManifestVersion: 2
Bundle-SymbolicName: com.pragprog.HelloWorld
Bundle-Name: HelloWorld
Bundle-Version: 1.0.0
Bundle-Activator: com.pragprog.hello.HelloWorld
Import-Package: org.osgi.framework
```

There are several important things being said in these headers, so let's examine each of them:

Bundle-ManifestVersion

This header gives the OSGi specification to use to read the bundle. Oddly enough, the default value of 1 indicates OSGi release 3, while 2 indicates OSGi release 4 and later. Confusing? You bet! To keep it simple, just remember that it should always be 2.

Bundle-SymbolicName

This header is the only required header and specifies a unique identifier for the bundle. The value can be virtually anything, but it is strongly recommended that you follow a reverse domain name convention (just like Java package names) when deciding on a bundle's symbolic name—to help ensure its uniqueness.

Bundle-Name

This header specifies a human-readable name for the bundle that is easier to read than the symbolic name. You can name your bundles anything you like, as long as it doesn't contain any spaces.

Bundle-Version

This is the version of the bundle. We'll talk more about versioning later.

Bundle-Activator

This is the fully qualified class name of a special bundle life-cycle class called an *activator*. This class implements the BundleActivator interface, and its start() and stop() methods will be invoked when the bundle is started and stopped (respectively). We'll see what com.pragprog.hello.HelloWorld looks like in a moment.

Import-Package

> This header lists one or more packages (contained in other bundles) that this bundle requires. Since our bundle activator depends on a couple of items in the org.osgi.framework package and since that package is defined in another bundle, we had to import it here.

Simply adding the Bundle-SymbolicName header to the manifest makes any JAR file an OSGi bundle. But in this specific bundle that we're creating, we've specified a Bundle-Activator, so we have a bit more work to do.

A bundle activator is a special class in the bundle that gets hooked into a portion of the bundle's life cycle and is triggered when a bundle is started and stopped. Using a bundle activator, we can develop startup and shutdown behavior for a bundle. To qualify as a bundle activator, the class must implement the org.osgi.framework.BundleActivator interface, which defines start() and stop() methods that are invoked when a bundle is started and stopped. As for our HelloWorld activator, it looks like this:

hello/src/main/java/com/pragprog/hello/HelloWorld.java

```java
package com.pragprog.hello;

import org.osgi.framework.BundleActivator;
import org.osgi.framework.BundleContext;

public class HelloWorld implements BundleActivator {
  public void start(BundleContext ctx) throws Exception {
    System.out.println("Hello World!");
  }

  public void stop(BundleContext ctx) throws Exception {
    System.out.println("Goodbye World!");
  }
}
```

In the interest of keeping things simple (a tenet of all good *Hello World* examples), the start() method simply prints "Hello World!" when the bundle is started (as illustrated in Figure 2.1, on the following page). Likewise, the stop() method prints "Goodbye World!" as the bundle is stopped. Notice that both methods are given a BundleContext that can be used to interact with the OSGi container. We'll see how to use the BundleContext a little later, but we won't need it in this example.

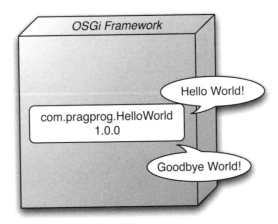

Figure 2.1: THE HELLOWORLD ACTIVATOR SAYS "HELLO WORLD!" WHEN THE BUNDLE STARTS AND "GOODBYE WORLD!" WHEN THE BUNDLE IS STOPPED.

We're almost ready to see the bundle in action. But first, we must create the bundle JAR file. To do that, compile HelloWorld.java, and then create a JAR file having the structure illustrated in Figure 2.2, on the next page. Since I'm using Maven, you can create the JAR file with the Maven's package goal:

```
hello% mvn package
[INFO] Scanning for projects...
[INFO] ------------------------------------------------------------------
[INFO] Building Hello World - OSGi Activator
[INFO]    task-segment: [package]
[INFO] ------------------------------------------------------------------
...
[INFO] ------------------------------------------------------------------
[INFO] BUILD SUCCESSFUL
[INFO] ------------------------------------------------------------------
[INFO] Total time: 5 seconds
[INFO] Finished at: Tue Mar 03 00:19:56 CST 2009
[INFO] Final Memory: 7M/13M
[INFO] ------------------------------------------------------------------
hello%
```

The example code that accompanies this book[4] can be built into a bundle JAR file using Maven 2.

---

4. http://pragprog.com/titles/cwosg/source_code

Joe Asks...

Do I Have to Use Maven?

There's nothing about OSGi that requires Maven. However, I think that there's a lot of synergy between Maven's compile-time dependency management and OSGi's runtime dependency management. Thus, it seems quite natural to use Maven to build OSGi bundle projects.

If you're not a Maven expert, rest easy. There's not much about Maven you'll need to know to work through the examples in this book. We'll be using only the following handful of Maven goals:

- test: Compiles all Java code and runs unit tests.

- package: Compiles and tests Java code and then packages project classes and resources in a JAR or WAR file.

- install: Same as package, but also installs the JAR/WAR in the local Maven repository.

If you want to learn more about Maven, then I suggest Sonatype's *Maven: The Definitive Guide* (Com08).*

∗.   http://www.sonatype.com/products/maven/documentation/book-defguide

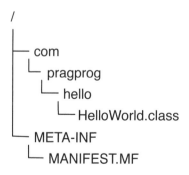

Figure 2.2: THE STRUCTURE OF THE *Hello World* ACTIVATOR BUNDLE

Installing the Bundle

With the JAR bundle created, we're now ready to start an OSGi container and try using it. Throughout this book, I'll be using Equinox. I chose Equinox primarily as a matter of personal preference. But also, we'll be working with OSGi fragments later, and Felix doesn't yet support fragments.[5] Even so, you're welcome to use Felix or any other OSGi container you want.

First, let's fire up Equinox. As you'll recall from earlier, you can start Equinox in console mode like this:

```
equinox% java -jar org.eclipse.osgi_3.4.0.v20080605-1900.jar -console

osgi>
```

Next, from the Equinox prompt, we'll install the *Hello World* bundle:

```
osgi> install file:target/hello-activator-1.0.0.jar
Bundle id is 1

osgi> ss

Framework is launched.

id      State       Bundle
0       ACTIVE      org.eclipse.osgi_3.4.0.v20080605-1900
1       INSTALLED   com.pragprog.HelloWorld_1.0.0

osgi>
```

After issuing the ss command, we see that our bundle is sitting there in INSTALLED state, waiting to be started. So, let's not keep it waiting. To start it, issue the start command:

```
osgi> start 1
Hello World!

osgi>
```

The start command takes a bundle ID as its argument. Notice that once we started the bundle, the familiar "Hello World!" greeting was printed. What's more is that our humble little bundle is now in ACTIVE state, as proven by issuing the ss command again:

```
osgi> ss

Framework is launched.
```

---

5. See FELIX-29 in the Felix issue-tracking system for the status on fragments in Felix.

```
id      State       Bundle
0       ACTIVE      org.eclipse.osgi_3.4.0.v20080605-1900
1       ACTIVE      com.pragprog.HelloWorld_1.0.0

osgi>
```

That was pretty cool. But it shows only half of what our bundle can do. Now let's stop the bundle and see what happens:

```
osgi> stop 1
Goodbye World!

osgi>
```

As expected, stopping the bundle yielded a "Goodbye World!" message on the screen. And if we issue an ss command again, we'll see that its status is no longer in ACTIVE state:

```
osgi> ss

Framework is launched.

id      State       Bundle
0       ACTIVE      org.eclipse.osgi_3.4.0.v20080605-1900
1       RESOLVED    com.pragprog.HelloWorld_1.0.0

osgi>
```

Were you a little surprised to see the bundle in RESOLVED state? Maybe you were expecting it to go back to INSTALLED state. For now, don't worry too much about bundle states—it's enough to just know that the bundle is no longer active. We'll examine the bundle life cycle in more detail later in Section 4.3, *Following the Bundle Life Cycle*, on page 72.

I couldn't be more excited! We've just built our first OSGi bundle, deployed it to an OSGi container, and seen it do its stuff. If you'd like, you can kick it around some more. Feel free to start it and stop it again as many times as you like. But don't get too carried away. . . there's more fun in store for the *Hello World* example.

2.3 A *Hello World* Service Bundle

A bundle can do a lot of things. It can simply act as a library, providing classes and interfaces for other bundles to use. Or, as we've already seen with the previous example, a bundle can contain an activator that performs some action when the bundle is started and stopped.

Another thing that a bundle can do is publish services to be consumed by other bundles. To illustrate, let's rip our *Hello World* example into two parts: a bundle that publishes a service that provides greetings and another bundle that contains a consumer of the service and prints those greetings.

Publishing a Hello Service

The first step in creating a service is deciding what its interface will look like. In OSGi, a service's interface defines not only how other components can interact with the service but also how the other components find the service. For our *Hello World* service, we'll need two methods: one to return some hello message and one to return a goodbye message. The following interface should do the trick:

`hello-service/src/main/java/com/pragprog/hello/service/HelloService.java`

```
package com.pragprog.hello.service;

public interface HelloService {
    String getHelloMessage();

    String getGoodbyeMessage();
}
```

Now we write the service implementation class. To keep things interesting, the following service implementation has an international flair:

`hello-service/src/main/java/com/pragprog/hello/service/impl/HelloImpl.java`

```
package com.pragprog.hello.service.impl;

import com.pragprog.hello.service.HelloService;

public class HelloImpl implements HelloService {
    public String getHelloMessage() {
        return "Bonjour!";
    }

    public String getGoodbyeMessage() {
        return "Arrivederci!";
    }
}
```

Take notice of the service implementation's package and how it differs from the interface's package. Although both could reside in the same package, it's a good practice to keep them separate. As we'll soon see, keeping them separate will make it possible to publish the service under an exported interface for other bundles to use, while keeping the implementation of the service hidden from its consumers.

In OSGi, services are published to a service registry within the container and are identified by the interface(s) that they implement. So, we'll need some way to register HelloImpl with the service registry. For that, let's create HelloPublisher:

hello-service/src/main/java/com/pragprog/hello/service/impl/HelloPublisher.java

```java
package com.pragprog.hello.service.impl;

import org.osgi.framework.BundleActivator;
import org.osgi.framework.BundleContext;
import org.osgi.framework.ServiceRegistration;

import com.pragprog.hello.service.HelloService;

public class HelloPublisher implements BundleActivator {
    private ServiceRegistration registration;

    public void start(BundleContext context) throws Exception {
        registration = context.registerService(HelloService.class.getName(),
                        new HelloImpl(), null);
    }

    public void stop(BundleContext context) throws Exception {
        registration.unregister();
    }
}
```

HelloPublisher is a bundle activator, much like the HelloWorld activator we created earlier. This activator, however, uses the BundleContext that it is given to register an instance of HelloImpl as a service. It does this by calling the BundleContext's registerService() method, passing the service's interface (as the String returned from a call to the interface's class.getName() method), an instance of HelloImpl, and a set of service properties to associate with the service (which, for our purposes, can be null).

The last thing we need to create is the bundle's META-INF/MANIFEST.MF file:

hello-service/src/main/resources/META-INF/MANIFEST.MF

```
Bundle-ManifestVersion: 2
Bundle-SymbolicName: com.pragprog.HelloWorldService
Bundle-Name: HelloWorldService
Bundle-Version: 1.0.0
Bundle-Activator: com.pragprog.hello.service.impl.HelloPublisher
Import-Package: org.osgi.framework
Export-Package: com.pragprog.hello.service
```

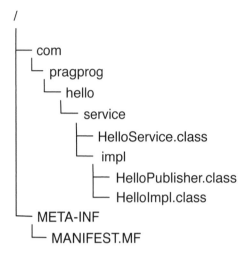

Figure 2.3: The structure of the HelloWorld service bundle

This bundle's manifest isn't dramatically different from the manifest we created before, but there is one new header to take note of. The Export-Package header publishes the contents of one or more packages for other bundles to use. Here, we've exported the com.pragprog.hello.service package so that consumers of our service can see and use the HelloService interface.

What's particularly interesting about Export-Package is the package that it doesn't export. Specifically, we're not exporting the com.pragprog. hello.service.impl package. That's because the service's implementation (and HelloPublisher, for that matter) are implementation details that are best kept secret. By not exporting them, we're effectively declaring them to be private, or unpublished. This prevents undesirable coupling that may occur if another bundle were to try to use HelloImpl directly instead of through its interface.

Now we're ready to compile and package everything up in a JAR file. In Figure 2.3, we can see the structure of the bundled JAR.

Finally, let's install it in Equinox:

```
osgi> install file:target/hello-service-1.0.0.jar
Bundle id is 2

osgi> ss
```

```
Framework is launched.

id      State       Bundle
0       ACTIVE      org.eclipse.osgi_3.4.0.v20080605-1900
1       ACTIVE      com.pragprog.HelloWorld_1.0.0
2       INSTALLED   com.pragprog.HelloWorldService_1.0.0

osgi>
```

The service bundle is now installed, alongside our first *Hello World* bundle that we deployed earlier. But the service won't be of any use to us until we start the bundle:

```
osgi> start 2

osgi> ss

Framework is launched.

id      State       Bundle
0       ACTIVE      org.eclipse.osgi_3.4.0.v20080605-1900
1       ACTIVE      com.pragprog.HelloWorld_1.0.0
2       ACTIVE      com.pragprog.HelloWorldService_1.0.0

osgi>
```

When the service bundle is started, Equinox will invoke the start() method in HelloPublisher, consequently publishing the service in the service registry. To prove that the service has been published, we can issue Equinox's bundle command:

```
osgi> bundle 2
file:target/hello-service-1.0.0-SNAPSHOT.jar [2]
  Id=2, Status=ACTIVE
      Data Root=/Users/wallsc/osgi/configuration/org.eclipse.osgi/bundles/2/data
  Registered Services
    {com.pragprog.hello.service.HelloService}={service.id=21}
  No services in use.
  Exported packages
    com.pragprog.hello.service; version="0.0.0"[exported]
  Imported packages
    org.osgi.framework; version="1.4.0"<System Bundle [0]>
  No fragment bundles
  Named class space
    com.pragprog.HelloWorldService; bundle-version="1.0.0"[provided]
  No required bundles

osgi>
```

Notice that our service is found under the *Registered Services* heading. Also, notice that com.pragprog.hello.service is under the *Exported packages* heading.

Before we move on, it's worth noting that although HelloPublisher makes liberal use of the OSGi API in order to publish the service, HelloImpl and HelloService are completely OSGi-free.

At this point, the service has been deployed, but nobody is using it. Our original *Hello World* bundle is still in the container, but its activator is still printing hard-coded greetings. Let's put the service bundle to work by giving it a client.

Consuming the Service

Rather than create a new bundle to consume the hello service, let's revisit the original HelloWorld activator that we created earlier and change it to use the HelloWorld service:

`hello-consumer/src/main/java/com/pragprog/hello/HelloWorld.java`

```java
package com.pragprog.hello;

import org.osgi.framework.BundleActivator;
import org.osgi.framework.BundleContext;
import org.osgi.framework.ServiceReference;

import com.pragprog.hello.service.HelloService;

public class HelloWorld implements BundleActivator {

    public void start(BundleContext context) throws Exception {
        HelloService helloService = getHelloService(context);
        System.out.println(helloService.getHelloMessage());
    }

    public void stop(BundleContext context) throws Exception {
        HelloService helloService = getHelloService(context);
        System.out.println(helloService.getGoodbyeMessage());
    }

    private HelloService getHelloService(BundleContext context) {
        ServiceReference ref = context.getServiceReference(HelloService.class
                        .getName());

        HelloService helloService = (HelloService) context.getService(ref);
        return helloService;
    }
}
```

This new HelloWorld activator is a bit more interesting than the first one. Rather than printing hard-coded greetings, the new start() and stop() methods use the HelloService returned from getHelloService(). The getHelloService() method is just a convenience method that looks up the service in the OSGi service registry. It does this by using the service's class

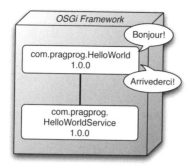

Figure 2.4: THE NEW SERVICE-ORIENTED HELLOWORLD ACTIVATOR RELIES ON A SERVICE (DEPLOYED IN A SEPARATE BUNDLE) TO PROVIDE ITS GREETINGS.

name to get a service reference. With the service reference in hand, it then asks the BundleContext for the service, as shown in Figure 2.4.

It may not be apparent at first glance, but the getHelloService() method is rather naive. In OSGi, services can come and go as bundles are installed, updated, started, stopped, and uninstalled. What will the BundleContext's getService() return if the service's bundle isn't active or installed? As it turns out, if the service isn't available, then getHelloService() will return null, and the calls to getHelloMessage() and getGoodbyeMessage() will fail in a splendid fashion with a NullPointerException.

For now we'll just pretend that the service will always be available. We'll examine some strategies for dealing with missing services more gracefully in Chapter 5, *OSGi Services*, on page 75.

The only thing left to do is modify the manifest to account for the changes made to the HelloWorld activator. Since the activator now uses the HelloService interface, we must add its package to the Import-Package header:

hello-consumer/src/main/resources/META-INF/MANIFEST.MF

```
Bundle-ManifestVersion: 2
Bundle-SymbolicName: com.pragprog.HelloWorld
Bundle-Name: HelloWorld
Bundle-Version: 1.0.1
Bundle-Activator: com.pragprog.hello.HelloWorld
Import-Package: org.osgi.framework,
 org.osgi.util.tracker,
 com.pragprog.hello.service
```

In addition to importing the service's interface package, I have also bumped up the Bundle-Version to 1.0.1, just to indicate that this is a slightly different bundle than the one we've already installed.

All the pieces are now in place. To see it in action, first compile and JAR up the bundle, and then install it to Equinox. Assuming that the new version of the JAR file is in the same location as before, we can issue the update command:

```
osgi> update 1
Goodbye World!
Bonjour!
```

A lot of stuff happens when we ask Equinox to update the bundle. It first stops the bundle—that's why we see the "Goodbye World!" message. Then it uninstalls the old bundle and reinstalls the new bundle from the original location. Finally, it starts the bundle, resulting in the hello message being printed. And, it does all of this without having to restart Equinox!

Did you notice that the hello message is now "Bonjour!"? That proves that the activator is using the service and not simply printing the old hard-coded "Hello World!" message. If you need any further evidence that the bundle has been updated, check the status by issuing the ss command:

```
osgi> ss

Framework is launched.

id      State        Bundle
0       ACTIVE       org.eclipse.osgi_3.4.0.v20080605-1900
1       ACTIVE       com.pragprog.HelloWorld_1.0.1
2       ACTIVE       com.pragprog.HelloWorldService_1.0.0

osgi>
```

The thing to spot is that the version number is now 1.0.1 and not 1.0.0 as it was previously.

For proof that the activator is actually using the service, the bundle command again comes in handy:

```
osgi> bundle 1
file:../hello/target/hello-activator-1.0.0.jar [1]
  Id=1, Status=ACTIVE
      Data Root=/Users/wallsc/osgi/configuration/org.eclipse.osgi/bundles/1/d
  No registered services.
```

```
Services in use:
  {com.pragprog.hello.service.HelloService}={service.id=21}
No exported packages
Imported packages
  org.osgi.framework; version="1.4.0"<System Bundle [0]>
  org.osgi.util.tracker; version="1.3.3"<System Bundle [0]>
  com.pragprog.hello.service; version="0.0.0"
            <file:../hello-service/target/hello-service-1.0.0.jar [2]>
No fragment bundles
Named class space
  com.pragprog.HelloWorld; bundle-version="1.0.1"[provided]
No required bundles

osgi>
```

If you look under the *Services in use:* heading, you'll find that this bundle is using the service published by the service bundle. And, it imports the com.pragprog.hello.service package that is exported by the service bundle.

We've seen the hello message. Now let's complete the story by stopping the bundle and seeing the goodbye message:

```
osgi> stop 1
Arrivederci!

osgi> ss

Framework is launched.

id      State        Bundle
0       ACTIVE       org.eclipse.osgi_3.4.0.v20080605-1900
1       RESOLVED     com.pragprog.HelloWorld_1.0.1
2       ACTIVE       com.pragprog.HelloWorldService_1.0.0

osgi>
```

With that, we conclude our first adventure in OSGi. Although we've kept things simple, we've covered a lot of ground. We've become acquainted with two different OSGi containers (Equinox and Felix). We've also deployed a simple *Hello World* bundle in an OSGi container and seen it in action. And, we've expanded the *Hello World* example to be split across two bundles, one consuming a service published by the other. All of this serves as the basis for more OSGi adventure to come.

Chapter 3

Dude, Where's My JAR?

As much fun as it has been to build *Hello World* bundles, those simplistic examples do not serve well in demonstrating the full extent of OSGi's power. If we are to get a real sense of what it is like to build real-world applications that are based on OSGi, then we'll need to work on a more realistic example.

We could build the umpteenth pet store application or perhaps another MySpace knockoff and, in the end, have nothing to show for our efforts other than the remnants of another academic exercise. Wouldn't it be great if in the course of learning OSGi we could develop something that we might actually *use*?

To that end, the primary example throughout the rest of this book will be a search engine with Java developers as the target user base. We'll call it *Dude, Where's My JAR?* In this short chapter, we'll map out the basic design for the application and start thinking about how we can use OSGi to realize that plan.

3.1 Searching for JAR Files

How many times have you spent several moments crafting the next great piece of software only to be confronted with the enigmatic ClassNotFoundException upon submitting your work to the compiler.

You're a skilled Java programmer. You know what to do, right? The solution required here is simply a matter of adding some JAR file to your classpath. But which one? There are so many Java classes scattered across so many Java libraries, how can you know for sure which JAR file you should add? And even if you think you know which JAR file is needed, where do you go to get it?

That's where *Dude, Where's My JAR?* comes to the rescue. It is a search engine for Java libraries. Given a class, interface, enum, or annotation name, it will search Maven repositories for all matching JAR files. It will then help you include the JAR in a Maven 2 build by providing you with the proper *<dependency>* and repository information to add to your project's pom.xml file.

What's more, if you're an OSGi developer, *Dude, Where's My JAR?* will index information contained within a JAR's META-INF/MANIFEST.MF file so that you can find just the right OSGi bundle to fit your needs.

3.2 Designing the Application Components

To get started, let's think about the features that the application needs. At a very basic level, we're going to need the following:

- Something that crawls around one or more Maven repositories, finding JAR files to add to the index
- A means of indexing meta-information about a JAR file so that it can be found later
- Some domain object(s) that represent the JAR file by holding the meta-information
- A way to query for JAR files that match certain criteria
- A web front end so that the Java-developing masses can use the application to find their libraries

Let's flesh each of these items out more, starting with the repository crawler.

The Maven Repository Spider

If your favorite bookstore had nothing but empty shelves every time you visited it, it probably wouldn't be your favorite bookstore for very long. Likewise, a search engine that doesn't have any information to present in its results isn't a very good search engine. Therefore, we need a way to stock the application's index. For that, we'll need to develop a spider that crawls around one or more Maven repositories looking for JAR files.

As the spider finds a JAR file, it will collect meta-information about the JAR file (such as its Maven group, artifact, and version, and the names of the classes it contains). It will send the meta-information to the index service (more on that in a moment) to be added to the index and then continue looking for more JAR files.

A JAR-File Domain

JAR files can get rather large, so it's not desirable (nor necessary) for *Dude, Where's My JAR?* to keep the JAR files once it has indexed them. Instead, we only need to collect a set of basic information about each JAR to be searched upon later.

Some of the information that may be interesting about a JAR is the following:

- The URL of the Maven repository where the JAR was found.
- The Maven group ID, artifact ID, and version of the JAR.
- A list of the JAR's contents (e.g., a list of the .class files contained within the JAR).
- It might be nice to know whether the JAR is a proper OSGi bundle (that is, does its META-INF/MANIFEST.MF have a Bundle-SymbolicName header?).

This information can be collected into a simple domain object.

The Index Service

Once the spider has collected meta-information about a JAR file, it'll need to hand it off to some service to be indexed. Later, when a user searches for a JAR file, we'll also need a way to search that index and produce a result set.

For both indexing and searching, we'll create an index service. It'll offer two functions:

- Given JAR file meta-information, it will add the information to an index.
- Given a search string, it will produce a collection of JAR file meta-information that matches the search criteria.

Under the covers, the index service uses Compass (an object-mapping abstraction over Lucene) to populate and search the index.

The Web Application

Finally, we need a way for users to tell *Dude, Where's My JAR?* what we're looking for and for the application to respond with a set of matching JAR files.

To build the application front end, we'll use Spring MVC, a simple and capable web framework that is based on the Spring Framework. The controllers in the web application will interact with the index service to search for JARs that match a user's criteria.

3.3 Bundling the Application Components for OSGi

If this were a typical application, we'd probably give each of the components its own package within the overall application structure and call that modularity. If we're in a particularly enlightened frame of mind, we might even package each component into its own JAR file that is ultimately encased in the web application's WAR file.

But this isn't a typical application. In order to benefit from ease of deployment, versioning, parallel development, testability, and the other virtues of modularity, we're going to build this application as a collection of OSGi bundles.[1]

More specifically, we're going to define the following bundles, as illustrated in Figure 3.1, on the facing page:

- *A domain bundle*: This rather simple bundle will contain the domain class that defines a JAR file. This bundle will simply export the single domain package for all the other bundles to use. It will not consume or publish any services. We'll start working on this bundle in Chapter 4, *Working with Bundles*, on page 53.

- *A spider bundle*: This bundle will contain the repository-crawling spider component. It will not export any packages, and it will not publish any services. The spider works almost autonomously, importing only the domain package from the domain bundle and making calls to the index service to add JAR file data to the index. We'll take a first pass at bundling up the spider component in Chapter 5, *OSGi Services*, on page 75 and then revisit it again in Chapter 6, *Spring and OSGi*, on page 107 when we look at Spring-DM and how to use dependency injection with OSGi services.

---

1. Besides... this *is* an OSGi book, right? Why would we do it any other way?

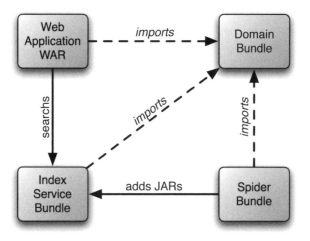

Figure 3.1: THE COMPONENTS OF THE *Dude, Where's My JAR?* APPLICA-
TION WILL BE BUILT AND DEPLOYED AS OSGI BUNDLES.

- *An index bundle*: This bundle is the centerpiece of *Dude, Where's My JAR?*, containing the index service that both indexes JAR file metadata and searches the index on behalf of a user. It will import the domain package and will publish the index service. We'll start building the index bundle in Chapter 5, *OSGi Services*, on page 75 and then revisit it in Chapter 6, *Spring and OSGi*, on page 107 to see how Spring-DM simplifies publication of OSGi services.

- *A web bundle*: This bundle is the most unusual of all the bundles we'll create. That's because it will bear more of a resemblance to a traditional WAR file than an OSGi bundle. But we'll see in Chapter 7, *Creating Web Bundles*, on page 127 how to deploy a WAR file as an OSGi bundle.

Along the way, we'll also see how to extend bundles with fragments (in Chapter 8, *Extending Bundles*, on page 157), how to test bundles (in Chapter 4, *Working with Bundles*, on page 53), and how to do other OSGi techniques such as versioning and hot deployment.

But before we get too carried away, we need to do a little setup of the project structure that we'll be building on throughout the book.

> **Getting to Know the Pax Tools**
>
> Pax Construct is just one of many tools under the Pax umbrella project. The Pax project* includes more than a dozen subprojects that provide tools and utility bundles for OSGi development.
>
> In this chapter, you'll be introduced to Pax Construct, a development toolkit for OSGi. Before the end of the book, you'll have seen a few other Pax projects, including the following:
>
> - Pax Exam: An extension to JUnit for testing bundles within an OSGi framework
>
> - Pax Logging: An implementation of the OSGi Logging Service
>
> - Pax Runner: A utility for starting an OSGi framework with a predefined set of bundles installed
>
> - Pax ConfMan: An implementation of the OSGi Configuration Admin Service
>
> ---
> *. http://wiki.ops4j.org/display/ops4j/Pax

3.4 Setting Up the Project

Since we're building four separate bundles, it seems logical that we'll probably need to create four different project directories, each with their own build instructions. Furthermore, so that we can build the entire set of bundles together, we may want to organize those projects all under a parent project.

Setting up such a project structure is a fairly straightforward effort, involving the creation of a project directory and four subdirectories (one for each of the individual bundle projects). Then, in each directory we'd need to determine where our source code goes, where the build output goes, and where other resources related to the project will go. And, we'd need to create build instructions, using either Ant or Maven, for the parent project and each of the bundle subprojects.

It's not all too complicated to create a project directory and write build instructions. But it's also quite tedious and prone to error—and it sounds like a lot of work. I've got a better idea. . . .

 **Joe Asks. . .**

Do I Have to Use Pax Construct?

You really don't need many tools to build OSGi bundles. In fact, all that you really need is a text editor, a Java compiler, and the Java jar utility. But if you want to save yourself some trouble, you should consider taking advantage of some of the OSGi-oriented tools.

I like to use Pax Construct because it simplifies a lot of what goes into building OSGi bundles and because it leverages Maven, which, as I've already stated, has a lot of synergy with OSGi. I also really like the scripted Rails-like development model of Pax Construct. Finally, my decision to use Pax Construct doesn't preclude the possibility of using Eclipse PDE or most other OSGi development tools.

If Pax Construct isn't your style, then feel free to find an OSGi tool that better fits you.

Allow me to introduce you to Pax Construct,[2] one of the handiest tools that OSGi developers can have at their disposal. Pax Construct is a set of scripts, backed by a Maven plugin, that automates the creation, building, and execution of OSGi projects. In many ways, the scripts provided by Pax Construct are similar to the scripts used when developing Ruby on Rails (or Grails) applications. It not only sets up a project for you, but it also helps you manage your bundles' manifests and deal with third-party dependencies, and it even deploys your bundles into an OSGi framework.

Installing Pax Construct

To get started with Pax Construct, you'll need to download the scripts and install them in your system path. As I write this, the current version of Pax Construct is 1.4.[3]

After downloading the distribution file, unzip it to a folder on your system. Then, add the unzipped folder's bin directory to your system path.

---

2. http://wiki.ops4j.org/display/ops4j/Pax+Construct
3. http://repo1.maven.org/maven2/org/ops4j/pax/construct/scripts/1.4/scripts-1.4.zip

Script	What It Does
pax-add-repository	Adds a Maven repository to the project's list of repositories.
pax-clone	Clones an existing Pax Construct project so that it can be re-created elsewhere.
pax-create-bundle	Creates a new bundle project within an OSGi project or within a module.
pax-create-module	Creates a new module within another module or an OSGi project. Modules are an organizational entity to group related bundles together.
pax-create-project	Creates a new parent OSGi project. This is the first Pax Construct script you'll use. Within the project that it creates, you'll use the other scripts to create new bundle subprojects.
pax-embed-jar	Embeds a third-party JAR file within a bundle, ensuring that it is added to the bundle's classpath.
pax-import-bundle	Adds Import-Package instructions to ensure that a bundle imports a dependency bundle.
pax-move-bundle	Moves a bundle project to a new directory, updating the Maven POM as necessary.
pax-provision	Starts an OSGi framework (Felix by default), installs all of the project's bundles and dependencies, and starts the bundles.
pax-remove-bundle	Removes a bundle from the OSGi project.
pax-update	Checks for and installs a new version of Pax Construct.
pax-wrap-jar	Creates a bundle project within an OSGi project or a module that wraps a third-party JAR file as an OSGi bundle.

Figure 3.2: PAX CONSTRUCT PROVIDES SEVERAL SCRIPTS TO AUTOMATE DEVELOPMENT OF OSGI PROJECTS.

Now you're ready to start using Pax Construct. All the scripts made available by Pax Construct are described in Figure 3.2.

Since we haven't set up a project yet, the script that we'll need first is pax-create-project. We'll use it to create the foundation for the *Dude, Where's My JAR?* project.

Updating Pax Construct

While I was still writing this book, Pax Construct 1.4 was released, fixing a significant bug with regard to deploying web bundles (we'll talk more about that later in Chapter 7, *Creating Web Bundles*, on page 127). To take advantage of the bug fix, I needed to update Pax Construct from version 1.3 to version 1.4.

No problem. That's exactly what the pax-update script is for. It checks for a newer version of Pax Construct and automatically updates the version used by the current project. To use it, simply type pax-update at the command line of the Pax Construct–enabled project.

Creating the Top-Level Project

The simplest way to create a new project with Pax Construct is to run the pax-create-project script at the command line:

```
projects% pax-create-project

pax-create-project -g groupId -a artifactId [-v version] [-o] [-- mvnOpts ...]
groupId (examples) ? com.dudewheresmyjar
artifactId (myProject) ? dwmj
version (1.0-SNAPSHOT) ? 1.0.0-SNAPSHOT

[INFO] Scanning for projects...

[INFO] Scanning for projects...
[INFO] ------------------------------------------------------------------------
[INFO] Building Maven Default Project
[INFO]    task-segment: [org.ops4j:maven-pax-plugin:1.4:create-project]
         (aggregator-style)
[INFO] ------------------------------------------------------------------------
[INFO] Setting property: classpath.resource.loader.class =>
         'org.codehaus.plexus.velocity.ContextClassLoaderResourceLoader'.
[INFO] Setting property: velocimacro.messages.on => 'false'.
[INFO] Setting property: resource.loader => 'classpath'.
[INFO] Setting property: resource.manager.logwhenfound => 'false'.
...
[INFO] Archetype created in dir: /Users/wallsc/Projects/projects/dwmj
[INFO] ------------------------------------------------------------------------
[INFO] BUILD SUCCESSFUL
[INFO] ------------------------------------------------------------------------
[INFO] Total time: 5 seconds
[INFO] Finished at: Thu Mar 05 23:57:34 CST 2009
[INFO] Final Memory: 10M/19M
[INFO] ------------------------------------------------------------------------
projects%
```

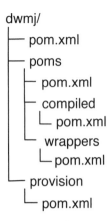

```
dwmj/
├── pom.xml
├── poms
│       ├── pom.xml
│       ├── compiled
│       │       └── pom.xml
│       └── wrappers
│               └── pom.xml
└── provision
        └── pom.xml
```

Figure 3.3: THE PAX-CREATE-PROJECT SCRIPT KICK STARTS OSGI PROJECT DEVELOPMENT WITH A BASIC PROJECT STRUCTURE AND MAVEN 2 POM FILES.

Under the covers, pax-create-project uses a Maven 2 archetype to create the project structure. Therefore, when you run pax-create-project without any arguments, it will prompt you for a Maven group ID, artifact ID, and version number to apply to the project it creates. If you'd rather not answer any questions, you could also provide those details on the command line:

```
projects% pax-create-project -g com.dudewheresmyjar -a dwmj -v 1.0.0-SNAPSHOT
```

When pax-create-project is finished, you'll find the top-level project for *Dude, Where's My JAR?* in the dwmj directory. Within this directory, you'll find the directory structure shown in Figure 3.3.

As you can see, there are several Maven 2 pom.xml files in the project. For the most part, the only one that matters right now is the one at the top level, just inside the dwmj directory—it is the one that is used to build the whole project. The pom.xml files under the poms directory will serve as parent POMs for the bundle subprojects that we'll create later.

As for the pom.xml file in the provision directory, Pax Construct will use it to decide what bundles to install when the OSGi framework is started with the pax-provision script. Since we've only just started, there's not much in there yet. But if you want to give it a spin, feel free to kick off pax-provision now.

```
projects% cd dwmj
dwmj% pax-provision
[INFO] Scanning for projects...
[INFO] Reactor build order:
[INFO]    com.dudewheresmyjar.dwmj (OSGi project)
[INFO]    dwmj - plugin configuration
[INFO]    dwmj - wrapper instructions
[INFO]    dwmj - bundle instructions
[INFO]    dwmj - imported bundles
[INFO] ------------------------------------------------------------------------
[INFO] Building com.dudewheresmyjar.dwmj (OSGi project)
[INFO]    task-segment: [org.ops4j:maven-pax-plugin:1.4:provision]
          (aggregator-style)
[INFO] ------------------------------------------------------------------------
[INFO] [pax:provision]
[INFO] ~~~~~~~~~~~~~~~~~~~
[INFO]  No bundles found!
[INFO] ~~~~~~~~~~~~~~~~~~~
[INFO] Installing /Users/wallsc/Projects/projects/dwmj/runner/deploy-pom.xml to
       /Users/wallsc/.m2/repository/com/dudewheresmyjar/dwmj/build/deployment/
       1.0.0-SNAPSHOT/deployment-1.0.0-SNAPSHOT.pom
[INFO] artifact org.ops4j.pax.runner:pax-runner: checking for updates from central

    _____   _____  __  __
   / _ / / /  _   / / / / /
  /  __/ /   _   / / _\ \ _/
 / /    / / / / / / / _\ \
/__/   /_/ /_/ /_/ /_/

Pax Runner (0.14.1) from OPS4J - http://www.ops4j.org
------------------------------------------------------

  -> Using config [classpath:META-INF/runner.properties]
  -> Provision from [/Users/wallsc/Projects/projects/dwmj/runner/deploy-pom.xml]
  -> Provision from [scan-pom:file:/Users/wallsc/Projects/projects/dwmj/runner/
            deploy-pom.xml]
  -> Using property [org.osgi.service.http.port=8080]
  -> Using property [org.osgi.service.http.port.secure=8443]
  -> Using default executor
  -> Downloading bundles...
  -> Felix 1.2.2 : 356815 bytes @ [ 641kBps ]
  -> org.osgi.compendium (4.1.0) : 514214 bytes @ [ 331kBps ]
  -> org.apache.felix.shell (1.0.2) : 51390 bytes @ [ 1167kBps ]
  -> org.apache.felix.shell.tui.plugin (1.0.2) : 12237 bytes @ [ 108kBps ]
  -> Execution environment [J2SE-1.5]
  -> Starting platform [Felix 1.2.2]. Runner has successfully finished his job!

Welcome to Felix.
=================

->
```

As you can see, pax-provision fires up Felix. The key thing to notice is the line that says "No bundles found!" That's because we haven't created any bundles in our project yet. We'll get to that soon. But first, I thought you might be interested in seeing a few ways that the project can be customized. (Be sure to issue the shutdown command to get out of Felix.)

Customizing the Project

All of the project's behavior is contained within the top-level pom.xml file. If you open that file up in your text editor, you'll find a handful of places where you can customize the project.

This is a standard Maven 2 POM file, so you can add pretty much anything to this file that you would add to any other pom.xml file. I'm not going to spend any time on basic Maven configuration, but I do want to make a few simple tweaks to the project so that it works the way I'd like it to work.

As we develop the code for *Dude, Where's My JAR?*, we're likely to use Java 5 language constructs, such as annotations and generics. By default, however, Maven compiles only Java 1.4–level source code. So, to bring Maven up to Java 5, we'll add the following configuration to the *<build>*/*<plugins>* section of pom.xml:

```
dwmj/pom.xml
<plugin>
  <artifactId>maven-compiler-plugin</artifactId>
  <configuration>
    <source>1.5</source>
    <target>1.5</target>
  </configuration>
</plugin>
```

This tells Maven to compile code containing Java 5 constructs and to compile targeting a Java 5 virtual machine.

Another change you may want to make is to use a different OSGi framework when running pax-provision. As we've already seen, pax-provision defaults to using Felix. But you can change it to use another implementation, such as Equinox, by tweaking the –platform parameter:

```
dwmj/pom.xml
<plugin>
  <groupId>org.ops4j</groupId>
  <artifactId>maven-pax-plugin</artifactId>
```

```
  <version>1.4</version>
  <configuration>
    <provision>
      <param>--platform=equinox</param>
      <param>--profiles=minimal</param>
    </provision>
  </configuration>
</plugin>
```

The –platform parameter tells Pax which OSGi framework to use. If you'd rather use Knopflerfish, then feel free to set it to *knopflerfish* (or *kf* for short).

Finally, if you're an Eclipse user, like myself, you'll want to uncomment the lines near the end of pom.xml that say "uncomment to auto-generate IDE files," leaving the following Maven declaration uncommented:

dwmj/pom.xml

```
<execution>
  <id>ide-support</id>
  <goals>
    <goal>eclipse</goal>
  </goals>
</execution>
```

These lines instruct Pax Construct to automatically generate Eclipse project files so that you can easily import the bundle projects into Eclipse. Aside from ensuring that all of the necessary dependencies are in the Eclipse project classpath, Pax Construct will also make sure that the project has Eclipse's plugin development environment (PDE) nature—so that package visibility will be limited to packages that are imported in the project's manifest.

The stage is now set for the rest of the book. We have identified a sample application to be developed using OSGi. And we've taken a moment to break it down along functional boundaries into pieces that we'll develop as OSGi bundles.

In preparation for what is to come, we've also created a top-level project structure for the *Dude, Where's My JAR?* application. We could've set up the project by hand, but instead we've generated it using scripts provided by the Pax Construct project, which is an open source toolkit for developing OSGi applications. We'll use Pax Construct more as we continue fleshing out the bundles that make up our application.

In fact, we're now ready to create the first bundle of our application. In the next chapter, we'll create a simple library bundle that contains the domain objects of the application. As we do that, we'll learn a few new tricks with Pax Construct, and we'll figure out how to deal with third-party libraries that aren't quite OSGi-ready.

Chapter 4

Working with Bundles

OSGi is all about modularity. And the unit of modularity in OSGi is a bundle. As we've already discussed, OSGi bundles are little more than good old-fashioned JAR files with a little bit of extra information in their manifests.

We've already created a few simple bundles. But now we're ready to turn it up a notch and develop a few more realistic bundles that will come together to form the *Dude, Where's My JAR?* application.

In this chapter we're going to create the first bundle for the application. It will be a simple bundle that exports only a single package and does not publish or consume any services. Even though it's simple, we'll face several interesting problems, including how to deal with dependencies on third-party JAR files that aren't OSGi-ready.

4.1 Creating the Domain Bundle

In the previous chapter, we used Pax Construct's pax-create-project script to create a top-level project for our application. Now we'll use the pax-create-bundle script to generate a bundle subproject to carry the domain objects in the application. From within the dwmj project directory, execute pax-create-bundle.[1]

---

1. For readability, I'm using a Unix shell trick to break long lines by ending them with a backslash (\). The question mark (?) on the subsequent lines indicates that the lines are continuations of the previous line. If you're on Windows (or if you just want to), you can type the command and its arguments in a single line. If you choose to use this trick, you must type the backslash, but the Unix shell will provide the question mark.

```
dwmj% pax-create-bundle -p dwmj.domain -n domain \
?                           -g com.dudewheresmyjar -v 1.0.0-SNAPSHOTs
[INFO] Scanning for projects...
[INFO] -----------------------------------------------------------------
[INFO] Building com.dudewheresmyjar.dwmj (OSGi project)
[INFO]    task-segment: [org.ops4j:maven-pax-plugin:1.4:create-bundle]
          (aggregator-style)
[INFO] -----------------------------------------------------------------
...
[INFO] Archetype created in dir: /Users/wallsc/Projects/projects/dwmj/domain
[INFO] -----------------------------------------------------------------
[INFO] BUILD SUCCESSFUL
[INFO] -----------------------------------------------------------------
[INFO] Total time: 5 seconds
[INFO] Finished at: Fri Mar 06 00:04:11 CST 2009
[INFO] Final Memory: 10M/19M
[INFO] -----------------------------------------------------------------
dwmj%
```

Here, I've specified the root package of the bundle with the -p argument, the name of the bundle with the -n argument, the bundle's Maven group ID with the -g argument, and the version number with the -v argument. Optionally, I could've left that information off the command line, but then the script would have prompted me for the bundle details.

In any event, once pax-create-bundle has finished, you'll find the domain bundle project in the domain directory under dwmj. If you dig around in the domain directory, you'll find several interesting items, including the following:

- A pom.xml file: This contains the Maven build instructions for building the bundle project. Notice that this project has the top-level *dwmj* project as its parent. What's more, if you look at the top-level project's pom.xml file, you'll see that the *domain* project has been added as a child project.

- An osgi.bnd file: Under the covers, Pax Construct leans on a tool called BND[2] to automatically generate manifests for bundle projects. The osgi.bnd file contains a set of instructions to guide BND as it generates the manifest. By allowing Pax Construct to generate the manifest (using BND), we free ourselves from the burden of maintaining the manifest file ourselves. For the domain bundle, this file starts out empty.

- A src directory structure that contains a few Java class files: When Pax Construct creates a new bundle project, it places a few bits of

---

2. http://www.aqute.biz/Code/Bnd

example code in there as placeholders. ExampleService.java defines an interface that fronts the OSGi service defined in ExampleServiceImpl.java. ExampleActivator.java contains an OSGi activator that registers the service in the OSGi service registry.

Feel free to take a look around in the generated *domain* project's directory. You may be interested in taking a close look at the Java source code to see another example of an OSGi service and how a bundle activator registers it with the service registry.

The example service and activator Java files are great for educational purposes. However, they serve no purpose in our domain bundle, so when you're finished looking around, go ahead and delete them. In their place, we'll need to create a domain class that represents a JAR file within the index.

Defining the Domain Class

As you'll recall from the previous chapter, the primary function of the application is to provide a search engine for JAR files. Internally, JAR files will be represented by a domain class named JarFile:

dwmj/domain/src/main/java/dwmj/domain/JarFile.java

```java
package dwmj.domain;

public class JarFile {
    private String repository;
    private String groupId;
    private String artifactId;
    private String version;
    private boolean snapshot;
    private String rawUrl;
    private boolean hasSource;
    private boolean hasJavadoc;
    private String bundleSymbolicName;

    private Set<String> packages;

    public String getPackageNames() {
        if(packages == null) return "";

        String packageNames = "";
        for (String p : packages) {
            packageNames += (p + " ");
        }
        return packageNames;
    }
```

```java
  private Set<String> classes;

  public String getClassNames() {
    if(classes == null) return "";

    String classNames = "";
    for (String c : classes) {
      classNames += (c + " ");
    }
    return classNames;
  }

  // NOTE: property setter/getter methods left out
  // for brevity's sake

}
```

As you can see, a JarFile carries around several useful bits of information about artifacts that it indexes. Since the application will be using Maven repositories as its source of JAR files, the JarFile class holds information that can be used to find the JAR file in a Maven repository: the repository, group ID, artifact ID, and version. In addition, JarFile has two boolean properties indicating whether the JAR file is a snapshot version and whether it is an OSGi bundle (that is, does it have a Bundle-SymbolicName header in its manifest).

As it stands, JarFile is a sufficient class for holding JAR file metadata. But ultimately we'll want to write the information kept in JarFile to an index that can be searched upon. In the next chapter, we'll build the index service, which uses an open source search framework known as Compass to do the indexing and searching. In the meantime, we can go ahead and annotate the class with information that Compass can use when indexing a JarFile.

dwmj/domain/src/main/java/dwmj/domain/JarFile.java

```java
@Searchable(alias = "jar")
public class JarFile {
  @SearchableProperty(store = Store.YES, index = Index.UN_TOKENIZED)
  private String repository;
  @SearchableProperty(store = Store.YES, index = Index.UN_TOKENIZED)
  private String groupId;
  @SearchableProperty(store = Store.YES, index = Index.UN_TOKENIZED)
  private String artifactId;
  @SearchableProperty(store = Store.YES, index = Index.UN_TOKENIZED)
  private String version;
  @SearchableProperty(store = Store.YES, index = Index.UN_TOKENIZED)
  private boolean snapshot;
  @SearchableProperty(store = Store.YES, index = Index.UN_TOKENIZED)
```

```java
    private String rawUrl;
    @SearchableProperty(store = Store.YES, index = Index.UN_TOKENIZED)
    private boolean hasSource;
    @SearchableProperty(store = Store.YES, index = Index.UN_TOKENIZED)
    private boolean hasJavadoc;
    @SearchableProperty(store = Store.YES, index = Index.UN_TOKENIZED)
    private String bundleSymbolicName;

    private Set<String> packages;

    @SearchableProperty(store = Store.YES, index = Index.TOKENIZED)
    public String getPackageNames() {
        if(packages == null) return "";

        String packageNames = "";
        for (String p : packages) {
            packageNames += (p + " ");
        }
        return packageNames;
    }

    private Set<String> classes;

    @SearchableProperty(store = Store.YES, index = Index.TOKENIZED)
    public String getClassNames() {
        if(classes == null) return "";

        String classNames = "";
        for (String c : classes) {
            classNames += (c + " ");
        }
        return classNames;
    }

    // NOTE: property setter/getter methods left out
    // for brevity's sake

    @SearchableId
    public String getRawUrl() {
        return rawUrl;
    }
}
```

I used the **@Searchable** annotation to indicate that I want JarFile to be searchable (and thus, indexed by Compass). I also annotated the member variables of JarFile with **@SearchableProperty** to tell Compass that these values are searchable. Finally, I annotated the getRawUrl() method with **@SearchableId** to indicate that the value returned from this method should be used as the unique identifier for the JarFile (think of it as a primary key).

Because Compass is outside of the scope of this book, I won't dwell on these annotations any further. We'll do a bit more Compass work in the next chapter as we develop the index service, but if you want to know more about Compass, you can visit the project home page.[3]

The JarFile class is the only class we'll need in the domain bundle. Since we've written all of the code that this bundle needs, we're ready to build it into a deployable bundle JAR file.

Building the Domain Bundle

Pax Construct–created projects are based on Maven. Therefore, we can build the domain bundle using ordinary Maven life-cycle goals. More specifically, let's use Maven's install goal to build the bundle and deploy it in our local Maven repository:

```
domain% mvn install
[INFO] Scanning for projects...
[INFO] ------------------------------------------------------------------------
[INFO] Building com.dudewheresmyjar.domain [dwmj.domain]
[INFO]    task-segment: [install]
[INFO] ------------------------------------------------------------------------
[INFO] [resources:resources]
[INFO] Using default encoding to copy filtered resources.
[INFO] [pax:compile]
[INFO] Compiling 1 source file to
      /Users/wallsc/Projects/projects/dwmj/domain/target/classes
[INFO] [recovering meta-data]
[INFO] ------------------------------------------------------------------------
[ERROR] BUILD FAILURE
[INFO] ------------------------------------------------------------------------
[INFO] Compilation failure

/Users/wallsc/Projects/projects/dwmj/domain/src/main/java/dwmj/domain/JarFile.ja
      [7,31] package org.compass.annotations does not exist
...
[INFO] ------------------------------------------------------------------------
[INFO] For more information, run Maven with the -e switch
[INFO] ------------------------------------------------------------------------
[INFO] Total time: 5 seconds
[INFO] Finished at: Fri Mar 06 00:06:51 CST 2009
[INFO] Final Memory: 12M/23M
[INFO] ------------------------------------------------------------------------
domain%
```

Oops! It seems we've already run into some trouble. It looks like Maven is having trouble compiling JarFile.java because it can't find the Compass

---

3. http://www.compass-project.org/

annotations. That's because we haven't added Compass as a dependency in the project. Let's fix that by adding Compass as a dependency in pom.xml. Open the domain bundle project's pom.xml in your editor, and add the following *<dependency>* to the *<dependencies>* block:

```
<dependency>
  <groupId>org.compass-project</groupId>
  <artifactId>compass</artifactId>
  <version>2.1.1</version>
</dependency>
```

You're probably wondering how I knew what the group and artifact IDs should be. Well, it certainly would be nice if there were some sort of search engine that would find these things for us. But since nobody has developed one of those quite yet, I figured it out by reading the Compass website.

At the same time, I also happened to learn that Compass isn't in the central Maven repository—Compass has its own repository. In typical Maven fashion, we could add the following *<repository>* entry to the pom.xml file:

```
<repository>
  <id>compass-project.org</id>
  <name>Compass</name>
  <url>http://repo.compass-project.org</url>
</repository>
```

Or, since we're using Pax Construct, we can use the pax-add-repository script:

```
dwmj% pax-add-repository -i compass -u http://repo.compass-project.org
[INFO] Scanning for projects...
[INFO] ------------------------------------------------------------------------
[INFO] Building com.dudewheresmyjar.dwmj (OSGi project)
[INFO]    task-segment: [org.ops4j:maven-pax-plugin:1.4:add-repository]
          (aggregator-style)
[INFO] ------------------------------------------------------------------------
[INFO] [pax:add-repository]
[INFO] Adding repository http://repo.compass-project.org to
          com.dudewheresmyjar:dwmj:pom:1.0.0-SNAPSHOT
[INFO] ------------------------------------------------------------------------
[INFO] BUILD SUCCESSFUL
[INFO] ------------------------------------------------------------------------
[INFO] Total time: 4 seconds
[INFO] Finished at: Fri Mar 06 00:08:57 CST 2009
[INFO] Final Memory: 9M/18M
[INFO] ------------------------------------------------------------------------
dwmj%
```

With Compass added as a dependency in Maven, we're ready to try the build again. This time, things seem to go a little bit better:

```
domain% mvn install
[INFO] Scanning for projects...
[INFO] ------------------------------------------------------------------
[INFO] Building com.dudewheresmyjar.domain [dwmj.domain]
[INFO]     task-segment: [install]
[INFO] ------------------------------------------------------------------
...
```

And with that we have built the first bundle for our application. But before we get too celebratory, we should probably deploy it to the OSGi framework to see what happens.

Deploying the Bundle

In Chapter 2, we created and deployed a bundle that contained an activator class. As a result, we were given instant feedback from the bundle when it was started (as well as when it was stopped). The domain bundle, on the other hand, is much simpler and doesn't include any executable code. But that won't stop us from deploying it into the container and poking at it to see what happens.

As it turns out, Pax Construct's repertoire isn't limited to creating projects and bundles. Pax Construct also comes with the pax-provision script, which will automatically start an OSGi framework and deploy all the bundles associated with the project. To give it a spin, run it from the top-level project directory:

```
dwmj% pax-provision
[INFO] Scanning for projects...
[INFO] Reactor build order:
[INFO]    com.dudewheresmyjar.dwmj (OSGi project)
[INFO]    dwmj - plugin configuration
[INFO]    dwmj - wrapper instructions
[INFO]    dwmj - bundle instructions
[INFO]    dwmj - imported bundles
[INFO]    com.dudewheresmyjar.domain [dwmj.domain]
[INFO] ------------------------------------------------------------------
[INFO] Building com.dudewheresmyjar.dwmj (OSGi project)
[INFO]     task-segment: [org.ops4j:maven-pax-plugin:1.4:provision]
           (aggregator-style)
[INFO] ------------------------------------------------------------------
[INFO] [pax:provision]
[INFO] Installing /Users/wallsc/Projects/projects/dwmj/runner/deploy-pom.xml to
       /Users/wallsc/.m2/repository/com/dudewheresmyjar/dwmj/build/
          deployment/1.0.0-SNAPSHOT/deployment-1.0.0-SNAPSHOT.pom
```

```
Pax Runner (0.14.1) from OPS4J - http://www.ops4j.org
----------------------------------------------------

 -> Using config [classpath:META-INF/runner.properties]
 -> Provision from [/Users/wallsc/Projects/projects/dwmj/runner/deploy-pom.xml]
 -> Provision from [scan-pom:file:/Users/wallsc/Projects/projects/dwmj/runner/
        deploy-pom.xml]
 -> Using property [org.osgi.service.http.port=8080]
 -> Using property [org.osgi.service.http.port.secure=8443]
 -> Installing bundle [{location=mvn:com.dudewheresmyjar/domain/1.0.0-SNAPSHOT,
        startlevel=null,shouldStart=true,shouldUpdate=false}]
 -> Installing bundle [{location=mvn:org.compass-project/compass/2.1.1,
        startlevel=null,shouldStart=true,shouldUpdate=false}]
 -> Using default executor
 -> Downloading bundles...
 -> mvn:com.dudewheresmyjar/domain/1.0.0-SNAPSHOT : 4186 bytes @ [ 2093kBps ]
 -> mvn:org.compass-project/compass/2.1.1 : 2195374 bytes @ [ 6290kBps ]
 -> Execution environment [J2SE-1.5]
 -> Starting platform [Equinox 3.4.1]. Runner has successfully finished his job!

osgi>
```

Under the covers, pax-provision uses another Pax project, Pax Runner, to do its dirty work. Pax Runner is responsible for downloading an OSGi framework (Equinox 3.4.0 in this case), starting it, and then installing and starting a set of bundles. When used with Pax Construct, that set of bundles is determined from the set of bundle projects and dependencies in the Pax Construct–managed OSGi project.

Notice that once Pax Runner has finished its job, we're presented with our old friend, the *osgi>* prompt. Let's use it to see what was deployed:

```
osgi> ss

Framework is launched.

id      State       Bundle
0       ACTIVE      org.eclipse.osgi_3.4.2.R34x_v20080826-1230
1       ACTIVE      org.eclipse.osgi.util_3.1.300.v20080303
2       ACTIVE      org.eclipse.osgi.services_3.1.200.v20070605
3       INSTALLED   com.dudewheresmyjar.domain_1.0.0.SNAPSHOT
4       ACTIVE      org.compass-project.compass_2.1.1

osgi>
```

It seems that in addition to a few core Equinox bundles, Pax Runner has installed our domain bundle (id=3) and Compass (id=4). Now that's smart: Pax Runner not only knew to install our bundle, but it was able to figure out, from the Maven POM, that we'd also need Compass.

Our bundle is installed and everything seems in order, that is, except for the fact that our bundle isn't active. Hmmm. Why didn't Pax Runner start it for us like it did for the other bundles? Oh well, let's start it ourselves:

```
osgi> start 3
org.osgi.framework.BundleException: The bundle could not be resolved. Reason:
  Missing Constraint: Import-Package: org.compass.annotations; version="0.0.0"
    at org.eclipse.osgi.framework.internal.core.BundleHost.startWorker
    at org.eclipse.osgi.framework.internal.core.AbstractBundle.start
    at org.eclipse.osgi.framework.internal.core.AbstractBundle.start
    at org.eclipse.osgi.framework.internal.core.FrameworkCommandProvider._start
    at sun.reflect.NativeMethodAccessorImpl.invoke0
    at sun.reflect.NativeMethodAccessorImpl.invoke
    at sun.reflect.DelegatingMethodAccessorImpl.invoke
    at java.lang.reflect.Method.invoke
...
osgi>
```

Whoa! That was unexpected. Apparently our bundle can't be started because it can't find the org.compass.annotations package. That's funny ...I don't remember adding an Import-Package: header to the bundle's manifest. In any event, if our bundle is importing that package, would you not think that the Compass bundle would export it? Let's check into it by seeing what the Compass bundle has to offer:

```
osgi> bundle 4
initial@reference:file:org.compass-project.compass_2.1.1.jar/ [4]
  Id=4, Status=ACTIVE  Data Root=/Users/wallsc/Projects/projects/dwmj/runner/
        equinox/org.eclipse.osgi/bundles/4/data
  No registered services.
  No services in use.
  No exported packages
  No imported packages
  No fragment bundles
  Named class space
    org.compass-project.compass; bundle-version="2.1.1"[provided]
  No required bundles

osgi>
```

The *No exported packages* line looks to be the root of our problem. In fact, the Compass bundle looks pretty much useless as is. It seems that we'll need to modify the Compass bundle's manifest so that we can get at its content.

4.2 Contending with Nonbundle Dependencies

In a perfect world, pizza would be categorized as health food, we'd power our notebook computers from a wireless power source, and all JAR files would already be OSGi bundles.

Unfortunately, this is not an ideal world, and not every JAR file you'll encounter is a full-fledged OSGi bundle. In fact, a great number of libraries that you'll probably want to use in your applications do not have a proper OSGi-enabling MANIFEST.MF file.

We've already run into an example of a JAR file that isn't an OSGi bundle: Compass. Actually, the Compass 2.1.1 JAR file does contain a manifest with a Bundle-SymbolicName: header (which satisfies the minimum requirements for an OSGi bundle). Oddly enough, however, while the Compass JAR has a proper OSGi manifest, it seems to be incomplete. That's because the Compass manifest doesn't export any packages. Therefore, even though we can install Compass as a bundle into the OSGi framework, we can't use any of the classes, interfaces, or annotations that it contains. So, despite the presence of a Bundle-SymbolicName: header, we'll need to treat Compass as if it were a nonbundle JAR file.

Although we don't develop software in a perfect world, hope is not lost if your OSGi-based application depends on a library that doesn't provide an OSGi bundle. One way to fix the Compass bundle is to expand it, edit its manifest, and then reconstitute the contents back into a new JAR file. But that seems a bit extreme, especially if it's a manual effort.

Instead, let's consider two less extreme ways to bring nonbundle JARs into our OSGi application:

- Embed the JAR files within the bundles that need them.
- Wrap the JAR files with an OSGi manifest.

Let's take a look at how to use each of these techniques to be able to use Compass in our application.

Embedding JARs

The first option for using nonbundle JARs in an OSGi application is to directly embed the JAR files into the bundle. But wait a minute. Isn't the bundle a JAR file? Am I suggesting that we package a JAR file within another JAR file?

Yes, I know it sounds weird, but embedding JAR files within OSGi bundles is a perfectly valid way to add nonbundle libraries to your OSGi application. This trick involves adding a Bundle-ClassPath: header to the domain bundle's manifest.

The Bundle-ClassPath: header defines a bundle's classpath. By default, it is set to "." which indicates that the bundle's own content is on the classpath (in addition to any packages that it may have imported from other bundles). But if we were to embed the Compass JAR file within the domain bundle JAR, then we could add a reference to the embedded JAR in Bundle-ClassPath:, and Compass would be included in the domain bundle's classpath. For example, if we placed Compass in the JAR file under a lib directory, then we could set Bundle-ClassPath: to ".,lib/compass-2.1.1.jar."

That all sounds well and good, but it also sounds like a lot of work. Never fear—Pax Construct is on the job with its pax-embed-jar script. This handy little script will take care of everything needed to embed a JAR file in a bundle. To embed the Compass JAR, run pax-embed-jar from within the domain directory:

```
domain% pax-embed-jar -g org.compass-project -a compass -v 2.1.1
[INFO] Scanning for projects...
[INFO] ------------------------------------------------------------------------
[INFO] Building com.dudewheresmyjar.domain [dwmj.domain]
[INFO]    task-segment: [org.ops4j:maven-pax-plugin:1.4:embed-jar]
          (aggregator-style)
[INFO] ------------------------------------------------------------------------
[INFO] [pax:embed-jar]
[INFO] Embedding org.compass-project:compass:2.1.1 in
          com.dudewheresmyjar:domain:bundle:1.0.0-SNAPSHOT
[INFO] ------------------------------------------------------------------------
[INFO] BUILD SUCCESSFUL
[INFO] ------------------------------------------------------------------------
[INFO] Total time: 4 seconds
[INFO] Finished at: Fri Mar 06 00:29:16 CST 2009
[INFO] Final Memory: 9M/17M
[INFO] ------------------------------------------------------------------------
domain%
```

And with that, Compass will be embedded in the domain bundle. But how? What did pax-embed-jar really do?

Actually, pax-embed-jar didn't really embed anything. Instead, it changed a few of the domain project's files so that Compass will be embedded when the domain bundle is built. More specifically, pax-embed-jar made the following changes:

- Added an Embed-Dependency entry to osgi.bnd. The Embed-Dependency entry declares that the manifest should have a proper Bundle-ClassPath: header pointing to the Compass JAR file that will be embedded within the domain bundle.

- Added a <dependency> entry to the POM file to ensure that Compass is counted as a dependency of the project.

Now when we build the domain bundle, it should contain not only our JarFile class but also the contents of the Compass library. Let's try building it:

```
domain% mvn install
[INFO] Scanning for projects...
[INFO] ------------------------------------------------------------------------
[INFO] Building com.dudewheresmyjar.domain [dwmj.domain]
[INFO]     task-segment: [install]
[INFO] ------------------------------------------------------------------------
...
[INFO] ------------------------------------------------------------------------
[INFO] BUILD SUCCESSFUL
[INFO] ------------------------------------------------------------------------
[INFO] Total time: 9 seconds
[INFO] Finished at: Fri Mar 06 00:30:13 CST 2009
[INFO] Final Memory: 14M/33M
[INFO] ------------------------------------------------------------------------
domain%
```

So far so good. Let's kick it off again and see whether adding the Compass bundle will enable the domain bundle to start:

```
dwmj% pax-provision
[INFO] Scanning for projects...
...
osgi> ss

Framework is launched.

id      State       Bundle
0       ACTIVE      org.eclipse.osgi_3.4.2.R34x_v20080826-1230
1       ACTIVE      org.eclipse.osgi.util_3.1.300.v20080303
2       ACTIVE      org.eclipse.osgi.services_3.1.200.v20070605
3       INSTALLED   com.dudewheresmyjar.domain_1.0.0.SNAPSHOT

osgi>
```

As you can see, the domain bundle is still not starting. To figure out what's going on, let's use Eclipse's diag command:

```
osgi> diag 3
initial@reference:file:com.dudewheresmyjar.domain_1.0.0.SNAPSHOT.jar/ [3]
  Direct constraints which are unresolved:
    Missing imported package com.gigaspaces.datasource_0.0.0.
    Missing imported package com.gigaspaces.events_0.0.0.
    Missing imported package com.gigaspaces.events.batching_0.0.0.
    Missing imported package com.ibatis.sqlmap.client_0.0.0.
    Missing imported package com.ibatis.sqlmap.client.event_0.0.0.
    Missing imported package com.ibatis.sqlmap.engine.impl_0.0.0.
    Missing imported package com.ibatis.sqlmap.engine.mapping.result_0.0.0.
    Missing imported package com.ibatis.sqlmap.engine.mapping.statement_0.0.0.
    Missing imported package com.j_spaces.core_0.0.0.
...
```

Wow! it seems that our domain bundle now depends on a lot of other packages, including packages in libraries such as Gigaspaces and iBATIS. But I don't remember making any changes that would cause the domain bundle to depend on these packages. What's going on?

It just so happens that even though our domain bundle doesn't need any of those packages, Compass does. And when we embedded Compass within the domain bundle, that meant that the domain bundle would have to declare those imports on behalf of the embedded Compass library. But does this mean that we must install those other libraries as bundles in the OSGi framework? Not necessarily. . . .

By default, Pax Construct instructs BND to generate a manifest that imports every package needed by a bundle (and, in this case, by any libraries embedded within a bundle). That's why Equinox couldn't start the domain bundle—the embedded Compass library was demanding packages that aren't being provided by other bundles.

The good news, however, is that most of Compass' dependencies are optional. Compass comes with support for Gigaspaces, TopLink, iBATIS, and a lot of other third-party libraries. But unless we're using those parts of Compass, we shouldn't need to install them in OSGi.

What we need is a way to tell the OSGi framework to not require those packages. To do that, we can add the following directive to the domain bundle BND instruction file (osgi.bnd):

dwmj/domain/osgi-embedded.bnd

```
Import-Package: *;resolution:=optional
```

This tells BND to import all packages that it needs but differs from the default in that it specifies the resolution of those packages to be optional. In other words, BND will produce a manifest that tells the OSGi framework to try to resolve the packages but not to complain if it can't find a bundle that exports them. This should make it possible for us to start the domain bundle. After rebuilding the domain bundle (using mvn install), let's give it a try:

```
dwmj% pax-provision
[INFO] Scanning for projects...
...
osgi> ss

Framework is launched.

id      State        Bundle
0       ACTIVE       org.eclipse.osgi_3.4.2.R34x_v20080826-1230
1       ACTIVE       org.eclipse.osgi.util_3.1.300.v20080303
2       ACTIVE       org.eclipse.osgi.services_3.1.200.v20070605
3       ACTIVE       com.dudewheresmyjar.domain_1.0.0.SNAPSHOT

osgi>
```

It looks like that did the trick. Our domain bundle is installed and started with Compass embedded within it. At this point, we are ready to move on and start developing the index service bundle.

Hold on! Embedding Compass within the domain bundle satisfied the domain bundle's dependency on Compass. But our index service bundle is also going to need to use Compass to add JarFile entries to the index and to search for them on behalf of a user. With Compass embedded in the domain bundle, the index service bundle won't be able to use it—that is, unless the domain bundle also exports the Compass packages.

There's no reason why the domain bundle couldn't export Compass packages. But it probably shouldn't because it would create an awkward arrangement of dependencies. If we decide later to upgrade to a newer version of Compass, we'll have to rebuild the domain bundle with the new version embedded in place of the older version. In short, we sacrificed a little modularity by embedding Compass in our domain bundle.

Before we settle on the approach of embedding Compass within the domain bundle, let's see how we can make Compass available to the domain bundle by wrapping it to be a proper OSGi bundle.

Joe Asks...

How Do I Decide Whether to Embed a JAR or to Wrap It?

This is a very good question. The answer comes down to a choice of simplicity vs. fine-grained control.

When you wrap a JAR file, you effectively turn it into an OSGi bundle. This means that you can install, start, stop, update, and uninstall it in the OSGi framework just like any other bundle. You need to install it only once for all depending bundles to be able to use it.

Embedded JARs, on the other hand, can be managed only within the scope of the bundle into which they are embedded. This means that you can't upgrade to a newer version of an embedded JAR file without rebuilding the hosting bundle. Also, if more than one bundle depends on a library, then that library's JAR file must be embedded within each bundle that needs it.

With that said, embedding JARs within bundles follows a familiar deployment model that is similar to web application WAR files that have JAR files embedded within them.

As a rule of thumb, if a library is needed by only one bundle and if you will only ever manage that library within the scope of the depending bundle, then you should probably embed it. But if the library is needed by several bundles and/or you want to manage that library independent of other bundles in the OSGi framework, then it may make more sense to wrap the library and deploy it as a full-fledged bundle.

Wrapping JARs

Another way to deal with JARs that aren't OSGi-ready is to wrap them so that they'll contain a proper OSGi manifest. In a Pax Construct project, the easiest way to do this is using the pax-wrap-jar script. To wrap the Compass JAR, run pax-wrap-jar from the top-level project directory (the dwmj directory) like this:

```
dwmj% pax-wrap-jar -g org.compass-project -a compass -v 2.1.1
[INFO] Scanning for projects...
[INFO] ------------------------------------------------------------------------
[INFO] Building com.dudewheresmyjar.dwmj (OSGi project)
[INFO]    task-segment: [org.ops4j:maven-pax-plugin:1.4:wrap-jar] (aggregator-sty
[INFO] ------------------------------------------------------------------------
...
```

```
[INFO] ---------------------------------------------------------------
[INFO] BUILD SUCCESSFUL
[INFO] ---------------------------------------------------------------
[INFO] Total time: 5 seconds
[INFO] Finished at: Fri Mar 06 00:37:50 CST 2009
[INFO] Final Memory: 10M/19M
[INFO] ---------------------------------------------------------------
dwmj%
```

Like most other Pax Construct scripts, pax-wrap-jar takes Maven artifact information at the command line (but will prompt you to enter the information if you don't enter it on the command line). In this case, I've specified the group ID (org.compass-project), the artifact ID (compass), and the version number (2.1.1).

Once pax-wrap-jar has finished, you'll find a new bundle project under the dwmj directory in org.compass-project.compass. You'll also find that this new project has been added as a module to the top-level pom.xml file. But what does this project contain?

Not much, really. It contains just a Maven pom.xml file and an osgi.bnd file. The most interesting of these two files is the osgi.bnd file:

dwmj/org.compass-project.compass/osgi.bnd

```
Embed-Dependency:\
 *;scope=compile|runtime;type=!pom;inline=true,\
 lucene-core;groupId=org.apache.lucene;inline=false
```

This file directs BND (by way of Pax Construct) to automatically unpack Compass into this bundle as the bundle is being created. Effectively, this means unpacking the Compass JAR file, adding a manifest, and then repacking it as an OSGi bundle.

Take note of the backslashes at the end of each line. These are used to split apart exceptionally long lines.

Now let's rebuild the bundle (with mvn install) and then try pax-provision again:

```
dwmj% pax-provision
[INFO] Scanning for projects...
[INFO] Reactor build order:
[INFO]    com.dudewheresmyjar.dwmj (OSGi project)
[INFO]    dwmj - plugin configuration
[INFO]    dwmj - wrapper instructions
[INFO]    dwmj - bundle instructions
[INFO]    dwmj - imported bundles
[INFO]    com.dudewheresmyjar.domain [dwmj.domain]
[INFO]    org.compass-project.compass 2.1.1 [osgi]
```

```
[INFO] ------------------------------------------------------------------
[INFO] Building com.dudewheresmyjar.dwmj (OSGi project)
[INFO]     task-segment: [org.ops4j:maven-pax-plugin:1.4:provision]
           (aggregator-style)
[INFO] ------------------------------------------------------------------
...
osgi> ss

Framework is launched.

id      State        Bundle
0       ACTIVE       org.eclipse.osgi_3.4.2.R34x_v20080826-1230
1       ACTIVE       org.eclipse.osgi.util_3.1.300.v20080303
2       ACTIVE       org.eclipse.osgi.services_3.1.200.v20070605
3       INSTALLED    com.dudewheresmyjar.domain_1.0.0.SNAPSHOT
4       INSTALLED    org.compass-project.compass_2.1.1

osgi>
```

It looks like the Compass bundle has been installed, but neither it nor the domain bundle is started. Let's use Equinox's diag command to see what the problem might be:

```
osgi> diag 3
initial@reference:file:com.dudewheresmyjar.domain_1.0.0.SNAPSHOT.jar/ [3]
  Direct constraints which are unresolved:
    Missing imported package dwmj.domain_1.0.0.SNAPSHOT.
    Missing imported package org.compass.annotations_0.0.0.
  Leaf constraints in the dependency chain which are unresolved:
    initial@reference:file:org.compass-project.compass_2.1.1.jar/ [4]
      Missing imported package com.ibatis.sqlmap.engine.mapping.result_0.0.0.
    initial@reference:file:org.compass-project.compass_2.1.1.jar/ [4]
      Missing imported package javax.jdo.listener_0.0.0.
    initial@reference:file:org.compass-project.compass_2.1.1.jar/ [4]
      Missing imported package org.hibernate.cfg_0.0.0.
    initial@reference:file:org.compass-project.compass_2.1.1.jar/ [4]
      Missing imported package com.gigaspaces.events.batching_0.0.0.
    initial@reference:file:org.compass-project.compass_2.1.1.jar/ [4]
      Missing imported package org.apache.openjpa.lib.log_0.0.0.
    initial@reference:file:org.compass-project.compass_2.1.1.jar/ [4]
      Missing imported package org.jdom.xpath_0.0.0.
    initial@reference:file:org.compass-project.compass_2.1.1.jar/ [4]
      Missing imported package net.jini.core.transaction_0.0.0.
    initial@reference:file:org.compass-project.compass_2.1.1.jar/ [4]
      Missing imported package org.dom4j.io_0.0.0.
    initial@reference:file:org.compass-project.compass_2.1.1.jar/ [4]
      Missing imported package com.j_spaces.core_0.0.0.
...
```

Hmmm...this looks familiar. It seems that the Compass bundle can't be started because it depends on several third-party packages that aren't being exported by any of the bundles already installed. As you'll recall, we encountered the same problem when we tried embedding Compass in the domain bundle. The solution here is the same as then, except that we'll declare the optional packages in the wrapped Compass bundle project's osgi.bnd file:

`dwmj/org.compass-project.compass/osgi.bnd`

```
Import-Package: *;resolution:=optional
```

Just like in the embedded Compass situation, this tells BND to create a manifest that tries to import packages but doesn't complain if it can't.

OK, let's try to build the bundle once more (with mvn install) and then cross our fingers and provision it:

```
dwmj% pax-provision
[INFO] Scanning for projects...
...
osgi> ss

Framework is launched.

id      State        Bundle
0       ACTIVE       org.eclipse.osgi_3.4.2.R34x_v20080826-1230
1       ACTIVE       org.eclipse.osgi.util_3.1.300.v20080303
2       ACTIVE       org.eclipse.osgi.services_3.1.200.v20070605
3       ACTIVE       com.dudewheresmyjar.domain_1.0.0.SNAPSHOT
4       ACTIVE       org.compass-project.compass_2.1.1

osgi>
```

Voilà! It looks like both the Compass bundle and our domain bundle have been successfully installed and started. Compass was able to start because the framework was able to resolve all of its required dependencies (of which there were none). And with Compass started, all of the domain bundle's required dependencies were resolved, and the domain bundle was started.

Since Compass is installed as a separate bundle from the domain bundle, we can manage it independently of any of the other bundles in our application, including the domain bundle. So, in contrast to embedding Compass, wrapping Compass gave us back the modularity that we had lost between the domain bundle and Compass. For that reason, I think we should stick with the wrapped Compass.

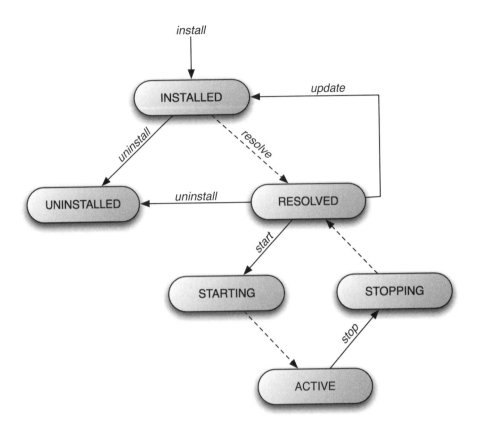

Figure 4.1: IN OSGI, THE BUNDLE LIFE CYCLE CONSISTS OF A WELL-
DEFINED SERIES OF STATES.

4.3 Following the Bundle Life Cycle

One thing that I've glossed over up until now is how a bundle moves
from one state to another. After we installed our bundles, the Equinox
ss command told us that they were in the INSTALLED state. Later, after
starting them, we saw that they were in the ACTIVE state. Then, when
we stopped them, they ended up in the RESOLVED state. But what do
these states mean, and what transitions take a bundle from one state
to another?

To help clear this up, consider the state diagram in Figure 4.1, which
traces the stages of a bundle's life cycle.

When you first install a bundle into the OSGi framework, its state is INSTALLED. If all the bundle's dependencies (imported packages or required bundles) are already available in the framework, it will automatically transition to the RESOLVED state. Otherwise, it will remain in INSTALLED state until all of its dependencies are met or until it is uninstalled.

If you choose to uninstall a bundle, it will be removed from the framework. Once it is removed, there'll be no trace of its existence in the framework. Therefore, it's unlikely that you'll ever see a bundle in the UNINSTALLED state. UNINSTALLED is merely a placeholder for bundles that are no longer available.

A bundle in the RESOLVED state has all of its dependencies satisfied, but it hasn't been started. As we've already seen, the start command starts a bundle, transitioning it to ACTIVE, via the STARTING state. Likewise, issuing the stop command on a bundle transitions it back to the RESOLVED state, by way of the STOPPING state. Starting and stopping a bundle is typically a quick activity. This means that although it's possible to see a bundle in STARTING or STOPPING state, it's unlikely that you'll be able to catch most bundles in one of those transitional states.

What's not apparent in the state diagram is that most OSGi framework implementations will allow you to uninstall an active bundle. But even if the bundle is in the ACTIVE state when it is uninstalled, it will still transition from ACTIVE through STOPPING to RESOLVED and then to UNINSTALLED. This series of transitions is important because it may be necessary for a bundle activator's stop() method to be invoked prior to uninstallation so that the bundle can free up resources or perform other shutdown activity.

Now we've constructed our application's first bundle. It doesn't do much, but it is, nonetheless, a critical module in the application. Along the way, we came to know Pax Construct a bit more, learned to deal with the inevitable nonbundle dependency, and came to understand the life cycle of a bundle.

Coming up in the next chapter, we'll add another bundle to *Dude, Where's My JAR?* as we build the heart of the application: the index service. In doing so, we'll see how to publish services from OSGi bundles.

Chapter 5

OSGi Services

In the previous chapter, we created and installed a simple OSGi bundle that defined a domain class for *Dude, Where's My JAR?*. Now we're going to put that domain class to work. Because the focus of this chapter is OSGi's service layer, we're going to continue fleshing out the application by building a bundle that publishes the index service. The index service, as you may recall, is responsible for both adding JarFile entries to an index and searching the index for any JarFiles that meet given search criteria. Then we'll create the spider bundle that will use the index service to index JAR files that it finds while scouring Maven repositories.

5.1 Creating an OSGi Service

To get started with the index service, we'll use Pax Construct's pax-create-bundle script to generate the index bundle subproject. From within the top-level dwmj directory, run pax-create-bundle, specifying the bundle project's name, base package, Maven group ID, and version:

```
dwmj% pax-create-bundle -n index -p dwmj.index -g com.dudewheresmyjar \
?                       -v 1.0.0-SNAPSHOT
[INFO] Scanning for projects...
[INFO] ------------------------------------------------------------------------
[INFO] Building com.dudewheresmyjar.dwmj (OSGi project)
[INFO]     task-segment: [org.ops4j:maven-pax-plugin:1.4:create-bundle]
          (aggregator-style)
[INFO] ------------------------------------------------------------------------
[INFO] ------------------------------------------------------------------------
[INFO] BUILD SUCCESSFUL
[INFO] ------------------------------------------------------------------------
[INFO] Total time: 7 seconds
[INFO] Finished at: Fri Mar 06 15:58:08 CST 2009
[INFO] Final Memory: 10M/19M
[INFO] ------------------------------------------------------------------------
dwmj%
```

Just as when we created the domain bundle, pax-create-bundle will create a sample activator, service class, and service interface. We won't be
needing these, so go ahead and delete them. In their place, we'll create
a new activator, service class, and interface for the index service. Let's
start with the IndexService interface:

dwmj/index/src/main/java/dwmj/index/IndexService.java

```java
package dwmj.index;

import java.util.List;

import dwmj.domain.JarFile;

public interface IndexService {
    void addJarFile(JarFile jarFile);

    List<JarFile> findJarFiles(String searchString);

    void removeJarFile(JarFile jarFile);
}
```

As reflected in the IndexService interface, the index service does three
basic things: it indexes JAR files, searches for JAR files, and removes
JAR files from the index. Later in this chapter, we'll see how the spider
bundle calls addJarFile() to add JAR file metadata to the index. As for
the findJarFiles() method, we'll use that when we build the web layer of
the application.

But first things first. The IndexService interface isn't very useful by itself.
We'll also need an implementation class:

dwmj/index/src/main/java/dwmj/index/internal/IndexServiceImpl.java

```java
package dwmj.index.internal;

import java.util.ArrayList;
import java.util.List;

import org.compass.core.Compass;
import org.compass.core.CompassException;
import org.compass.core.CompassHit;
import org.compass.core.CompassHits;
import org.compass.core.CompassSession;
import org.compass.core.CompassTransaction;

import dwmj.domain.JarFile;
import dwmj.index.IndexService;

public class IndexServiceImpl implements IndexService {
    private final Compass compass;
```

```
public IndexServiceImpl(Compass compass) {
   this.compass = compass;
}

public void addJarFile(JarFile jarFile) {
   CompassSession session = null;
   CompassTransaction transaction = null;
   try {
      session = compass.openSession();
      transaction = session.beginTransaction();

      session.create(jarFile);
      transaction.commit();
   }
   catch (CompassException e) {
      if (transaction != null) {
         transaction.rollback();
      }
   }
   finally {
      if (session != null) {
         session.close();
      }
   }
}

public List<JarFile> findJarFiles(String searchString) {
   CompassSession session = compass.openSession();
   CompassTransaction transaction = session.beginTransaction();
   CompassHits hits = session.find(searchString);

   List<JarFile> jarFiles = new ArrayList<JarFile>(hits.getLength());
   for (CompassHit hit : hits) {
      jarFiles.add((JarFile) hit.getData());
   }

   transaction.commit();
   session.close();
   return jarFiles;
}

public void removeJarFile(JarFile jarFile) {
   CompassSession session = null;
   CompassTransaction transaction = null;
   try {
      session = compass.openSession();
      transaction = session.beginTransaction();
      session.delete(jarFile);
      transaction.commit();
   }
```

```
      catch (CompassException e) {
        if (transaction != null) {
          transaction.rollback();
        }
      }
      finally {
        if (session != null) {
          session.close();
        }
      }
    }
  }
}
```

You're welcome to scrutinize the internal details of IndexServiceImpl if you'd like—for the most part they're not pertinent to our exploration of OSGi. But the main thing to take note of here is that IndexServiceImpl makes heavy use of Compass and the domain bundle's JarFile class. This means that this bundle will need to import the packages from those bundles in its manifest. And we'll need to add those bundles to the project's pom.xml file so that their classes will be available at compile time.

The good news is that Pax Construct's Maven plugin will automatically add the Import-Package: headers that we need when we build the bundle. But we'll still need to add the dependencies to the pom.xml file. For that, we'll use Pax Construct's pax-import-bundle script. First, the Compass bundle:

```
index% pax-import-bundle -g com.dudewheresmyjar.dwmj \
?                        -a org.compass-project.compass -v 2.1.1-001-SNAPSHOT
[INFO] Scanning for projects...
[INFO] ------------------------------------------------------------------------
[INFO] Building com.dudewheresmyjar.index [dwmj.index]
[INFO]    task-segment: [org.ops4j:maven-pax-plugin:1.4:import-bundle]
          (aggregator-style)
[INFO] ------------------------------------------------------------------------
[INFO] [pax:import-bundle]
[WARNING] Problem resolving project
     com.dudewheresmyjar.dwmj:org.compass-project.compass:pom:2.1.1-001-SNAPSHO
[INFO] ------------------------------------------------------------------------
[INFO] BUILD SUCCESSFUL
[INFO] ------------------------------------------------------------------------
[INFO] Total time: 4 seconds
[INFO] Finished at: Fri Mar 06 16:18:56 CST 2009
[INFO] Final Memory: 8M/15M
[INFO] ------------------------------------------------------------------------
index%
```

And then the domain bundle:

```
index% pax-import-bundle -g com.dudewheresmyjar -a domain -v 1.0.0-SNAPSHOT
[INFO] Scanning for projects...
[INFO] ------------------------------------------------------------------------
[INFO] Building com.dudewheresmyjar.index [dwmj.index]
[INFO]    task-segment: [org.ops4j:maven-pax-plugin:1.4:import-bundle]
          (aggregator-style)
[INFO] ------------------------------------------------------------------------
[INFO] [pax:import-bundle]
[INFO] Adding com.dudewheresmyjar.domain [dwmj.domain] as dependency to
          com.dudewheresmyjar:index:bundle:1.0.0-SNAPSHOT
[INFO] ------------------------------------------------------------------------
[INFO] BUILD SUCCESSFUL
[INFO] ------------------------------------------------------------------------
[INFO] Total time: 5 seconds
[INFO] Finished at: Fri Mar 06 16:20:32 CST 2009
[INFO] Final Memory: 8M/19M
[INFO] ------------------------------------------------------------------------
index%
```

Now we have a service interface and implementation class. But if you take another look at those classes, you'll see that there's nothing special about them that makes them an OSGi service. They're just a plain-old Java class and a plain-old Java interface (POJO/POJI). That's a good thing because it demonstrates the lightweight nature—the OSGi API hasn't crept into our service implementation. But it also means that just writing a service class doesn't do anything to make it an OSGi service. We need something more to publish the service.

Publishing the Service with a Bundle Activator

The key to publishing a service is a bundle activator. We've already seen one bundle activator earlier in this book (see Section 2.3, *Publishing a Hello Service*, on page 30). The activator that we'll create to publish the index service is remarkably similar to that activator:

`dwmj/index/src/main/java/dwmj/index/internal/IndexServiceActivator.java`

```java
package dwmj.index.internal;

import org.compass.core.Compass;
import org.compass.core.config.CompassConfiguration;
import org.compass.core.config.CompassEnvironment;
import org.osgi.framework.BundleActivator;
import org.osgi.framework.BundleContext;

import dwmj.domain.JarFile;
import dwmj.index.IndexService;
```

```java
public final class IndexServiceActivator implements BundleActivator {
    public void start(BundleContext bc) throws Exception {
        IndexService indexService = new IndexServiceImpl(getCompass());
        bc.registerService(IndexService.class.getName(), indexService, null);
    }

    public void stop(BundleContext bc) throws Exception {
    // nothing to do!
    }

    private Compass getCompass() {
        String tempDir = System.getProperty("java.io.tmpdir");
        CompassConfiguration config = new CompassConfiguration().setSetting(
                CompassEnvironment.CONNECTION, tempDir + "/dudeindex")
            .addClass(JarFile.class);

        return config.buildCompass();
    }
}
```

When the index bundle is installed into the OSGi framework and is started, the start() method on the activator will be called. In this case, the activator will use the BundleContext given to the start() method to register the index service.

The first parameter given to registerService() is the name under which we'll register the service. In reality, we could register the service under any name. But if we were to pick any arbitrary name, we increase the opportunity for a name collision with another service that just happens to be registered under the same arbitrary name. Therefore, the convention agreed upon is to register the service using the fully qualified name of the interface that the service implements. In addition to avoiding name collisions, this convention also provides a way for a service consumer to locate services by their function (as defined by the interface).

As for the second parameter, it is an instance of the service implementation. In this case, there's nothing special—just a new instance of IndexServiceImpl. But you could use this opportunity to inject references to other services into the service before registering it with the OSGi service registry.

The third parameter is an optional set of properties (java.util.Properties) that will be attached to the service as it's registered. In this case, we had no need for any additional properties. But if we had registered the service with properties, a service consumer could use those properties when looking up a service from the service registry.

Joe Asks...

Must I Develop to the OSGi API?

If importing OSGi-specific classes and interfaces is troubling to you, then hang tight. You're only one chapter away from learning how to eliminate OSGi from Java code.

There's just one more thing we need to do to ensure that our index service will be published: add a Bundle-Activator: header to the bundle's manifest. But since we're relying on Pax Construct's Maven plugin to automatically generate the manifest for us, we'll need to add the Bundle-Activator: entry to the osgi.bnd file instead:

`dwmj/index/osgi.bnd`

```
Bundle-Activator: dwmj.index.internal.IndexServiceActivator
```

While we are editing osgi.bnd, we'll also want to remove the existing Bundle-Activator: entry referencing dwmj.index.internal.ExampleActivator. It was just a leftover entry from when pax-create-bundle first created the subproject.

Using the Logging Service

Now it seems that all of the pieces are in place for our index service. So, let's build it (using mvn install) and provision it:

```
index% cd ..
dwmj% pax-provision
[INFO] Scanning for projects...
...
osgi> ss

Framework is launched.

id      State      Bundle
0       ACTIVE     org.eclipse.osgi_3.4.2.R34x_v20080826-1230
1       ACTIVE     org.eclipse.osgi.util_3.1.300.v20080303
2       ACTIVE     org.eclipse.osgi.services_3.1.200.v20070605
3       ACTIVE     com.dudewheresmyjar.domain_1.0.0.SNAPSHOT
4       ACTIVE     org.compass-project.compass_2.1.1
5       RESOLVED   com.dudewheresmyjar.index_1.0.0.SNAPSHOT

osgi>
```

Oops! The index service was installed into the framework, and while it resolved (which means that it found all of its explicit dependencies), it failed to start. And there's no obvious indication as to why it didn't start. What can we do?

Unfortunately, the answer is not all that obvious. There's nothing in the exceptions and stack traces that make it clear what's going on. But I do know one thing: Compass uses Jakarta Commons Logging. If we start using Compass and Commons Logging isn't available, we're going to have some trouble.

As it is, the Compass bundle doesn't explicitly import packages for Commons Logging, so it resolves and starts with no problems. But as our index service is starting, it creates an instance of IndexServiceImpl, which immediately starts using Compass. With no Commons Logging available, an exception is thrown, and our index bundle fails to start.

So, if my educated hunch is right, adding Commons Logging should solve our problem. . . right?

Yes. . . and no. You see, the way that Commons Logging (and other logging libraries, for that matter) loads its loggers makes using it in OSGi tricky at best. Even so, many third-party libraries (such as Compass) are already coded to use Commons Logging or Log4J.

Meanwhile, the OSGi specification defines a central logging service. But most implementations of the OSGi logging service are too minimalistic to be of any practical use. What's more, Compass and other libraries weren't developed to use the OSGi logging service.

If Commons Logging is not OSGi friendly and Compass doesn't know how to use the OSGi logging service, then are we at an impasse?

Absolutely not! Pax Logging, another open source OSGi offering from the OPS4J folks, comes to the rescue. Pax Logging is an implementation and extension of the OSGi logging service that also provides familiar logging interfaces such as those from Commons Logging and Log4J. In short, it is a better implementation of both the OSGi logging service (because it offers a familiar interface) and Jakarta Commons Logging (because it is OSGi-friendly). When I put it that way, it sounds just like something that might be useful in our current circumstance.

So, let's add it to our project. First, we'll need to add the Pax Logging API, which offers us the familiar Commons Logging interface we need.

Within the top-level dwmj directory we'll use pax-import-bundle to add
Pax Logging to our project.

```
dwmj% pax-import-bundle -g org.ops4j.pax.logging -a pax-logging-api -v 1.3.0
[INFO] Scanning for projects...
[INFO] ------------------------------------------------------------------------
[INFO] Building com.dudewheresmyjar.dwmj (OSGi project)
[INFO]    task-segment: [org.ops4j:maven-pax-plugin:1.4:import-bundle]
         (aggregator-style)
[INFO] ------------------------------------------------------------------------
[INFO] [pax:import-bundle]
[INFO] Importing OPS4J Pax Logging - API to
         com.dudewheresmyjar.dwmj.build:provision:pom:1.0.0-SNAPSHOT
[INFO] ------------------------------------------------------------------------
[INFO] BUILD SUCCESSFUL
[INFO] ------------------------------------------------------------------------
[INFO] Total time: 5 seconds
[INFO] Finished at: Fri Mar 06 16:31:37 CST 2009
[INFO] Final Memory: 8M/19M
[INFO] ------------------------------------------------------------------------
dwmj%
```

As for the Pax Logging's implementation of the OSGi logging service, it's
contained in a separate bundle. So, we'll also need to add the logging
service bundle to our project:

```
dwmj% pax-import-bundle -g org.ops4j.pax.logging -a pax-logging-service -v 1.3.0
[INFO] Scanning for projects...
[INFO] ------------------------------------------------------------------------
[INFO] Building com.dudewheresmyjar.dwmj (OSGi project)
[INFO]    task-segment: [org.ops4j:maven-pax-plugin:1.4:import-bundle]
         (aggregator-style)
[INFO] ------------------------------------------------------------------------
[INFO] [pax:import-bundle]
[INFO] Importing OPS4J Pax Logging - Service to
         com.dudewheresmyjar.dwmj.build:provision:pom:1.0.0-SNAPSHOT
[INFO] ------------------------------------------------------------------------
[INFO] BUILD SUCCESSFUL
[INFO] ------------------------------------------------------------------------
[INFO] Total time: 4 seconds
[INFO] Finished at: Fri Mar 06 16:32:29 CST 2009
[INFO] Final Memory: 9M/16M
[INFO] ------------------------------------------------------------------------
dwmj%
```

Now to see whether it worked, let's try building and provisioning the
index bundle again:

```
dwmj% pax-provision
[INFO] Scanning for projects...
...
[Start Level Event Dispatcher]
```

```
      DEBUG org.compass.core.util.reflection.ReflectionFactory -
Failed to generate ASM (should have worked...) for constructor
    [public dwmj.domain.JarFile()]
java.lang.NoSuchMethodException: Can't create ASM constructor reflection
    helper for [public dwmj.domain.JarFile()]
...
Caused by: java.lang.NoClassDefFoundError: org/apache/lucene/index/IndexWriter
        at org.compass.core.lucene.engine.LuceneSettings.configure()
        at org.compass.core.lucene.engine.LuceneSearchEngineFactory.<init>()
    at org.compass.core.impl.DefaultCompass.<init>()
    at org.compass.core.impl.DefaultCompass.<init>()
    at org.compass.core.config.CompassConfiguration.buildCompass()
    at dwmj.index.internal.IndexServiceActivator.getCompass()
    at dwmj.index.internal.IndexServiceActivator.start()
    at org.eclipse.osgi.framework.internal.core.BundleContextImpl$2.run()
    at java.security.AccessController.doPrivileged()
    at org.eclipse.osgi.framework.internal.core.
          BundleContextImpl.startActivator()
        ... 10 more
[Framework Event Dispatcher] DEBUG org.eclipse.osgi - FrameworkEvent STARTLEVEL
    CHANGED
```

```
osgi>
```

The good news is that it seems that adding Pax Logging addressed our concerns about logging. The bad news is that our index bundle still doesn't start. But this time it fails for a different reason and with an exception to work with. It seems that Compass is having trouble finding the IndexWriter class from Apache Lucene.

Embedding Lucene

It makes sense that Compass might complain that it can't find classes from Lucene. After all, Compass is an object-to-Lucene mapping framework. Under the hood, it uses Lucene to do the actual indexing and searching work. Since we've not installed Lucene into the OSGi framework, Compass won't be able to find it.

No problem! Let's use pax-wrap-jar to wrap the Lucene JAR as an OSGi bundle to be provisioned along with our other bundles.

But wait a minute. Before we get too carried away, let's give this a bit more thought. Compass does depend on Lucene—but our application does not (at least not directly). Moreover, Compass 2.1.1 was built and tested against a specific version of Lucene (2.4.0), making it unlikely that we'd ever want to use a different version of Lucene. Therefore, since Compass is the only bundle in our application that needs Lucene and since it is based on a specific version of Lucene, then why not embed Lucene within Compass instead of wrapping it? At very least, embedding Lucene will give us one less bundle to manage.

As you'll recall from the previous chapter, the pax-embed-jar script is the Pax Construct script used to embed a JAR within a bundle project. From within the org.compass-project.compass subproject directory, we ask pax-embed-jar to perform its magic:

```
org.compass-project.compass% pax-embed-jar -g org.apache.lucene -a lucene-core \
?                                          -v 2.4.0
[INFO] Scanning for projects...
[INFO] ------------------------------------------------------------------------
[INFO] Building org.compass-project.compass 2.1.1 [osgi]
[INFO]    task-segment: [org.ops4j:maven-pax-plugin:1.4:embed-jar]
          (aggregator-style)
[INFO] ------------------------------------------------------------------------
[INFO] [pax:embed-jar]
[INFO] Embedding org.apache.lucene:lucene-core:2.4.0 in
      com.dudewheresmyjar.dwmj:org.compass-project.compass:bundle:2.1.1-001-SNAPSHOT
[INFO] ------------------------------------------------------------------------
[INFO] BUILD SUCCESSFUL
[INFO] ------------------------------------------------------------------------
[INFO] Total time: 4 seconds
[INFO] Finished at: Fri Mar 06 16:34:40 CST 2009
[INFO] Final Memory: 8M/16M
[INFO] ------------------------------------------------------------------------
org.compass-project.compass%
```

After a few seconds, pax-embed-jar completes successfully. Lucene 2.4.0 should be contained within the Compass bundle. After building the Compass bundle (using mvn install), cross your fingers and try to provision all our application's bundles one more time:

```
dwmj% pax-provision
[INFO] Scanning for projects...
...
osgi> ss

Framework is launched.

id       State        Bundle
0        ACTIVE       org.eclipse.osgi_3.4.2.R34x_v20080826-1230
1        ACTIVE       org.eclipse.osgi.util_3.1.300.v20080303
2        ACTIVE       org.eclipse.osgi.services_3.1.200.v20070605
3        ACTIVE       org.ops4j.pax.logging.pax-logging-api_1.3.0
4        ACTIVE       org.ops4j.pax.logging.pax-logging-service_1.3.0
5        ACTIVE       com.dudewheresmyjar.domain_1.0.0.SNAPSHOT
6        ACTIVE       org.compass-project.compass_2.1.1
7        ACTIVE       com.dudewheresmyjar.index_1.0.0.SNAPSHOT

osgi>
```

Woo-hoo! As you can see, all of our bundles are active. But was the index service published? Let's use the bundle command in Equinox to find out:

```
osgi> bundle 7
initial@reference:file:com.dudewheresmyjar.index_1.0.0.SNAPSHOT.jar/ [7]
  Id=7, Status=ACTIVE      Data Root=/Users/wallsc/Projects/projects/dwmj/runner/
          equinox/org.eclipse.osgi/bundles/7/data
  Registered Services
    {dwmj.index.IndexService}={service.id=24}
  No services in use.
  Exported packages
    dwmj.index; version="1.0.0.SNAPSHOT"[exported]
  Imported packages
    dwmj.domain; version="1.0.0.SNAPSHOT"<initial@reference:file:
          com.dudewheresmyjar.domain_1.0.0.SNAPSHOT.jar/ [5]>
    org.compass.core; version="0.0.0"<initial@reference:file:
          org.compass-project.compass_2.1.1.jar/ [6]>
    org.compass.core.config; version="0.0.0"<initial@reference:file:
          org.compass-project.compass_2.1.1.jar/ [6]>
    org.osgi.framework; version="1.4.0"<System Bundle [0]>
  No fragment bundles
  Named class space
    com.dudewheresmyjar.index; bundle-version="1.0.0.SNAPSHOT"[provided]
  No required bundles

osgi>
```

And there you have it! Under the *Registered Services* header, we find that a service has, in fact, been registered with the fully qualified name of the IndexService interface. The index service is open for business.

Later in this chapter, we're going to build the spider bundle, a bundle that will consume the index service. And later, we'll build the web front end of the application that will use the index service to search for artifacts. But first, let's write an integration test to drive the index service and assert that it does what we want it to do.

5.2 Testing the Service

When testing the index service, we could (and perhaps should) write a unit test against IndexServiceImpl that mocks the Compass object given to the constructor. But that sort of test would only be able to confirm that IndexServiceImpl interacts with Compass in the way that we think it should. It does not assert that those interactions accomplish the functionality that we desire from the index service.

Pax Exam vs. Spring-DM's Testing Support

I should mention that Pax Exam isn't the only way to test OSGi bundles within an OSGi framework. Spring-DM also comes with bundle-level testing support that is conceptually very similar to what Pax Exam offers.

In fact, it could be argued that Spring-DM's testing support is better than Pax Exam because it takes advantage of Spring autowiring to eliminate the need to look up services from the OSGi service registry.

Although autowiring of services into tests is certainly a nice thing to have, Spring-DM's testing support is based on JUnit 3, which (in my opinion) makes it awkward to work with. Spring-DM has slated support for JUnit 4 (and TestNG) in version 2.0.0. But until then, I'll take Pax Exam's JUnit 4–style tests over Spring-DM's autowiring of services.

To be sure that index service is truly doing what we expect it to do, we should test the index service in a context that includes the other objects that it collaborates with. More specifically, we should test the index service bundle within the OSGi framework along with the other bundles that it depends upon. In short, we should write an integration test.

That's where we add Pax Exam to our OSGi toolbox. Pax Exam is an integration testing framework, based on JUnit, that enables in-framework testing of OSGi bundles. What's especially interesting about Pax Exam, as you'll soon see, is that instead of deploying bundles into the framework and then observing them from outside, Pax Exam test cases are actually deployed into the framework alongside the bundles it is testing.

As we'll soon see, Pax Exam test cases depend on ready-to-deploy bundles. Therefore, we can't add the test to the index service bundle project —the index service bundle will not have been built by the time the test case is run. Instead, we'll create a separate project to own the tests for the bundles.

Setting Up the Test Project

First, let's do some basic project setup, starting with the project directory structure. Because the tests will be run as part of a Maven 2 build, we'll need to set up the basic Maven 2 project structure to house the tests:

```
dwmj% mkdir -p bundle-tests/src/test/java
```

Next, let's create the Maven pom.xml file:

dwmj/bundle-tests/pom.xml

```
<project xsi:schemaLocation="http://maven.apache.org/POM/4.0.0
    http://maven.apache.org/maven-v4_0_0.xsd"
    xmlns="http://maven.apache.org/POM/4.0.0"
    xmlns:xsi="http://www.w3.org/2001/XMLSchema-instance">

  <parent>
    <relativePath>../poms/compiled/</relativePath>
    <groupId>com.dudewheresmyjar.dude.build</groupId>
    <artifactId>compiled-bundle-settings</artifactId>
    <version>1.0.0-SNAPSHOT</version>
  </parent>

  <modelVersion>4.0.0</modelVersion>
  <groupId>com.dudewheresmyjar</groupId>
  <artifactId>bundle-tests</artifactId>
  <version>1.0.0-SNAPSHOT</version>

  <packaging>jar</packaging>

  <dependencies>
    <dependency>
      <groupId>com.dudewheresmyjar</groupId>
      <artifactId>index</artifactId>
      <version>1.0.0-SNAPSHOT</version>
      <scope>test</scope>
    </dependency>
    <dependency>
      <groupId>com.dudewheresmyjar</groupId>
      <artifactId>domain</artifactId>
      <version>1.0.0-SNAPSHOT</version>
      <scope>test</scope>
    </dependency>
    <dependency>
      <groupId>com.dudewheresmyjar.dude</groupId>
      <artifactId>org.compass-project.compass</artifactId>
      <version>2.1.1-SNAPSHOT</version>
      <scope>test</scope>
    </dependency>
  </project>
```

The key pieces of this pom.xml file are the dependencies. Here I've included the two bundles that we've created so far (because the test will use classes from those bundles) and the Compass bundle (because there will be a transitive dependency between the test and Compass).

We'll also need to add Pax Exam. This includes the following Maven dependencies:

dwmj/bundle-tests/pom.xml

```xml
  <dependency>
    <groupId>org.ops4j.pax.exam</groupId>
    <artifactId>pax-exam</artifactId>
    <version>0.3.0</version>
    <scope>test</scope>
  </dependency>
  <dependency>
    <groupId>org.ops4j.pax.exam</groupId>
    <artifactId>pax-exam-container-default</artifactId>
    <version>0.3.0</version>
    <scope>test</scope>
  </dependency>
  <dependency>
    <groupId>org.ops4j.pax.exam</groupId>
    <artifactId>pax-exam-junit</artifactId>
    <version>0.3.0</version>
    <scope>test</scope>
  </dependency>
  <dependency>
    <groupId>org.ops4j.pax.exam</groupId>
    <artifactId>pax-exam-junit-extender-impl</artifactId>
    <version>0.3.0</version>
    <scope>test</scope>
  </dependency>
  <dependency>
    <groupId>org.ops4j.pax.url</groupId>
    <artifactId>pax-url-dir</artifactId>
    <version>0.4.0</version>
    <scope>test</scope>
  </dependency>
</dependencies>

<repositories>
  <repository>
    <id>OPS4J</id>
    <url>http://repository.ops4j.org/maven2</url>
    <snapshots>
      <enabled>true</enabled>
    </snapshots>
  </repository>
</repositories>
```

Testing the Bundle Context

Now the basic project structure has been set up, and we're ready to write the bundle test, IndexServiceBundleTest:

`dwmj/bundle-tests/src/test/java/dwmj/index/test/IndexServiceBundleTest.java`

```java
package dwmj.index.test;

import static org.junit.Assert.assertEquals;
import static org.junit.Assert.assertNotNull;
import static org.ops4j.pax.exam.CoreOptions.equinox;
import static org.ops4j.pax.exam.CoreOptions.mavenBundle;
import static org.ops4j.pax.exam.CoreOptions.options;
import static org.ops4j.pax.exam.CoreOptions.provision;

import java.util.List;

import org.junit.Test;
import org.junit.runner.RunWith;
import org.ops4j.pax.exam.Inject;
import org.ops4j.pax.exam.Option;
import org.ops4j.pax.exam.junit.Configuration;
import org.ops4j.pax.exam.junit.JUnit4TestRunner;
import org.osgi.framework.BundleContext;
import org.osgi.util.tracker.ServiceTracker;

import dwmj.domain.JarFile;
import dwmj.index.IndexService;

@RunWith(JUnit4TestRunner.class)
public class IndexServiceBundleTest {
    @Inject
    private BundleContext bundleContext;
// ...
}
```

Pax Exam test cases are just JUnit 4 test cases that use a special test runner called JUnit4TestRunner. This test runner is designed to fire up one or more OSGi framework implementations, install a set of bundles, and then wrap up the test class itself within an on-the-fly bundle that runs inside the OSGi framework alongside the bundles that are being tested.

The first element of this test class is a private BundleContext variable that's annotated with @Inject. The @Inject annotation tells Pax Exam to automatically inject the on-the-fly bundle's BundleContext so that we can use it in our tests.

To tell Pax Exam how to set up the OSGi framework and bundles, we must create a method that returns an array of Options and annotate it with @Configuration. For our test case, we're going to run the test in Equinox with our domain and index bundles. We'll also need the wrapped Compass bundle and Pax Logging installed. Here's a configuration method that sets up the test case:

`dwmj/bundle-tests/src/test/java/dwmj/index/test/IndexServiceBundleTest.java`

```java
@Configuration
public static Option[] configuration()
{
    return options(equinox(), provision(
        mavenBundle().groupId("org.ops4j.pax.logging").
            artifactId("pax-logging-service"),
        mavenBundle().groupId("org.ops4j.pax.logging").artifactId("pax-logging-api"),
        mavenBundle().groupId("com.dudewheresmyjar").artifactId("domain"),
        mavenBundle().groupId("com.dudewheresmyjar").artifactId("index"),
        mavenBundle().groupId("com.dudewheresmyjar.dude").
            artifactId("org.compass-project.compass").version("2.1.1-SNAPSHOT")
        ));
}
```

Pax Exam provides for test configuration through a fluent interface that starts with the options() method. This method takes one or more configuration items.

In this case, we're giving it two such items: a call to equinox() to indicate that we want the test to run in the latest supported version of Equinox and a call to provision() to itemize the bundles to install. As parameters to provision(), we're using mavenBundle(), which identifies bundles to install given their Maven group ID, artifact ID, and (optionally) version.

What's not shown here is that we could also run these tests in Felix or Knopflerfish by adding felix() and/or knopflerfish() as parameters to options(). For example:

`dwmj/bundle-tests/src/test/java/dwmj/index/test/IndexServiceBundleTest.java`

```java
@Configuration
public static Option[] configuration()
{
    return options(equinox(), felix(), knopflerfish(), provision(
        ...
        ));
}
```

With the configuration method in place, let's write the first test method. We'll start slow with a test that asserts that the BundleContext was injected:

```
dwmj/bundle-tests/src/test/java/dwmj/index/test/IndexServiceBundleTest.java
@Test
public void bundleContextShouldNotBeNull() {
    assertNotNull(bundleContext);
}
```

As with any JUnit 4 test case, test methods in a Pax Exam test case are annotated with @Test. The bundleContextShouldNotBeNull() method simply asserts that the BundleContext isn't **null**. Had the test setup failed for any reason, the on-the-fly bundle would not be created and installed, and this test would fail.

This humble little test method doesn't really test much at all—and it certainly doesn't make any assertions about the index service. But before we write any more test methods, let's get some quick gratification by running the test and seeing it pass. The test should run in the IDE of your choice, but I'll leave it up to you to try it in the IDE. Instead, I'll run the test through Maven with Maven's test goal:

```
bundle-tests% mvn test
[INFO] Scanning for projects...
...
[PaxRunnerTestContainer] - Starting up the test container (Pax Runner 0.17.2 )
[     ConfigurationImpl] - Using config [classpath:META-INF/runner.properties]
[                  Run] - Using only arguments from command line
...
[           PlatformImpl] - Preparing framework [Equinox 3.4.1]
[           PlatformImpl] - Downloading bundles...
[            StreamUtils] - Equinox 3.4.1 (v20080826) : downloading...
[            StreamUtils] - Equinox 3.4.1 (v20080826) : 997883 bytes @ [ 6929kBps
...
Tests run: 1, Failures: 0, Errors: 0, Skipped: 0, Time elapsed: 17.551 sec

Results :

Tests run: 1, Failures: 0, Errors: 0, Skipped: 0

[INFO] ------------------------------------------------------------------------
[INFO] BUILD SUCCESSFUL
[INFO] ------------------------------------------------------------------------
[INFO] Total time: 21 seconds
[INFO] Finished at: Fri Mar 06 16:54:53 CST 2009
[INFO] Final Memory: 10M/23M
[INFO] ------------------------------------------------------------------------
bundle-tests%
```

It looks like the test passed with flying colors. But if you look close, you'll see something even more interesting. As the test is run, Pax Exam starts the OSGi framework (in this case, Equinox) and then installs and starts several bundles. Among the bundles started is one that Pax Exam generates on the fly that contains IndexServiceBundleTest. As a result, IndexServiceBundleTest will be able to interact with the index service through the OSGi framework, the same way that the real consumers of the index service will.

Speaking of testing the index service, we need to write another test method to assert that the index service is actually doing its job.

Testing the Index Service

To test the index service, we'll need to write a test method that retrieves a reference to the service through the OSGi service registry and then exercises the methods on the index service. The following test method does just that:

dwmj/bundle-tests/src/test/java/dwmj/index/test/IndexServiceBundleTest.java

```java
@Test
public void shouldIndexAndFindAJarFileObject() throws Exception {
    IndexService indexService = retrieveIndexService();

    JarFile jarFile = new JarFile();
    jarFile.setRepository("http://repo1.maven.org/maven2");
    jarFile.setGroupId("com.dudewheresmyjar");
    jarFile.setArtifactId("domain");
    jarFile.setVersion("1.0.0");
    jarFile.setRawUrl(
            "http://repo1.maven.org/maven2/com/dudewheresmyjar/domain/1.0.0");

    indexService.addJarFile(jarFile);

    List<JarFile> foundJarFiles = indexService.findJarFiles("domain");
    assertEquals(1, foundJarFiles.size());

    JarFile foundJarFile = foundJarFiles.get(0);
    assertEquals(jarFile.getRepository(), foundJarFile.getRepository());
    assertEquals(jarFile.getGroupId(), foundJarFile.getGroupId());
    assertEquals(jarFile.getArtifactId(), foundJarFile.getArtifactId());
    assertEquals(jarFile.getVersion(), foundJarFile.getVersion());

    indexService.removeJarFile(foundJarFile);
    foundJarFiles = indexService.findJarFiles("domain");
    assertEquals(0, foundJarFiles.size());
}
```

This test method is a bit more interesting than the first. It starts by retrieving a reference to the index service (by calling retrieveIndexService(), which we'll see in a moment) and asserting that it isn't null. Then it creates a test JarFile instance and asks the index service to index it. Next, it searches the index and asserts that the JarFile that was originally indexed can be found. Finally, it cleans up after itself by removing the JarFile from the index and then asserting that it won't be found if searched for again.

As for the retrieveIndexService() method, it looks like this:

```
dwmj/bundle-tests/src/test/java/dwmj/index/test/IndexServiceBundleTest.java
```

```java
private IndexService retrieveIndexService() throws InterruptedException {
    ServiceTracker tracker = new ServiceTracker(bundleContext,
            IndexService.class.getName(), null);
    tracker.open();
    IndexService indexService = (IndexService) tracker.waitForService(5000);
    tracker.close();
    assertNotNull(indexService);
    return indexService;
}
```

This method uses a service tracker to look up the index service from the OSGi service repository. We'll talk a bit more about service trackers in Section 5.3, *Using Service Trackers*, on page 96.

But for now, the only thing left to do is to see this test pass. So, let's kick off the Maven test goal again:

```
bundle-tests% mvn test
[INFO] Scanning for projects...
...

Tests run: 2, Failures: 0, Errors: 0, Skipped: 0, Time elapsed: 22.442 sec

Results :

Tests run: 2, Failures: 0, Errors: 0, Skipped: 0

[INFO] ------------------------------------------------------------------------
[INFO] BUILD SUCCESSFUL
[INFO] ------------------------------------------------------------------------
[INFO] Total time: 26 seconds
[INFO] Finished at: Fri Mar 06 16:59:08 CST 2009
[INFO] Final Memory: 10M/22M
[INFO] ------------------------------------------------------------------------
bundle-tests%
```

For brevity's sake, I've cut out most of the output produced when running the test. But the punch line is the same: the test passes. Therefore, we know that our index service is working correctly (or at least within the expectations of the shouldIndexAndFindAJarFileObject() method). As we continue to develop the application, we'll know whether the changes we make break the index service, because this test will be the first to complain.

Our application is really starting to take shape. In this chapter, we added another bundle to the mix—this time with a service published in the OSGi service registry. And even though we haven't yet developed any bundles that consume that service, we've been able to test drive it with an integration test driven by Pax Exam.

But a service isn't any good unless someone uses it. Let's build something that uses the index service.

5.3 Consuming OSGi Services

As you'll recall from Chapter 3, *Dude, Where's My JAR?*, on page 39, the index service will ultimately have two consumers: the web front end and the repository spider. The web front end will use the index service to look search for JAR files that meet a user's criteria. The spider will use the index service to stock the search engine's index with the JAR files that it finds in Maven repositories. We'll get to the web front end later in Chapter 7, *Creating Web Bundles*, on page 127. But we'll go ahead and build the spider now.

First things first...the repository spider represents another module of our application and thus will be contained within its own bundle. Therefore, we'll need to create a new bundle project. Once again, we call on the pax-create-bundle script:

```
dwmj% pax-create-bundle -g com.dudewheresmyjar -p dwmj.spider -n spider \
?                       -v 1.0.0-SNAPSHOT
[INFO] Scanning for projects...
...
[INFO] Archetype created in dir: /Users/wallsc/Projects/projects/dwmj/spider
[INFO] ------------------------------------------------------------------------
[INFO] BUILD SUCCESSFUL
[INFO] ------------------------------------------------------------------------
[INFO] Total time: 8 seconds
[INFO] Finished at: Sat Mar 07 16:43:22 CST 2009
[INFO] Final Memory: 10M/19M
[INFO] ------------------------------------------------------------------------
dwmj%
```

As usual, pax-create-bundle adds an example service, service interface, and activator to the generated project. Go ahead and remove them, and we'll be ready to develop the spider bundle.

Using Service Trackers

The first thing we'll need to do is to create the spider implementation class. Spidering a Maven repository is quite involved. For the purposes of our application, this involves several steps such as parsing POM files, reading a JAR file's contents, and extracting information from a JAR's META-INF/MANIFEST.MF file. For the most part, however, the functionality of the spider has nothing to do with OSGi. Therefore, in the interest of saving space and to keep our focus on consuming services, I'm going to show only the parts of the spider that are pertinent to the topic of consuming OSGi services.[1]

`dwmj/spider/src/main/java/dwmj/spider/internal/MavenSpider.java`

```java
package dwmj.spider.internal;

import java.io.IOException;
import java.io.InputStream;
import java.io.InputStreamReader;
import java.net.URL;

import javax.swing.text.MutableAttributeSet;
import javax.swing.text.html.HTML;
import javax.swing.text.html.HTMLEditorKit;
import javax.swing.text.html.HTML.Tag;
import javax.swing.text.html.HTMLEditorKit.Parser;
import javax.swing.text.html.HTMLEditorKit.ParserCallback;

import org.osgi.util.tracker.ServiceTracker;

import dwmj.domain.JarFile;
import dwmj.index.IndexService;

public class MavenSpider implements Runnable {
    private JarFilePopulator[] jarFilePopulators = new JarFilePopulator[] {};
    private final ServiceTracker indexServiceTracker;
    private String repositoryUrl;
    private boolean active;

    public MavenSpider(ServiceTracker indexServiceTracker) {
        this.indexServiceTracker = indexServiceTracker;
    }
```

---

1. Remember, you can download the complete source code from http://www.pragprog.com/titles/cwosg/source_code.

```java
    public void setRepositoryUrl(String repositoryUrl) {
        this.repositoryUrl = repositoryUrl;
    }

    // ...
    private void handleJarFile(String jarUrl) {
        // ...
            IndexService indexService =
                (IndexService) indexServiceTracker.getService();

            if(indexService != null) {
                indexService.addJarFile(jarFile);
            }
    }

    // ...
}
```

The MavenSpider class is constructed by passing in a service tracker. You're probably wondering what this odd little class is for. Ultimately, doesn't MavenSpider need the index service? Why not just give it the index service straightaway? Why all of the indirection?

OSGi services are a tricky bunch. They can come and go at any time. There's no way to be sure that if we give an index service to the MavenSpider at creation that the index service will still be around when we're ready to use it. For that matter, there's no guarantee that the index service is even available when we create the MavenSpider.

Rather than putting MavenSpider in the awkward position of having to manage the comings and goings of the index service, we will use a service tracker. Service trackers contain all of the magic to keep track of whether a service is available, and they hide away the complexity of dealing with the OSGi service registry through lower-level APIs. MavenSpider is given a service tracker that keeps track of the index service and, upon request through the getService() method, provides the index service so that we can add a JarFile to the index.

Even though the service tracker abstracts away any unpleasantness of dealing with the service registry's low-level APIs, getService() could still return null if the service is unavailable. So, we will need to check for a null service before calling addJarFile(). But if you'd rather wait for the service to become available, we could call waitForService() instead of getService().

> **Caution: Don't Dawdle in an Activator**
>
> The waitForService() method will block until a service is available or the specified timeout has passed. For that reason, avoid specifying a long timeout when using waitForService() in an activator's start() or stop() method. If the service isn't available, the bundle will get stuck in STARTING or STOPPING state while transitioning to or from an ACTIVE state.

dwmj/spider/src/main/java/dwmj/spider/internal/MavenSpider.java

```java
try {
    IndexService indexService =
        (IndexService) indexServiceTracker.waitForService(10000);

    // ...
}
catch (InterruptedException e) {
    // handle exception
}
```

Unlike getService(), which returns immediately, waitForService() will wait for a service to become available, up to a specified timeout (in milliseconds). In this case, waitForService() will wait up to ten seconds for the service to become available before giving up. A timeout of zero tells waitForService() to wait indefinitely.

Now that we've spent some time looking at how to use a service tracker to look up a service from the OSGi registry, you're probably wondering where that service tracker comes from. For the answer to that, look no further than SpiderActivator, the spider bundle's activator:

dwmj/spider/src/main/java/dwmj/spider/internal/SpiderActivator.java

```java
package dwmj.spider.internal;

import org.osgi.framework.BundleActivator;
import org.osgi.framework.BundleContext;
import org.osgi.util.tracker.ServiceTracker;

import dwmj.index.IndexService;

public final class SpiderActivator implements BundleActivator {
    private ServiceTracker indexServiceTracker;

    private static String[] REPOSITORIES = new String[] {
        "http://www.dudewheresmyjar.com/repo/" };
```

```
private static JarFilePopulator[] POPULATORS = new JarFilePopulator[] {
    new PomBasedJarFilePopulator(), new JarContentBasedJarFilePopulator()
};

private final MavenSpider[] spiders = new MavenSpider[REPOSITORIES.length];

public void start(BundleContext context) throws Exception {
    indexServiceTracker = new ServiceTracker(context, IndexService.class
                .getName(), null);
    indexServiceTracker.open();

    for (int i = 0; i < REPOSITORIES.length; i++) {
        MavenSpider spider = new MavenSpider(indexServiceTracker);
        spider.setRepositoryUrl(REPOSITORIES[i]);
        spider.setJarFilePopulators(POPULATORS);

        Thread thread = new Thread(spider);
        thread.start();
    }
}

public void stop(BundleContext context) throws Exception {
    for (int i = 0; i < spiders.length; i++) {
        spiders[i].stop();
    }
    indexServiceTracker.close();
}
}
```

SpiderActivator's main job is to create an instance of MavenSpider for each
Maven repository that will be crawled (in this case, an artificial repos-
itory). But first, it creates a service tracker to track the index service.
The constructor for ServiceTracker takes three parameters:

- The bundle context

- The name of the service to be tracked

- An optional service tracker customizer (org.osgi.util.tracker.
  ServiceTrackerCustomizer)

Since we need to track the index service, we pass in the bundle context
and the fully qualified name of the IndexService interface.

As for the third parameter, ServiceTrackerCustomizer is an odd little interface that lets us hook into the service tracker to monitor when services
are added, removed, or modified. We won't need a service tracker customizer, though—so we'll give it a null service tracker customizer.

The last thing that the activator does is create a MavenSpider instance
for each of the repositories and sends them off to crawl. So that the

Please Don't Crawl IBiblio

As a consequence of crawling a repository, the spider generates a lot of traffic. Maven repositories are geared toward serving occasional requests for Java libraries but may not be prepared to handle a barrage of requests from our spider.

Please be a good citizen, and do not configure the spider to crawl the central repository at IBiblio or any other repository that you do not have express permission to crawl. Or better yet, set up a local repository, and set the spider bundle to crawl it.

start() method can finish without waiting for the crawlers (Maven repositories are large—it might take awhile), SpiderActivator fires off a thread for each spider to crawl in.

The spider bundle is almost complete. The only thing left to do is to register SpiderActivator as the bundle's activator by adding a line in the BND instruction file:

dwmj/spider/osgi.bnd

```
Bundle-Activator: dwmj.spider.internal.SpiderActivator
```

All of the bundle's pieces are in place. We're almost ready to build and deploy the spider bundle and watch it crawl a repository.

Deploying the Spider Bundle

There's only one more thing to do before we can build the spider bundle. Since the spider directly depends on classes and interfaces from the domain and index bundles, we'll need to make sure that they're in the compile-time classpath. For that, we'll use Pax Construct's pax-add-dependency script. First, we'll add the domain bundle as a dependency to the spider bundle:

```
spider% pax-import-bundle -g com.dudewheresmyjar -a domain -v 1.0.0-SNAPSHOT
[INFO] Scanning for projects...
[INFO] ------------------------------------------------------------------------
[INFO] Building com.dudewheresmyjar.spider [dwmj.spider]
[INFO]    task-segment: [org.ops4j:maven-pax-plugin:1.4:import-bundle]
          (aggregator-style)
[INFO] ------------------------------------------------------------------------
[INFO] [pax:import-bundle]
[INFO] Adding com.dudewheresmyjar.domain [dwmj.domain] as dependency to
          com.dudewheresmyjar:spider:bundle:1.0.0-SNAPSHOT
```

```
[INFO] ------------------------------------------------------------------------
[INFO] BUILD SUCCESSFUL
[INFO] ------------------------------------------------------------------------
[INFO] Total time: 5 seconds
[INFO] Finished at: Sat Mar 07 21:52:40 CST 2009
[INFO] Final Memory: 8M/18M
[INFO] ------------------------------------------------------------------------
spider%
```

Then we'll add the index bundle:

```
spider% pax-import-bundle -g com.dudewheresmyjar -a index -v 1.0.0-SNAPSHOT
[INFO] Scanning for projects...
[INFO] ------------------------------------------------------------------------
[INFO] Building com.dudewheresmyjar.spider [dwmj.spider]
[INFO]    task-segment: [org.ops4j:maven-pax-plugin:1.4:import-bundle]
          (aggregator-style)
[INFO] ------------------------------------------------------------------------
[INFO] [pax:import-bundle]
[INFO] Adding com.dudewheresmyjar.index [dwmj.index] as dependency to
          com.dudewheresmyjar:spider:bundle:1.0.0-SNAPSHOT
[INFO] ------------------------------------------------------------------------
[INFO] BUILD SUCCESSFUL
[INFO] ------------------------------------------------------------------------
[INFO] Total time: 5 seconds
[INFO] Finished at: Sat Mar 07 21:53:00 CST 2009
[INFO] Final Memory: 8M/18M
[INFO] ------------------------------------------------------------------------
spider%
```

The pax-add-dependency script should have added the domain and index bundles as <dependency>s in the spider bundle's pom.xml file. Now
that the spider bundle is set dependency-wise, let's try building it:

```
spider% mvn install
[INFO] Scanning for projects...
[INFO] ------------------------------------------------------------------------
[INFO] Building com.dudewheresmyjar.spider [dwmj.spider]
[INFO]    task-segment: [install]
[INFO] ------------------------------------------------------------------------
...
[INFO] ------------------------------------------------------------------------
[INFO] BUILD SUCCESSFUL
[INFO] ------------------------------------------------------------------------
[INFO] Total time: 9 seconds
[INFO] Finished at: Sat Mar 07 22:01:03 CST 2009
[INFO] Final Memory: 14M/31M
[INFO] ------------------------------------------------------------------------
spider%
```

Good deal! The spider bundle was successfully built.

Now we're ready to provision it and see whether it works:

```
dwmj% pax-provision
[INFO] Scanning for projects...
...
osgi> ss

Framework is launched.

id      State       Bundle
0       ACTIVE      org.eclipse.osgi_3.4.2.R34x_v20080826-1230
1       ACTIVE      org.eclipse.osgi.util_3.1.300.v20080303
2       ACTIVE      org.eclipse.osgi.services_3.1.200.v20070605
3       ACTIVE      org.ops4j.pax.logging.pax-logging-api_1.3.0
4       ACTIVE      org.ops4j.pax.logging.pax-logging-service_1.3.0
5       ACTIVE      com.dudewheresmyjar.domain_1.0.0.SNAPSHOT
6       ACTIVE      org.compass-project.compass_2.1.1
7       ACTIVE      com.dudewheresmyjar.index_1.0.0.SNAPSHOT
8       ACTIVE      com.dudewheresmyjar.spider_1.0.0.SNAPSHOT

osgi>
```

After running pax-provision and using the Equinox ss command, you'll
see that the spider bundle was installed and started. Moreover, if you
issue the bundle command to view the spider bundle's information. . .

```
osgi> bundle 8
initial@reference:file:com.dudewheresmyjar.spider_1.0.0.SNAPSHOT.jar/ [8]
  Id=8, Status=ACTIVE      Data Root=/Users/wallsc/Projects/projects/dwmj/runne
          equinox/org.eclipse.osgi/bundles/8/data
  No registered services.
  Services in use:
    {dwmj.index.IndexService}={service.id=24}
  Exported packages
    dwmj.spider.impl; version="1.0.0.SNAPSHOT"[exported]
  Imported packages
    dwmj.domain; version="1.0.0.SNAPSHOT"<initial@reference:file:
            com.dudewheresmyjar.domain_1.0.0.SNAPSHOT.jar/ [5]>
    dwmj.index; version="1.0.0.SNAPSHOT"<initial@reference:file:
            com.dudewheresmyjar.index_1.0.0.SNAPSHOT.jar/ [7]>
    javax.swing.text; version="0.0.0"<System Bundle [0]>
    javax.swing.text.html; version="0.0.0"<System Bundle [0]>
    javax.xml.parsers; version="0.0.0"<System Bundle [0]>
    javax.xml.xpath; version="0.0.0"<System Bundle [0]>
    org.osgi.framework; version="1.4.0"<System Bundle [0]>
    org.osgi.util.tracker; version="1.3.3"<System Bundle [0]>
    org.w3c.dom; version="0.0.0"<System Bundle [0]>
  No fragment bundles
  Named class space
    com.dudewheresmyjar.spider; bundle-version="1.0.0.SNAPSHOT"[provided]
  No required bundles

osgi>
```

. . . you'll find that the spider bundle uses the service identified as dwmj. index.IndexService (look under the *Services in use:* header). Also, if you wait a moment or two, you'll see the spider interacting with the index service as it finds JAR files in the Maven repository.

Finally, as one more bit of proof that the index service is indexing JarFiles on behalf of the spider, go dig around in the index directory (probably /tmp/dudeindex on Unix or c:\temp\dudeindex on Windows). This directory contains a set of files that comprise a Lucene index. While the spider is running, the selection of files and the sizes of those files will fluctuate, indicating that new entries are being written to the index.

In this chapter, we've developed two of the central bundles of our application. The index bundle publishes a service through which consumers can add and search for JarFile entries in an index. The spider bundle is one such consumer of the index service, crawling a Maven repository and submitting what it finds to the index service for indexing.

We'll write some code to search that index when we develop the web front end in Chapter 7, *Creating Web Bundles*, on page 127. But before we get there, let's push rewind on the project and see how Spring Dynamic Modules for OSGi (Spring-DM) brings a POJO-based programming model to OSGi, simplifying some of the OSGi plumbing code we've written so far.

Part II

Spring Dynamic Modules and Web Bundles

Chapter 6

Spring and OSGi

We're making great progress on the *Dude, Where's My JAR?* application. In the previous chapter, we developed a great deal of the application's functionality. We created the index bundle, which publishes a service to the OSGi service registry. And we consumed that service from within the spider bundle that crawls Maven repositories looking for JAR files.

It would seem that we have most of the pieces in place and that the only thing left to do is to build the web front end to present the application to its users.

But first, let's think about what we had to do to publish and consume services. Publishing the index service wasn't so bad—we had to create a bundle activator, but at least our work with the OSGi API was confined to the activator class. However, if you're like me, you felt a bit dirty writing the MavenSpider class that dealt with a ServiceTracker to look up the index service.

If only there were some way to write our application code as POJOs and then declare that they are to consume or to be published as OSGi services.

In this chapter, we're going to see how to use Spring Dynamic Modules for OSGi (Spring-DM) to eliminate all of that OSGi-specific code that we used to publish and consume services. At the same time we'll bring all the power of the Spring Framework to OSGi. Instead of programming to the OSGi API, as we did in the previous chapter, this time we'll *declare* Spring beans to be OSGi services and inject services into other beans.

Native OSGi Services vs. Spring-DM

As you'll see in this chapter, Spring-DM greatly simplifies working with OSGi services. But that doesn't mean that our exercise in managing services natively through the OSGi API was a waste of time. Having gone through that experience, you'll be able to make sense of any bundle you encounter that works with services that way. And you'll be able to fully appreciate what Spring-DM offers.

6.1 Introducing Spring-DM

Unless you've been living under a rock or involved in some sort of multiyear solitary confinement exercise, you've probably heard about the Spring Framework. You may have even worked on a project or two that is based on Spring. It's a fact that Spring has made a tremendous impact on enterprise Java development.

Spring brings a lot to the table for any application, including:

- Spring's support for dependency injection promotes loose coupling and high testability of application objects.
- Spring's support for aspect-oriented programming offers developers an opportunity to separate cross-cutting concerns such as transactions, security, and caching from core application code.
- Spring makes it easy to work with JDBC and other persistence frameworks such as Hibernate, JPA, and iBATIS for data persistence.
- Spring supports declarative creation and consumption of remote services using a variety of remoting options, including RMI, Hessian, Burlap, and web services.
- Spring cleanly integrates POJOs with many pieces of the enterprise Java stack, including Enterprise JavaBeans (EJB), Java Messaging Service (JMS), Java Naming and Directory Interface (JNDI), and JavaMail.
- Spring provides a very simple yet capable MVC framework for building web applications.
- And Spring offers much, much more than I could possibly list here.

> ### Getting to Know the Spring Framework
>
> Our focus in this chapter will be on Spring-DM, an OSGi extension to the Spring Framework. I'll assume that you are already familiar with Spring, so I will not be going into any detail on how to declare any wire beans in a Spring application context. However, if you need a bit more introduction to Spring, many great books are available on the subject, including my personal favorite: *Spring in Action, Second Edition* (Wal07).

Although it'd be unusual that you'd use every part of Spring in a given application, it's quite likely that you could find a use for some subset of Spring in any application.

The Synergy of OSGi and Spring

Spring and OSGi have a lot to offer each other.

Spring does a lot of things, but at its core Spring is a framework that promotes loose coupling through dependency injection and interface-oriented design. However, even though Spring's dependency injection goes a long way toward decoupling application objects, it provides little for working with application modules.

Meanwhile, as we've seen already, OSGi is great for factoring applications into several modules. But when it comes to publishing and consuming services, OSGi ends up being a little bit cumbersome. And OSGi offers nothing for wiring together the objects within a bundle.

Spring-DM is the blending of OSGi's support for modularity with Spring's dependency injection model. Using Spring-DM, not only will we be able to wire together objects within our bundles, but we'll also be able to declaratively publish and consume OSGi services. What's more, because it's Spring, we'll have the full power of Spring at our disposal as we develop OSGi applications.

The Spring-DM Extender

At the center of Spring-DM is the Spring-DM extender. The Spring-DM extender's purpose in life is to watch for other bundles to be started,

> ## \}// Joe Asks...
> ### What About OSGi Declarative Services? Or iPOJO?
>
> When it comes to declaring OSGi services, Spring-DM is not the only game in town. In addition to Spring-DM, there are at least two other options for declarative services. One such option is appropriately named *Declarative Services* (or DS for short) and is part of the OSGi Compendium Specification (section 112). The other is part of the Apache Felix project and is called iPOJO.
>
> There's nothing inherently wrong with either DS or iPOJO. They both have their merits and are worth consideration in any OSGi project. However, although DS and iPOJO are focused on declaring services, Spring-DM also provides for dependency injection among the beans that make up a service. Not only that, but Spring-DM also brings the full power of Spring and its related projects to the table. If you want to exploit the other features of Spring in your OSGi project, then I recommend Spring-DM over the other options.

and if they are Spring-enabled, it will create a Spring application context for them. Here, Spring-enabled means that the bundle contains one or more Spring context definition files.

By default, the Spring-DM extender looks for Spring context definition files in the META-INF/spring directory. It assumes that all XML files in that folder are Spring context definition files and will use those files to create beans in the bundle's Spring application context.

As illustrated in Figure 6.1, on the facing page, the Spring-DM extender creates a separate Spring application context for each Spring-enabled bundle. That means that beans from one bundle can't see beans from any other bundles. This is consistent with the encapsulation espoused by OSGi.

Setting Up Spring-DM

Spring-DM is delivered in the form of a handful of OSGi bundles, including the bundle that contains the Spring-DM extender.

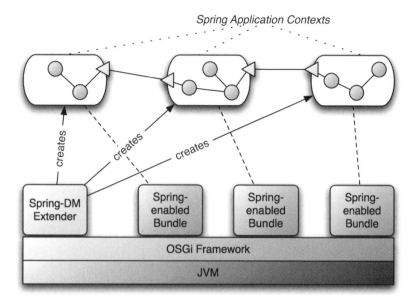

Figure 6.1: SPRING-DM'S <*osgix:cm-properties*> PULLS CONFIGURATION DETAILS FROM THE OSGI CONFIGURATION ADMIN SERVICE AND MAKES IT AVAILABLE TO SPRING'S PROPERTY PLACEHOLDER FACILITY.

Moving the Spring Context Files

If you don't want to place your Spring context definition files under META-INF/spring, that's OK. But you'll have to tell Spring-DM where they are by supplying the Spring-Context: header in the manifest (by way of osgi.bnd since we're using Pax Construct).

For example, if you'd rather place them in a directory called spring-config at the root of the bundle JAR, then add the following to the bundle's META-INF/MANIFEST.MF file:

```
Spring-Context: spring-config/*.xml
```

Or, if you prefer, you may explicitly list which XML files to use in defining the Spring context:

```
Spring-Context: spring-config/some-beans.xml, \
  spring-config/some-more-beans.xml
```

To get started with Spring-DM, we'll need to add these bundles to our project:

```
dwmjs% pax-import-bundle -g org.springframework.osgi -a spring-osgi-extender \
?                        -v 1.2.0 -- -DimportTransitive -DwidenScope
[INFO] Scanning for projects...
...
[INFO] ------------------------------------------------------------------------
[INFO] BUILD SUCCESSFUL
[INFO] ------------------------------------------------------------------------
[INFO] Total time: 8 seconds
[INFO] Finished at: Fri Mar 20 15:33:34 CDT 2009
[INFO] Final Memory: 9M/18M
[INFO] ------------------------------------------------------------------------
dwmjs%
```

Here we've asked Pax Construct to add version 1.2.0 of the Spring-DM extender bundle (identified with a group ID of org.springframework.osgi and an artifact ID of org.springframework.osgi.extender) to the project. In addition to the Spring-DM extender bundle itself, we've also asked that pax-import-bundle also pull in transitive dependencies (-DimportTransitive) and to consider all compile and runtime dependencies as potential bundles (-DwidenScope).

The Spring-DM bundles are now in place and are ready to help us declaratively publish the index service.

6.2 Declaring Services

The first step in declaring a service in Spring-DM is to wire a bean in the Spring application context. In Spring, a bean is any object (not necessarily a JavaBean) that is instantiated and managed by the Spring Framework. A common way of configuring the beans that Spring creates is to define a Spring application context in an XML file. For example, consider this Spring configuration XML (index-context.xml) that we'll use to define an application context for the index service bundle:

```
dwmjs/index/src/main/resources/META-INF/spring/index-context.xml
```

```xml
<beans xmlns="http://www.springframework.org/schema/beans"
    xmlns:xsi="http://www.w3.org/2001/XMLSchema-instance"
    xmlns:compass="http://www.compass-project.org/schema/spring-core-config"
    xsi:schemaLocation="http://www.springframework.org/schema/beans
        http://www.springframework.org/schema/beans/spring-beans-2.5.xsd
        http://www.compass-project.org/schema/spring-core-config
        http://www.compass-project.org/schema/spring-compass-core-config-2.0.xsd"
  <bean id="indexService"
      class="dwmj.index.internal.IndexServiceImpl">
    <constructor-arg ref="compass" />
  </bean>
```

```
<compass:compass name="compass" >
  <compass:connection>
    <compass:file path="/tmp/dudeindex" />
  </compass:connection>
  <compass:mappings>
    <compass:class name="dwmj.domain.JarFile"/>
  </compass:mappings>
</compass:compass>

<compass:session id="compassSession" />
</beans>
```

Here we've declared two beans. The first is defined with the <bean> element. This bean tells Spring to create an instance of IndexServiceImpl and to give it an ID of *indexService*. What's especially interesting about this bean is that we're telling Spring to instantiate it by calling a single-argument constructor and passing in a reference to another bean. Specifically, Spring should construct IndexServiceImpl with a reference to a bean whose ID is *compass*.

That brings us to the second bean. Instead of using a generic <bean> element to declare the *compass* bean, we're using elements from a Compass-specific configuration namespace provided as part of the Compass library. Ultimately, this declaration creates a bean of type org.compass.core.Compass, suitable for the first argument of the IndexServiceImpl constructor.

As mentioned before, Spring-DM creates an application context by reading all XML files in the META-INF/spring directory. Since we're building the bundle using Maven, we'll need to place index-context.xml in the src/main/resources/META-INF/spring directory of the index bundle project.

But it won't be alone. In addition to the core Spring configuration file, we'll also create a separate Spring configuration file (index-osgi.xml) that tells Spring-DM to publish the indexService bean to the OSGi service registry:

dwmjs/index/src/main/resources/META-INF/spring/index-osgi.xml

```
<beans:beans xmlns="http://www.springframework.org/schema/osgi"
  xmlns:beans="http://www.springframework.org/schema/beans"
  xmlns:xsi="http://www.w3.org/2001/XMLSchema-instance"
  xsi:schemaLocation="http://www.springframework.org/schema/osgi
      http://www.springframework.org/schema/osgi/spring-osgi.xsd
      http://www.springframework.org/schema/beans
      http://www.springframework.org/schema/beans/spring-beans-2.5.xsd">

  <service ref="indexService"
      interface="dwmj.index.IndexService" />

</beans:beans>
```

Using Spring-DM with Java 1.4

In Spring-DM, it's common for beans from different application contexts to interact with each other concurrently. To avoid deadlocks when beans are requested from the application contexts, Spring-DM needs concurrent collections. Java 1.5 and later provide concurrent collections out of the box. But Java 1.4 does not.

To add concurrent collection classes for Java 1.4, you'll need to add the Backport bundle. First, because the Backport libraries in the central Maven repository aren't OSGi-ready bundles, you'll need to add the Spring-DM repository:

```
dwmjs% pax-add-repository -i spring-osgi -u \
?       http://s3.amazonaws.com/maven.springframework.org/osgi \
?       -- -Dsnapshots
```

Then import the Backport bundle into the project:

```
dwmjs% pax-import-bundle -g org.springframework.osgi -a \
?       backport-util-concurrent.osgi -v 3.0-SNAPSHOT -- \
?       "-DimportPackage=sun.misc;resolution:=optional,*"
...
dwmjs%
```

To keep the OSGi-specific configuration separate from the generic bean definitions, I've placed this service declaration in a separate configuration file. The <service> element declares that the bean referenced by the ref= attribute should be published to the OSGi service registry with the interface specified in the interface= attribute. In this case, it's the index service bean that we declared in index-context.xml, which should be published with the dwmj.index.IndexService interface.

And that simple bit of Spring configuration is all we need to do to declare the index service bean as an OSGi service. You've no doubt noticed that this is simpler than programmatically publishing it using a bundle activator. All of the hassles of working directly with the OSGi API go away and are replaced with a simple entry in a Spring application context configuration file.

Speaking of not having to deal with the OSGi API, we no longer need the index bundle's activator. We needed it only to create and publish the index service.

But since Spring-DM's handling that for us now, we can get rid of it:

```
dwmjs% cd index
index% rm src/main/java/dwmj/index/internal/IndexServiceActivator.java
index%
```

We'll also need to delete the Bundle-Activator: entry from the osgi.bnd file.

Now that we've swapped out the bundle activator for a Spring-DM service declaration, let's rebuild the index service...

```
index% mvn install
[INFO] Scanning for projects...
...
[INFO] ------------------------------------------------------------------------
[INFO] BUILD SUCCESSFUL
[INFO] ------------------------------------------------------------------------
[INFO] Total time: 7 seconds
[INFO] Finished at: Fri Mar 20 15:47:34 CDT 2009
[INFO] Final Memory: 13M/31M
[INFO] ------------------------------------------------------------------------
index%
```

...and then provision it:

```
index% cd ..
dwmjs% pax-provision
[INFO] Scanning for projects...
...
Caused by: java.lang.ClassNotFoundException:
    org.compass.core.config.binding.metadata.AsmMetaDataReader
        not found from bundle [com.dudewheresmyjar.index]
...
osgi>
```

Oops! It looks like our index bundle had a little trouble getting started. Now that we're using Compass' configuration namespace for Spring, our bundle needs to import some packages that we're not currently importing. But wait—the index service is already using Compass in some capacity, and we haven't had to import any Compass packages before. Why must we import Compass packages now?

The answer is a bit nonobvious. As you'll recall, our build is using the BND tool to generate the MANIFEST.MF file from the osgi.bnd file. When we were programmatically working with Compass in the bundle activator, BND was able to figure out what packages to import by analyzing the activator and the service classes. But now the activator class has gone away, and we're declaring much of the Compass stuff in the Spring configuration file.

Unfortunately, BND doesn't analyze the Spring configuration file when putting together its list of packages to import. So, we'll have to add those imports to osgi.bnd ourselves:

dwmjs/index/osgi.bnd

```
Import-Package: *, \
  org.compass.core.engine.naming, \
  org.compass.core.executor.concurrent, \
  org.compass.core.cache.first, \
  org.compass.core.lucene.engine.analyzer, \
  org.compass.core.lucene.engine.optimizer, \
  org.compass.core.transaction, \
  org.apache.lucene.index, \
  org.apache.lucene, \
  org.apache.lucene.document, \
  org.apache.lucene.queryParser, \
  org.apache.lucene.search, \
  org.apache.lucene.store, \
  org.apache.lucene.util,\
  org.compass.core.config.binding.metadata,\
  org.compass.core.json.impl.converter
```

The first item in the import list is *, which tells BND to import all packages that it finds while analyzing Java classes—the default import behavior. What follows are the packages that are needed by Compass.[1] Let's build the index bundle and try provisioning it again:

```
dwmjs% pax-provision
[INFO] Scanning for projects...
...
Caused by: java.lang.NoClassDefFoundError:
        org/springframework/transaction/PlatformTransactionManager
...
osgi>
```

We have one more hurdle to overcome. It seems that Spring can't create the *compass* bean because it can't find org.springframework.transaction. PlatformTransactionManager. What? Spring cannot find one of its own classes?

As it turns out, PlatformTransactionManager resides in a separate bundle from the Spring bundles that we've already installed. To get past this problem, we're going to need to add Spring's transaction support bundle to our project.

---

1. I figured out what packages are needed by a tedious trial and error effort. I'm sparing you the effort of walking you through that exercise. But if you'd like to try it yourself, you can start by importing org.compass.core.engine.naming—the package containing the class that was the subject of the ClassNotFoundException we encountered—and following the breadcrumbs from there.

```
dwmjs% pax-import-bundle -g org.springframework -a spring-tx -v 2.5.6
[INFO] Scanning for projects...
[INFO] ------------------------------------------------------------------------
[INFO] Building com.dudewheresmyjar.dwmj (OSGi project)
[INFO]    task-segment: [org.ops4j:maven-pax-plugin:1.4:import-bundle]
          (aggregator-style)
[INFO] ------------------------------------------------------------------------
[INFO] [pax:import-bundle]
[INFO] Importing Spring Framework: Transaction to
          com.dudewheresmyjar.dwmj.build:provision:pom:1.0.0-SNAPSHOT
[INFO] ------------------------------------------------------------------------
[INFO] BUILD SUCCESSFUL
[INFO] ------------------------------------------------------------------------
[INFO] Total time: 5 seconds
[INFO] Finished at: Fri Mar 20 15:54:07 CDT 2009
[INFO] Final Memory: 8M/18M
[INFO] ------------------------------------------------------------------------
dwmjs%
```

With the Spring transaction support bundle in place, let's try to provision all of our bundles one more time:

```
dwmjs% pax-provision
[INFO] Scanning for projects...
...
osgi> ss

Framework is launched.

id     State       Bundle
0      ACTIVE      org.eclipse.osgi_3.4.2.R34x_v20080826-1230
1      ACTIVE      org.eclipse.osgi.util_3.1.300.v20080303
2      ACTIVE      org.eclipse.osgi.services_3.1.200.v20070605
3      ACTIVE      org.ops4j.pax.logging.pax-logging-api_1.3.0
4      ACTIVE      org.ops4j.pax.logging.pax-logging-service_1.3.0
5      ACTIVE      org.springframework.osgi.extender_1.2.0
6      ACTIVE      org.springframework.osgi.core_1.2.0
7      ACTIVE      org.springframework.osgi.io_1.2.0
8      ACTIVE      com.springsource.slf4j.org.apache.commons.logging_1.5.0
9      ACTIVE      com.springsource.slf4j.api_1.5.0
                   Fragments=10
10     RESOLVED    com.springsource.slf4j.log4j_1.5.0
                   Master=9
11     ACTIVE      org.springframework.aop_2.5.6
12     ACTIVE      org.springframework.beans_2.5.6
13     ACTIVE      org.springframework.context_2.5.6
14     ACTIVE      org.springframework.core_2.5.6
15     ACTIVE      org.springframework.test_2.5.6
16     ACTIVE      com.springsource.org.aopalliance_1.0.0
17     ACTIVE      org.springframework.transaction_2.5.6
18     ACTIVE      com.dudewheresmyjar.domain_1.0.0.SNAPSHOT
```

```
19      ACTIVE      org.compass-project.compass_2.1.1
20      ACTIVE      com.dudewheresmyjar.index_1.0.0.SNAPSHOT
21      ACTIVE      com.dudewheresmyjar.spider_1.0.0.SNAPSHOT

osgi>
```

So far so good. There were no exceptions thrown that time, and all of our bundles are active. Let's use the bundle command to dig a little deeper into the index bundle to see whether it is publishing the index service:

```
osgi> bundle 20
initial@reference:file:com.dudewheresmyjar.index_1.0.0.SNAPSHOT.jar/ [20]
  Id=20, Status=ACTIVE      Data Root=/Users/wallsc/Projects/projects/dwmjs/
                                    runner/equinox/org.eclipse.osgi/bundles/20/data
  Registered Services
▶ {dwmj.index.IndexService}={org.springframework.osgi.bean.name=indexService,
▶     Bundle-SymbolicName=com.dudewheresmyjar.index,
▶     Bundle-Version=1.0.0.SNAPSHOT, service.id=26}
  {org.springframework.osgi.context.DelegatedExecutionOsgiBundleApplicationConte
   org.springframework.osgi.context.ConfigurableOsgiBundleApplicationContext,
   org.springframework.context.ConfigurableApplicationContext,
   org.springframework.context.ApplicationContext,
   org.springframework.context.Lifecycle,
   org.springframework.beans.factory.ListableBeanFactory,
   org.springframework.beans.factory.HierarchicalBeanFactory,
   org.springframework.context.MessageSource,
   org.springframework.context.ApplicationEventPublisher,
   org.springframework.core.io.support.ResourcePatternResolver,
   org.springframework.beans.factory.BeanFactory,
   org.springframework.core.io.ResourceLoader,
   org.springframework.beans.factory.DisposableBean}=
   {org.springframework.context.service.name=com.dudewheresmyjar.index,
       Bundle-SymbolicName=com.dudewheresmyjar.index,
       Bundle-Version=1.0.0.SNAPSHOT, service.id=27}
...

osgi>
```

It looks like that worked, as evidenced by the first entry under the *Registered Services* header. Notice that there's a lot of information about the service, including the interface that it's published under, the bundle that publishes the service, and the Spring bean that provides the service.

You may have noticed that there's another entry under *Registered Services*—where'd that come from? In addition to publishing the services declared using the <*service*> element, Spring-DM also publishes the Spring application context as a service. And, it's published under a

---

How to Not Publish the Spring Context as a Service

If you'd rather not have a bundle's Spring context published as a service, you'll need to say so with the Spring-Context: header:

```
Spring-Context: META-INF/spring/*.xml;publish-context:=false
```

By setting the publish-context directive to false, we're asking Spring-DM to go ahead and load the Spring context using XML files in META-INF/spring, but not to publish the context in the OSGi service registry.

---

baker's dozen of interfaces, any of which you can use to retrieve the bundle's Spring context.

Now that we've converted the index bundle to use Spring-DM, let's turn our attention to the spider bundle to see whether Spring-DM can help us eliminate all of the code that we wrote to consume the index service.

6.3 Injecting Services into Consumers

As you'll recall, there's much more to consuming a service than publishing it. A service consumer must carefully deal with the transitivity of services to make sure that it's not trying to use a service that has gone away or that has been replaced with a newer version. All of that service management resulted in a lot of code in both the spider bundle's activator and in the spider implementation class.

Spring-DM was able to eliminate OSGi-specific code in our index bundle. Can it do the same for the spider bundle? You bet! In fact, as you'll soon see, consuming a service with Spring-DM isn't much different from publishing a service.

First things first... just as with the index bundle, we're no longer going to need the bundle activator for the spider bundle. So, let's go ahead and ditch it:

```
dwmjs% cd spider
spider% rm src/main/java/dwmj/spider/impl/SpiderActivator.java
```

Be sure to remove the Bundle-Activator: entry from osgi.bnd, too.

Now that the spider's bundle activator is gone, we no longer have a way to give the MavenSpider a service tracker to look up the index service.

But that's OK, because instead of giving MavenSpider a way to get the index service, we're going to inject the index service into MavenSpider:

```
dwmjs/spider/src/main/java/dwmj/spider/internal/MavenSpider.java
public class MavenSpider {
   private static final Logger LOGGER = Logger.getLogger("MavenSpider");
   private JarFilePopulator[] jarFilePopulators = new JarFilePopulator[] {};
   private String repositoryUrl;
   private boolean active = true;
   private IndexService indexService;

   public MavenSpider(IndexService indexService) {
      this.indexService = indexService;
   }

}
```

We've traded a ServiceTracker for a reference to an IndexService. Actually, we're going to inject MavenSpider with a proxy to the index service (that automatically handles the transitive nature of services). But for all intents and purposes, you can pretend that it's the real index service—MavenSpider won't know the difference.

Notice that MavenSpider no longer implements java.lang.Runnable. Originally, we had to start MavenSpider in a separate thread so that it would not hold up the spider bundle from starting. But now Spring is going to start MavenSpider, so it no longer needs to implement Runnable.

There's just one more tweak we must make to MavenSpider to make it ready for Spring-DM. Now that we're injecting an IndexService reference into MavenSpider, we'll need to change it to just use the IndexService and not try to look it up from the ServiceTracker. Previously, MavenSpider had a snippet of code that looked like this:

```
dwmj/spider/src/main/java/dwmj/spider/internal/MavenSpider.java
if (jarFile.isIndexable()) {
   IndexService indexService =
         (IndexService) indexServiceTracker.getService();

   if(indexService != null) {
      indexService.addJarFile(jarFile);
   }
}
```

But with the ServiceTracker gone, it's much simpler:

```java
if(jarFile.isIndexable()) {
    indexService.addJarFile(jarFile);
}
```

Awesome! We've managed to turn MavenSpider into a POJO, eliminating all hints of the OSGi API. To wrap up the conversion of the spider bundle to use Spring-DM, we need to wire MavenSpider as a Spring bean, injecting it with a reference to the index service. First, we'll configure a reference to the index service:

```xml
<?xml version="1.0" encoding="UTF-8"?>
<beans:beans xmlns="http://www.springframework.org/schema/osgi"
      xmlns:beans="http://www.springframework.org/schema/beans"
      xmlns:xsi="http://www.w3.org/2001/XMLSchema-instance"
      xsi:schemaLocation="http://www.springframework.org/schema/osgi
          http://www.springframework.org/schema/osgi/spring-osgi.xsd
          http://www.springframework.org/schema/beans
          http://www.springframework.org/schema/beans/spring-beans-2.5.xsd">

  <reference id="indexService"
      interface="dwmj.index.IndexService" />

</beans:beans>
```

The <reference> element isn't much different from the <service> element, only in reverse. The interface= attribute tells Spring to look up a service from the OSGi service registry with the dwmj.index.IndexService interface. The id= attribute is effectively the flipside of the <service> element's ref= element—but, instead of referencing another Spring bean, the id= attribute gives the index service proxy a name with which we can inject it into the MavenSpider.

Speaking of injecting the index service into the MavenSpider, let's wire up the spider bean:

```xml
<beans xmlns="http://www.springframework.org/schema/beans"
   xmlns:xsi="http://www.w3.org/2001/XMLSchema-instance"
   xsi:schemaLocation="http://www.springframework.org/schema/beans
       http://www.springframework.org/schema/beans/spring-beans-2.5.xsd">

  <bean class="dwmj.spider.internal.MavenSpider"
      init-method="run" destroy-method="stop">
    <constructor-arg ref="indexService" />
```

```
        <property name="repositoryUrl" value="http://repo2.maven.org/maven2/" />
        <property name="jarFilePopulators">
          <list>
            <bean class=
              "dwmj.spider.internal.PomBasedJarFilePopulator" />
            <bean class=
              "dwmj.spider.internal.JarContentBasedJarFilePopulator" />
          </list>
        </property>
  </bean>
</beans>
```

The third *<constructor-arg>* injects the bean named *indexService* into
the MavenSpider as it's constructed. Once it has been constructed,
Spring will start the spider by calling the run() method, as indicated
by the *<bean>* element's init-method= attribute. Later, when the Spring
context is shut down (when the bundle is stopped), Spring will invoke
the stop() method to stop the spider, as indicated by the destroy-method=
attribute.

The spider bundle is now converted from a bundle whose Java code is
strewn with bits of the OSGi API to one containing simple POJOs that
are managed by Spring. Before we move on, there's one more thing left
to do... let's build the spider bundle and see whether it works. First,
the build...

```
spider% mvn install
[INFO] Scanning for projects...
...
[INFO] ------------------------------------------------------------------------
[INFO] BUILD SUCCESSFUL
[INFO] ------------------------------------------------------------------------
[INFO] Total time: 7 seconds
[INFO] Finished at: Fri Mar 20 18:00:13 CDT 2009
[INFO] Final Memory: 14M/31M
[INFO] ------------------------------------------------------------------------
spider%
```

... and then the provision:

```
spider% cd ..
dwmjs% pax-provision
[INFO] Scanning for projects...
...
osgi> ss

Framework is launched.
```

Joe Asks...

What If a Service Isn't Available?

When we used the <*reference*> element to consume the index service, we assumed that the service would be readily available. But what if it isn't?

By default, Spring-DM will wait five minutes for the service to become available before an unchecked ServiceUnavailableException is thrown. If you want to change the timeout period, you have two options.

First, you can set the timeout= attribute on the <*reference*> element to adjust the timeout on a reference-by-reference basis:

```
<reference id="indexService"
  interface="com.dudewheresmyjar.index.IndexService"
  timeout="60000"/>
```

Or you can change the default timeout value by setting the osgi:default-timeout= at the root of the XML file:

```
<beans:beans xmlns="http://www.springframework.org/schema/osgi"
    xmlns:osgi="http://www.springframework.org/schema/osgi"
    xmlns:beans="http://www.springframework.org/schema/beans"
    xmlns:xsi="http://www.w3.org/2001/XMLSchema-instance"
    xsi:schemaLocation="http://www.springframework.org/schema/osgi
      http://www.springframework.org/schema/osgi/spring-osgi.xsd
      http://www.springframework.org/schema/beans
      http://www.springframework.org/schema/beans/
            spring-beans-2.5.xsd"
    osgi:default-timeout="60000">

  <reference id="indexService"
      interface="com.dudewheresmyjar.index.IndexService" />

</beans:beans>
```

```
id       State      Bundle
0        ACTIVE     org.eclipse.osgi_3.4.2.R34x_v20080826-1230
1        ACTIVE     org.eclipse.osgi.util_3.1.300.v20080303
2        ACTIVE     org.eclipse.osgi.services_3.1.200.v20070605
3        ACTIVE     org.ops4j.pax.logging.pax-logging-api_1.3.0
4        ACTIVE     org.ops4j.pax.logging.pax-logging-service_1.3.0
5        ACTIVE     org.springframework.osgi.extender_1.2.0
6        ACTIVE     org.springframework.osgi.core_1.2.0
7        ACTIVE     org.springframework.osgi.io_1.2.0
8        ACTIVE     com.springsource.slf4j.org.apache.commons.logging_1.5.0
9        ACTIVE     com.springsource.slf4j.api_1.5.0
                    Fragments=10
10       RESOLVED   com.springsource.slf4j.log4j_1.5.0
                    Master=9
11       ACTIVE     org.springframework.aop_2.5.6
12       ACTIVE     org.springframework.beans_2.5.6
13       ACTIVE     org.springframework.context_2.5.6
14       ACTIVE     org.springframework.core_2.5.6
15       ACTIVE     org.springframework.test_2.5.6
16       ACTIVE     com.springsource.org.aopalliance_1.0.0
17       ACTIVE     org.springframework.transaction_2.5.6
18       ACTIVE     com.dudewheresmyjar.domain_1.0.0.SNAPSHOT
19       ACTIVE     org.compass-project.compass_2.1.1
20       ACTIVE     com.dudewheresmyjar.index_1.0.0.SNAPSHOT
21       ACTIVE     com.dudewheresmyjar.spider_1.0.0.SNAPSHOT

osgi>
```

So far so good. There were no exceptions thrown, and everything seems
to be working. Let's check the spider bundle to make sure that it's using
the index service:

```
osgi> bundle 21
initial@reference:file:com.dudewheresmyjar.spider_1.0.0.SNAPSHOT.jar/ [21]
  Id=21, Status=ACTIVE      Data Root=/Users/wallsc/Projects/projects/dwmjs/runne
      equinox/org.eclipse.osgi/bundles/21/data
  No registered services.
  Services in use:
    {org.springframework.beans.factory.xml.NamespaceHandlerResolver}={service.id=
    {org.xml.sax.EntityResolver}={service.id=25}
    {dwmj.index.IndexService}={org.springframework.osgi.bean.name=indexService,
      Bundle-SymbolicName=com.dudewheresmyjar.index, Bundle-Version=1.0.0.SNAPSHO
      service.id=26}
  Exported packages
    dwmj.spider.impl; version="1.0.0.SNAPSHOT"[exported]
  Imported packages
    dwmj.domain; version="1.0.0.SNAPSHOT"<initial@reference:file:
        com.dudewheresmyjar.domain_1.0.0.SNAPSHOT.jar/ [18]>
    dwmj.index; version="1.0.0.SNAPSHOT"<initial@reference:file:
        com.dudewheresmyjar.index_1.0.0.SNAPSHOT.jar/ [20]>
    javax.swing.text; version="0.0.0"<System Bundle [0]>
```

Spring-DM to Become Part of the OSGi Specification

As I write this, a draft of the OSGi 4.2 Specification is available. Within this specification is RFC 124: A Component Model for OSGi. It's commonly being referred to as the Blueprint Service.

What's curious about the Blueprint Service is that it looks suspiciously like Spring-DM. A few names and terms have been changed, but for the most part, Blueprint Service is Spring-DM. This should come as no surprise to anyone who looks closely as the specification—it is written by employees of SpringSource, the company behind the Spring Framework and Spring-DM.

See Appendix C, on page 215, for more information on how the Blueprint Service compares to Spring-DM.

```
    javax.swing.text.html; version="0.0.0"<System Bundle [0]>
    javax.xml.parsers; version="0.0.0"<System Bundle [0]>
    javax.xml.xpath; version="0.0.0"<System Bundle [0]>
    org.w3c.dom; version="0.0.0"<System Bundle [0]>
  No fragment bundles
  Named class space
    com.dudewheresmyjar.spider; bundle-version="1.0.0.SNAPSHOT"[provided]
  No required bundles

osgi>
```

And there it is. The third entry under the *Services in use:* header tells us that the spider bundle is using the index service—thanks to Spring-DM and the *<reference>* element.

At this point we've developed all the bundles of the *Dude, Where's My JAR?* application twice: once using the core OSGi API and again using Spring-DM. Before we move on, let's take a moment to reflect on what Spring-DM has done for us.

Without Spring-DM, both publication and consumption of a service required writing directly to the OSGi API. In both cases, we had to write an activator class to either register or retrieve a service in the OSGi service registry. On the other hand, with Spring-DM we were able to publish and consume services in a declarative fashion, with no need to interact directly with the OSGi API.

Now we're ready to put a face on this application. Coming up in the next chapter, we're going to develop the web front end of the application.

Chapter 7

Creating Web Bundles

Up until now, all of the modules that we've created have been the basic garden-variety OSGi bundle. They are all JAR files with some extra metadata in their MANIFEST.MF to guide the OSGi framework in deploying and starting them. And in some cases they publish and/or consume services.

Now as we begin to put a face on our application, we're going to be creating a different flavor of OSGi bundle. In this chapter, we're going to build a web bundle—a bundle that looks like a WAR file (or is it a WAR file that looks like a bundle?).

But before we build our web bundle, the first order of business is setting up an environment for it to run in. Let's start by adding web server capabilities to the OSGi framework.

7.1 Assembling a Web Server

If we were building an everyday, run-of-the-mill Java web application, we might deploy our application into a web container, such as those included in virtually every Java application server. But we're building an OSGi web application, so things are going to be a little different. Instead of deploying our application into a web container, we're going to install a web container into our application—or, more accurately, we're going to deploy a web container alongside our application in the OSGi framework.

When installing a web container in OSGi, we have two choices: Tomcat and Jetty. Let's look at how to assemble a small collection of bundles to make an OSGi-ready web application server.

Installing Tomcat Bundles

Tomcat is easily one of the most popular Java web application servers. So, it'd be no surprise if that's the server you'd want to use to host web applications. Unfortunately, the JAR files that make up the Tomcat server don't come ready-made for OSGi. That is, they aren't OSGi bundles, and therefore we can't use them as is in an OSGi context.

But we're not going to let that stop us.

The silver lining behind this seemingly dark Tomcat-in-OSGi cloud is that the Spring-DM team has converted the Tomcat JAR files into OSGi bundles and has made them available in the Spring-DM bundle repository. If you haven't already added the Spring-DM repository to the project for Java 1.4 support (see the sidebar on page 114), then you'll need to add it now to be able to use the OSGi-ified Tomcat bundles. Here's how to add the Spring-DM repository:

```
dwmjs% pax-add-repository -i spring-osgi \
?       -u http://s3.amazonaws.com/maven.springframework.org/osgi \
?       -- -Dsnapshots
[INFO] Scanning for projects...
[INFO] ------------------------------------------------------------
[INFO] Building com.dudewheresmyjar.dwmj (OSGi project)
[INFO]    task-segment: [org.ops4j:maven-pax-plugin:1.4:add-repository]
          (aggregator-style)
[INFO] ------------------------------------------------------------
[INFO] [pax:add-repository]
[INFO] Adding repository http://s3.amazonaws.com/maven.springframework.org/osgi
          com.dudewheresmyjar:dwmj:pom:1.0.0-SNAPSHOT
[INFO] ------------------------------------------------------------
[INFO] BUILD SUCCESSFUL
[INFO] ------------------------------------------------------------
[INFO] Total time: 5 seconds
[INFO] Finished at: Fri Mar 20 20:25:41 CDT 2009
[INFO] Final Memory: 8M/16M
[INFO] ------------------------------------------------------------
dwmjs%
```

Note that we've declared the Spring-DM repository as being a SNAP-SHOT repository. That's because many of the bundles that the Spring-DM team have converted from nonbundle JARs are versioned as SNAP-SHOT versions to differentiate them from their nonbundle counterparts.

Now we're ready to add bundles. The first bundle we'll need for Tomcat support is the one that contains the servlet engine—the Catalina bundle.

The Future of the Spring-DM Repository

You should know that the Spring-DM team refers to their own repository as a temporary repository. That's because Spring-Source has another Maven repository that's chock-full of OSGi bundles known as the SpringSource Enterprise Bundle Repository* or by its nickname of BRITS (short for Bundle Repository in the Sky).

Because of the temporary nature of the Spring-DM repository, the Spring-DM team recommends that you use BRITS instead of the Spring-DM repository. However, as I write this, there are still a few of the bundles missing in BRITS that we need to make our application work. Specifically, it's missing the Tomcat and Jetty starter bundles.

So, I'm going to go ahead and use the temporary repository in the examples but recommend that you keep an eye on both repositories and be prepared to switch when the missing bundles are available in BRITS.

*. http://www.springsource.com/repository/app/

```
dwmjs% pax-import-bundle -g org.springframework.osgi \
?                       -a catalina.osgi -v 6.0.16-SNAPSHOT
[INFO] Scanning for projects...
[INFO] ------------------------------------------------------------
[INFO] Building com.dudewheresmyjar.dwmj (OSGi project)
[INFO]    task-segment: [org.ops4j:maven-pax-plugin:1.4:import-bundle]
          (aggregator-style)
[INFO] ------------------------------------------------------------
[INFO] [pax:import-bundle]
[INFO] Importing Apache Tomcat Catalina Container (OSGi version) to
          com.dudewheresmyjar.dwmj.build:provision:pom:1.0.0-SNAPSHOT
[INFO] ------------------------------------------------------------
[INFO] BUILD SUCCESSFUL
[INFO] ------------------------------------------------------------
[INFO] Total time: 6 seconds
[INFO] Finished at: Fri Mar 20 20:26:42 CDT 2009
[INFO] Final Memory: 9M/16M
[INFO] ------------------------------------------------------------
dwmjs%
```

In support of the Catalina servlet engine, we'll also need to import a bundle containing the Java Servlet API.

```
dwmjs% pax-import-bundle -g org.springframework.osgi -a servlet-api.osgi \
?                              -v 2.5-SNAPSHOT
[INFO] Scanning for projects...
[INFO] ------------------------------------------------------------------------
[INFO] Building com.dudewheresmyjar.dwmj (OSGi project)
[INFO]     task-segment: [org.ops4j:maven-pax-plugin:1.4:import-bundle]
           (aggregator-style)
[INFO] ------------------------------------------------------------------------
[INFO] [pax:import-bundle]
[INFO] Importing Servlet API 2.5 (OSGi version) to
          com.dudewheresmyjar.dwmj.build:provision:pom:1.0.0-SNAPSHOT
[INFO] ------------------------------------------------------------------------
[INFO] BUILD SUCCESSFUL
[INFO] ------------------------------------------------------------------------
[INFO] Total time: 5 seconds
[INFO] Finished at: Fri Mar 20 20:27:34 CDT 2009
[INFO] Final Memory: 9M/16M
[INFO] ------------------------------------------------------------------------
dwmjs%
```

When we develop the web portion of our application, we're going to use JSP to develop the view. Therefore, we'll also need to add Jasper, Tomcat's JSP engine:

```
dwmjs% pax-import-bundle -g org.springframework.osgi -a jasper.osgi \
?                              -v 6.0.16-SNAPSHOT
[INFO] Scanning for projects...
[INFO] ------------------------------------------------------------------------
[INFO] Building com.dudewheresmyjar.dwmj (OSGi project)
[INFO]     task-segment: [org.ops4j:maven-pax-plugin:1.4:import-bundle]
           (aggregator-style)
[INFO] ------------------------------------------------------------------------
[INFO] [pax:import-bundle]
[INFO] Importing Tomcat 6.x JSP Jasper (OSGi version) to
          com.dudewheresmyjar.dwmj.build:provision:pom:1.0.0-SNAPSHOT
[INFO] ------------------------------------------------------------------------
[INFO] BUILD SUCCESSFUL
[INFO] ------------------------------------------------------------------------
[INFO] Total time: 6 seconds
[INFO] Finished at: Fri Mar 20 20:28:24 CDT 2009
[INFO] Final Memory: 8M/18M
[INFO] ------------------------------------------------------------------------
dwmjs%
```

As the JSP engine, Jasper depends on the JSP API. So, we'll need to add a bundle for that, as well:

```
dwmjs% pax-import-bundle -g org.mortbay.jetty -a jsp-api-2.1 -v 6.1.14
[INFO] Scanning for projects...
[INFO] ------------------------------------------------------------------------
[INFO] Building com.dudewheresmyjar.dwmj (OSGi project)
[INFO]     task-segment: [org.ops4j:maven-pax-plugin:1.4:import-bundle]
           (aggregator-style)
```

```
[INFO] ----------------------------------------------------------------
[INFO] [pax:import-bundle]
[INFO] Importing Glassfish Jasper API to
           com.dudewheresmyjar.dwmj.build:provision:pom:1.0.0-SNAPSHOT
[INFO] ----------------------------------------------------------------
[INFO] BUILD SUCCESSFUL
[INFO] ----------------------------------------------------------------
[INFO] Total time: 5 seconds
[INFO] Finished at: Fri Mar 20 20:28:58 CDT 2009
[INFO] Final Memory: 8M/18M
[INFO] ----------------------------------------------------------------
dwmjs%
```

If you look closely, you'll see that we're using the JSP API bundle provided by Jetty. Even though it may seem odd to use Jetty's JSP API with Tomcat, rest assured that there's nothing Jetty-specific about it and that it will work fine with Tomcat. The reason we're using Jetty's JSP API is that it is the only one available in version 2.1, which is the version that Jasper 6.0.16 depends on.

Next, to support JSP expression language syntax, we'll need the expression language API:

```
dwmjs% pax-import-bundle -g org.springframework.osgi -a el-api.osgi \
?                       -v 2.1-SNAPSHOT
[INFO] Scanning for projects...
[INFO] ----------------------------------------------------------------
[INFO] Building com.dudewheresmyjar.dwmj (OSGi project)
[INFO]    task-segment: [org.ops4j:maven-pax-plugin:1.4:import-bundle]
           (aggregator-style)
[INFO] ----------------------------------------------------------------
[INFO] [pax:import-bundle]
[INFO] Importing EL API (OSGi version) to
           com.dudewheresmyjar.dwmj.build:provision:pom:1.0.0-SNAPSHOT
[INFO] ----------------------------------------------------------------
[INFO] BUILD SUCCESSFUL
[INFO] ----------------------------------------------------------------
[INFO] Total time: 5 seconds
[INFO] Finished at: Fri Mar 20 20:29:33 CDT 2009
[INFO] Final Memory: 8M/18M
[INFO] ----------------------------------------------------------------
dwmjs%
```

All of the core pieces of a Tomcat server are now in place. There's only one more bundle we'll need to add to our project if we want to use Tomcat as our web server. In addition to converting Tomcat JARs into OSGi bundles, the Spring-DM team has also provided a bundle that contains an activator that starts Tomcat. Let's add it to the mix.

```
dwmjs% pax-import-bundle -g org.springframework.osgi -a catalina.start.osgi \
?                             -v 1.0.0
[INFO] Scanning for projects...
[INFO] ------------------------------------------------------------------------
[INFO] Building com.dudewheresmyjar.dwmj (OSGi project)
[INFO]    task-segment: [org.ops4j:maven-pax-plugin:1.4:import-bundle]
          (aggregator-style)
[INFO] ------------------------------------------------------------------------
[INFO] [pax:import-bundle]
[INFO] Importing Tomcat Catalina OSGi Activator to
          com.dudewheresmyjar.dwmj.build:provision:pom:1.0.0-SNAPSHOT
[INFO] ------------------------------------------------------------------------
[INFO] BUILD SUCCESSFUL
[INFO] ------------------------------------------------------------------------
[INFO] Total time: 5 seconds
[INFO] Finished at: Fri Mar 20 20:30:22 CDT 2009
[INFO] Final Memory: 8M/18M
[INFO] ------------------------------------------------------------------------
dwmjs%
```

Now, if you were to fire up the application (using pax-provision) and then point your browser to http://localhost:8080, you'd see a blank page. The fact that you didn't get an error about being unable to connect to the server indicates that Tomcat is listening for requests on port 8080. The blank page indicates that there are no servlets available to respond to the request. Don't worry about that; by the time we finish this chapter, there'll be plenty for Tomcat to serve up.

But first, let's set Tomcat aside and look at Jetty, the other web server that we can use in OSGi.

Installing Jetty Bundles

Jetty is special in that it is already distributed in the form of OSGi bundles. So, there's not much to do other than add the Jetty bundles to our project. Specifically, there are six bundles we'll need to import, starting with the Jetty server bundle:

```
dwmjs% pax-import-bundle -g org.mortbay.jetty -a jetty -v 6.1.14
[INFO] Scanning for projects...
[INFO] ------------------------------------------------------------------------
[INFO] Building com.dudewheresmyjar.dwmj (OSGi project)
[INFO]    task-segment: [org.ops4j:maven-pax-plugin:1.4:import-bundle]
          (aggregator-style)
[INFO] ------------------------------------------------------------------------
[INFO] [pax:import-bundle]
[INFO] Importing Jetty Server to
          com.dudewheresmyjar.dwmj.build:provision:pom:1.0.0-SNAPSHOT
[INFO] ------------------------------------------------------------------------
[INFO] BUILD SUCCESSFUL
```

```
[INFO] -----------------------------------------------------------------------
[INFO] Total time: 4 seconds
[INFO] Finished at: Fri Mar 20 20:33:15 CDT 2009
[INFO] Final Memory: 8M/18M
[INFO] -----------------------------------------------------------------------
dwmjs%
```

The Jetty server bundle depends on a few utility classes contained in a separate Jetty utilities bundle, so we'll also need to add that:

```
dwmjs% pax-import-bundle -g org.mortbay.jetty -a jetty-util -v 6.1.14
[INFO] Scanning for projects...
[INFO] -----------------------------------------------------------------------
[INFO] Building com.dudewheresmyjar.dwmj (OSGi project)
[INFO]    task-segment: [org.ops4j:maven-pax-plugin:1.4:import-bundle]
          (aggregator-style)
[INFO] -----------------------------------------------------------------------
[INFO] [pax:import-bundle]
[INFO] Importing Jetty Utilities to
          com.dudewheresmyjar.dwmj.build:provision:pom:1.0.0-SNAPSHOT
[INFO] -----------------------------------------------------------------------
[INFO] BUILD SUCCESSFUL
[INFO] -----------------------------------------------------------------------
[INFO] Total time: 5 seconds
[INFO] Finished at: Fri Mar 20 20:33:49 CDT 2009
[INFO] Final Memory: 8M/18M
[INFO] -----------------------------------------------------------------------
dwmjs%
```

The two bundles that we've added thus far constitute the bulk of the Jetty server. But the server won't start by itself. Fortunately, the Spring-DM folks have provided an activator bundle to kick off Jetty:

```
dwmjs% pax-import-bundle -g org.springframework.osgi -a jetty.start.osgi \
?                       -v 1.0.0
[INFO] Scanning for projects...
[INFO] -----------------------------------------------------------------------
[INFO] Building com.dudewheresmyjar.dwmj (OSGi project)
[INFO]    task-segment: [org.ops4j:maven-pax-plugin:1.4:import-bundle]
          (aggregator-style)
[INFO] -----------------------------------------------------------------------
[INFO] [pax:import-bundle]
[INFO] Importing Jetty OSGi Activator to
          com.dudewheresmyjar.dwmj.build:provision:pom:1.0.0-SNAPSHOT
[INFO] -----------------------------------------------------------------------
[INFO] BUILD SUCCESSFUL
[INFO] -----------------------------------------------------------------------
[INFO] Total time: 5 seconds
[INFO] Finished at: Fri Mar 20 20:34:19 CDT 2009
[INFO] Final Memory: 8M/18M
[INFO] -----------------------------------------------------------------------
dwmjs%
```

Next, just as we did with Tomcat, we'll need to install the bundle containing the Java Servlet API:

```
dwmjs% pax-import-bundle -g org.springframework.osgi -a servlet-api.osgi \
?                          -v 2.5-SNAPSHOT
[INFO] Scanning for projects...
[INFO] ------------------------------------------------------------------------
[INFO] Building com.dudewheresmyjar.dwmj (OSGi project)
[INFO]    task-segment: [org.ops4j:maven-pax-plugin:1.4:import-bundle]
           (aggregator-style)
[INFO] ------------------------------------------------------------------------
[INFO] [pax:import-bundle]
[INFO] Importing Servlet API 2.5 (OSGi version) to
           com.dudewheresmyjar.dwmj.build:provision:pom:1.0.0-SNAPSHOT
[INFO] ------------------------------------------------------------------------
[INFO] BUILD SUCCESSFUL
[INFO] ------------------------------------------------------------------------
[INFO] Total time: 5 seconds
[INFO] Finished at: Fri Mar 20 20:35:11 CDT 2009
[INFO] Final Memory: 8M/18M
[INFO] ------------------------------------------------------------------------
dwmjs%
```

Finally, we'll need to add a JSP engine. As it turns out, Jetty also uses Jasper, so we'll need to add Jasper...

```
dwmjs% pax-import-bundle -g org.springframework.osgi -a jasper.osgi \
?                          -v 6.0.16-SNAPSHOT
[INFO] Scanning for projects...
[INFO] ------------------------------------------------------------------------
[INFO] Building com.dudewheresmyjar.dwmj (OSGi project)
[INFO]    task-segment: [org.ops4j:maven-pax-plugin:1.4:import-bundle]
           (aggregator-style)
[INFO] ------------------------------------------------------------------------
[INFO] [pax:import-bundle]
[INFO] Importing Tomcat 6.x JSP Jasper (OSGi version) to
           com.dudewheresmyjar.dwmj.build:provision:pom:1.0.0-SNAPSHOT
[INFO] ------------------------------------------------------------------------
[INFO] BUILD SUCCESSFUL
[INFO] ------------------------------------------------------------------------
[INFO] Total time: 5 seconds
[INFO] Finished at: Fri Mar 20 20:35:48 CDT 2009
[INFO] Final Memory: 8M/18M
[INFO] ------------------------------------------------------------------------
dwmjs%
```

...and the JSP API...

```
dwmjs% pax-import-bundle -g org.mortbay.jetty -a jsp-api-2.1 -v 6.1.14
[INFO] Scanning for projects...
[INFO] ------------------------------------------------------------------------
[INFO] Building com.dudewheresmyjar.dwmj (OSGi project)
```

```
\//  Joe Asks...
;f
~    Tomcat or Jetty?
```

It really doesn't matter whether you choose to use Tomcat or Jetty to serve your web applications in OSGi. Either one should work well; the decision mostly boils down to a matter of personal preference.

I'll be assuming Jetty throughout the rest of the book. But if you'd prefer to use Tomcat, then go right ahead. There should be very few differences (and I'll note them along the way).

```
[INFO]    task-segment: [org.ops4j:maven-pax-plugin:1.4:import-bundle]
          (aggregator-style)
[INFO] -------------------------------------------------------------
[INFO] [pax:import-bundle]
[INFO] Importing Glassfish Jasper API to
          com.dudewheresmyjar.dwmj.build:provision:pom:1.0.0-SNAPSHOT
[INFO] -------------------------------------------------------------
[INFO] BUILD SUCCESSFUL
[INFO] -------------------------------------------------------------
[INFO] Total time: 4 seconds
[INFO] Finished at: Fri Mar 20 20:36:15 CDT 2009
[INFO] Final Memory: 8M/18M
[INFO] -------------------------------------------------------------
dwmjs%
```

Let's start it up to see whether it works. First, use pax-provision to start Equinox, all of our application's bundles, and the Jetty bundles. Point your web browser to http://localhost:8080, and you will see... an HTTP 404 error.

Don't panic. The fact that we get an HTTP 404 error is a good sign. It proves that the web server is running and responding to browser requests. The only reason we get an error message is because there aren't any web applications deployed to the Jetty server. We'll address that problem before this chapter is done.

7.2 The Spring-DM Web Extender

While most of the bundles we'll deploy in the OSGi framework are just JAR files with some OSGi metadata in the META-INF/MANIFEST.MF

\\/ Joe Asks. . .

Do I Need Spring-DM to Deploy Web Applications in OSGi?

The short answer is no.

In fact, the OSGi Services Compendium defines an HTTP Service that enables deployment of servlets in an OSGi framework. The problem with the HTTP Service, however, is that it requires you to deploy servlets programmatically through the OSGi API. That approach is very unnatural for most Java web developers who are accustomed to registering servlets via a web.xml file.

What's more, the HTTP Service is defined to support only servlets and not the full capability of the Java Servlet specification. That means it doesn't support filters, listeners, or even JSP.

What's nice about Spring-DM's web extender is that it allows you to deploy web applications in a bundle that resembles a traditional WAR file, right down to the web.xml file that registers servlets. And because it deploys your web application to a real web application server such as Tomcat or Jetty, you are welcome to use whatever parts of the servlet specification you would like.

file, web bundles are WAR files with some OSGi metadata in the META-INF/MANIFEST.MF file.

I know what you're thinking—what's the difference? Well, there are a few subtle factors to consider when developing web bundles:

- The class space of a JAR bundle is rooted at the root of the JAR file. But the class space of a WAR file is rooted at WEB-INF/classes (and, WEB-INF/lib if there are any embedded libraries).

- JAR files are libraries that merely need to be available in an application's class space to be useful. WAR files, however, are of little use unless they are installed into a servlet container.

We'll address the first difference when we get around to building our web bundle. It's the second difference—deploying a WAR bundle to a servlet container—that we'll need to think about now. For that, we'll use Spring-DM's web extender.

How It Works

When a WAR file is installed into the OSGi framework, the framework only knows to treat it like any other bundle. That is, the framework will manage its life cycle and, if directed to do so by the manifest, import and export packages. But the OSGi framework doesn't know much about how to serve web applications. And, even though we may have Tomcat or Jetty installed, the OSGi framework doesn't know how to hand the WAR file off to the servlet container.

That's where Spring-DM's web extender comes in. The web extender is a bundle that has an activator whose job is to watch for bundles to be installed into the OSGi framework and, if it sees a web bundle, to deploy that bundle to either Tomcat or Jetty.

Installing the Web Extender

Spring-DM's support for web applications comes in the form of two bundles that we'll need to add to our application. The first is the Spring-DM web extender itself:

```
dwmjs% pax-import-bundle -g org.springframework.osgi \
?                        -a spring-osgi-web-extender -v 1.2.0
[INFO] Scanning for projects...
[INFO] ------------------------------------------------------------------------
[INFO] Building com.dudewheresmyjar.dwmj (OSGi project)
[INFO]    task-segment: [org.ops4j:maven-pax-plugin:1.4:import-bundle]
          (aggregator-style)
[INFO] ------------------------------------------------------------------------
[INFO] [pax:import-bundle]
[INFO] Importing Spring OSGi Web Extender to
         com.dudewheresmyjar.dwmj.build:provision:pom:1.0.0-SNAPSHOT
[INFO] ------------------------------------------------------------------------
[INFO] BUILD SUCCESSFUL
[INFO] ------------------------------------------------------------------------
[INFO] Total time: 4 seconds
[INFO] Finished at: Fri Mar 20 20:39:42 CDT 2009
[INFO] Final Memory: 9M/16M
[INFO] ------------------------------------------------------------------------
dwmjs%
```

The web extender bundle only watches for WAR bundles to be installed in the OSGi framework. For the real work—deploying the WAR to a web container and creating a Spring application context—the extender delegates to classes contained in a separate Spring-DM web support bundle.

```
dwmjs% pax-import-bundle -g org.springframework.osgi -a spring-osgi-web \
?                          -v 1.2.0
[INFO] Scanning for projects...
[INFO] ------------------------------------------------------------------------
[INFO] Building com.dudewheresmyjar.dwmj (OSGi project)
[INFO]     task-segment: [org.ops4j:maven-pax-plugin:1.4:import-bundle]
           (aggregator-style)
[INFO] ------------------------------------------------------------------------
[INFO] [pax:import-bundle]
[INFO] Importing Spring OSGi Web Support to
           com.dudewheresmyjar.dwmj.build:provision:pom:1.0.0-SNAPSHOT
[INFO] ------------------------------------------------------------------------
[INFO] BUILD SUCCESSFUL
[INFO] ------------------------------------------------------------------------
[INFO] Total time: 4 seconds
[INFO] Finished at: Fri Mar 20 20:40:38 CDT 2009
[INFO] Final Memory: 9M/18M
[INFO] ------------------------------------------------------------------------
dwmjs%
```

This web support bundle contains, among other things, a special OSGi-ready implementation of Spring's WebApplicationContext interface. This means that this bundle depends on the web bundle from the Spring Framework. So, we'll also need to be sure to add that bundle:

```
dwmjs% pax-import-bundle -g org.springframework -a spring-web -v 2.5.6
[INFO] Scanning for projects...
[INFO] ------------------------------------------------------------------------
[INFO] Building com.dudewheresmyjar.dwmj (OSGi project)
[INFO]     task-segment: [org.ops4j:maven-pax-plugin:1.4:import-bundle]
           (aggregator-style)
[INFO] ------------------------------------------------------------------------
[INFO] [pax:import-bundle]
[INFO] Importing Spring Framework: Web to
           com.dudewheresmyjar.dwmj.build:provision:pom:1.0.0-SNAPSHOT
[INFO] ------------------------------------------------------------------------
[INFO] BUILD SUCCESSFUL
[INFO] ------------------------------------------------------------------------
[INFO] Total time: 4 seconds
[INFO] Finished at: Fri Mar 20 20:41:12 CDT 2009
[INFO] Final Memory: 8M/18M
[INFO] ------------------------------------------------------------------------
dwmjs%
```

The Spring-DM web extender is now in place and is ready to deploy WAR bundles to Tomcat. But what if you chose to use Jetty instead of Tomcat?

Configuring the Web Extender for Jetty

By default, the web extender assumes that you're using Tomcat to serve web applications. But if Jetty is more your cup of tea, then you'll need to tell the web extender to deploy web bundles to Jetty instead. The trick to configuring the web extender for Jetty is to install a special kind of bundle known as a *fragment*. We'll talk more about fragments in the next chapter, but for now just know that fragments are a mechanism for extending OSGi bundles with additional content.

In this case, the fragment needs two things:

- Its manifest must include a Fragment-Host: that is set to org. springframework.bundle.osgi.web.extender. This tells the OSGi framework that the fragment is to be hosted by the web extender bundle.

- There must be a Spring context definition file in META-INF/spring/ extender that defines a *warDeployer* bean of type org.springframework.osgi.web.deployer.jetty.JettyWarDeployer. This overrides the default TomcatWarDeployer used by the web extender.

I could show you how to build a fragment that fits this bill. But why bother building one yourself if you can just install a ready-made fragment from the Spring-DM repository? Importing the Jetty web extender fragment should do the trick:

```
dwmjs% pax-import-bundle -g org.springframework.osgi \
?                       -a jetty.web.extender.fragment.osgi -v 1.0.1
[INFO] Scanning for projects...
[INFO] ------------------------------------------------------------------
[INFO] Building com.dudewheresmyjar.dwmj (OSGi project)
[INFO]    task-segment: [org.ops4j:maven-pax-plugin:1.4:import-bundle]
          (aggregator-style)
[INFO] ------------------------------------------------------------------
[INFO] [pax:import-bundle]
[INFO] Importing Jetty Spring-DM Web Fragment (OSGi version) to
          com.dudewheresmyjar.dwmj.build:provision:pom:1.0.0-SNAPSHOT
[INFO] ------------------------------------------------------------------
[INFO] BUILD SUCCESSFUL
[INFO] ------------------------------------------------------------------
[INFO] Total time: 5 seconds
[INFO] Finished at: Fri Mar 20 20:48:30 CDT 2009
[INFO] Final Memory: 8M/16M
[INFO] ------------------------------------------------------------------
dwmjs%
```

There's just one more bundle you'll need to set up the web extender to deploy to Jetty. Internally, the Jetty WAR deployer uses CGLIB to create a proxy to the Jetty server. The details of that interaction aren't important, but it is important that we make CGLIB available to the Jetty WAR deployer. To do that, we'll add a CGLIB bundle to the mix:

```
dwmjs% pax-import-bundle -g org.springframework.osgi -a cglib-nodep.osgi \
?                          -v 2.1.3-SNAPSHOT
[INFO] Scanning for projects...
[INFO] ------------------------------------------------------------------------
[INFO] Building com.dudewheresmyjar.dwmj (OSGi project)
[INFO]    task-segment: [org.ops4j:maven-pax-plugin:1.4:import-bundle]
           (aggregator-style)
[INFO] ------------------------------------------------------------------------
[INFO] [pax:import-bundle]
[INFO] Importing cglib no dependencies (OSGi version) to
          com.dudewheresmyjar.dwmj.build:provision:pom:1.0.0-SNAPSHOT
[INFO] ------------------------------------------------------------------------
[INFO] BUILD SUCCESSFUL
[INFO] ------------------------------------------------------------------------
[INFO] Total time: 5 seconds
[INFO] Finished at: Fri Mar 20 20:49:53 CDT 2009
[INFO] Final Memory: 8M/18M
[INFO] ------------------------------------------------------------------------
dwmjs%
```

Now that we've set up all the infrastructure our application needs for web bundles, it's time to create the web bundle itself.

7.3 Developing a Web Bundle

As I've already mentioned, web bundles are a strange breed. In many ways, they resemble a traditional WAR file, but they also contain an OSGi-ready manifest to enable them to be deployed in an OSGi framework. But although adding a manifest to a WAR file may make it an OSGi bundle, that alone doesn't fully exploit the benefits of OSGi.

A typical WAR file contains not only the web portion of an application but also the complete functionality of the application. Even if the application is developed in a modular fashion, those modules end up as JAR files in the WEB-INF/lib directory of the WAR, as illustrated in Figure 7.1, on the next page.

An OSGi web bundle, on the other hand, doesn't need to carry anything more than the web portion of the application. The remaining functionality of the application is contained in separate bundles, as shown in Figure 7.2, on the facing page. The web bundle consumes services from the other bundles.

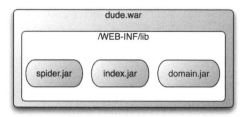

Figure 7.1: IN A CONVENTIONAL JAVA WEB APPLICATION, ALL OF THE APPLICATION'S MODULES END UP PACKAGED WITHIN A SINGLE WAR FILE.

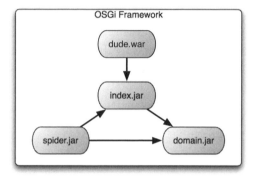

Figure 7.2: AN OSGI WEB BUNDLE RESEMBLES A WAR FILE BUT COLLABORATES WITH OTHER BUNDLES INSTEAD OF CARRYING ITS OWN DEPENDENCIES.

We're going to develop the web front end for our application using Spring's web MVC framework. It's a fairly lightweight framework, and it naturally integrates with Spring. Even so, much of what we'll do to create a web bundle is applicable to almost any Java web framework.

Let's start by setting up a new bundle project.

Setting Up a Web Bundle Project

The first step toward creating a web bundle is the same first step as with any other bundle. We must create the bundle project. So, from within the top-level directory of the *Dude* project, we'll once again use pax-create-bundle to set up a skeleton bundle project.

```
dwmjs% pax-create-bundle -p dwmj.web -n web -g com.dudewheresmyjar \
?                       -v 1.0.0-SNAPSHOT -- -Dspring
[INFO] Scanning for projects...
...
[INFO] ------------------------------------------------------------------------
[INFO] BUILD SUCCESSFUL
[INFO] ------------------------------------------------------------------------
[INFO] Total time: 5 seconds
[INFO] Finished at: Fri Mar 20 20:55:50 CDT 2009
[INFO] Final Memory: 10M/18M
[INFO] ------------------------------------------------------------------------
dwmjs%
```

You'll notice that this time I did one thing a little different from before. In addition to the standard set of group ID, artifact ID, and version information, I also specified that the project is a Spring-DM project by including --*Dspring* on the command line. The first two dashes indicate that what follows is a Maven option. The *-Dspring* option tells the Pax Construct Maven plugin to include Spring context configuration files in the META-INF/spring directory.

Just like before, pax-create-bundle places some sample classes in the project. We won't need those classes, so we'll erase them to get them out of our way:

```
dwmjs% cd web
web% rm src/main/java/dwmj/web/ExampleBean.java
web% rm src/main/java/dwmj/web/internal/ExampleBeanImpl.java
web%
```

But, what we will need are the bundles that our web bundle will depend on. We already know that the web portion of the application will use the index service to search for JAR files. So, let's import the index bundle:

```
web% pax-import-bundle -g com.dudewheresmyjar -a index -v 1.0.0-SNAPSHOT
[INFO] Scanning for projects...
[INFO] ------------------------------------------------------------------------
[INFO] Building com.dudewheresmyjar.web [dwmj.web]
[INFO]    task-segment: [org.ops4j:maven-pax-plugin:1.4:import-bundle]
          (aggregator-style)
[INFO] ------------------------------------------------------------------------
[INFO] [pax:import-bundle]
[INFO] Adding com.dudewheresmyjar.index [dwmj.index] as dependency to
          com.dudewheresmyjar:web:bundle:1.0.0-SNAPSHOT
[INFO] ------------------------------------------------------------------------
[INFO] BUILD SUCCESSFUL
[INFO] ------------------------------------------------------------------------
[INFO] Total time: 4 seconds
[INFO] Finished at: Fri Mar 20 20:57:29 CDT 2009
[INFO] Final Memory: 8M/18M
[INFO] ------------------------------------------------------------------------
web%
```

And the web bundle will also be dealing with JarFile instances, so we'll need to import the domain bundle:

```
web% pax-import-bundle -g com.dudewheresmyjar -a domain -v 1.0.0-SNAPSHOT
[INFO] Scanning for projects...
[INFO] ------------------------------------------------------------------------
[INFO] Building com.dudewheresmyjar.web [dwmj.web]
[INFO]    task-segment: [org.ops4j:maven-pax-plugin:1.4:import-bundle]
          (aggregator-style)
[INFO] ------------------------------------------------------------------------
[INFO] [pax:import-bundle]
[INFO] Adding com.dudewheresmyjar.domain [dwmj.domain] as dependency to
          com.dudewheresmyjar:web:bundle:1.0.0-SNAPSHOT
[INFO] ------------------------------------------------------------------------
[INFO] BUILD SUCCESSFUL
[INFO] ------------------------------------------------------------------------
[INFO] Total time: 5 seconds
[INFO] Finished at: Fri Mar 20 20:58:00 CDT 2009
[INFO] Final Memory: 8M/18M
[INFO] ------------------------------------------------------------------------
web%
```

Since we're going to be using the Spring MVC web framework, we also need to add it to the mix:

```
web% pax-import-bundle -g org.springframework -a spring-webmvc -v 2.5.6
[INFO] Scanning for projects...
[INFO] ------------------------------------------------------------------------
[INFO] Building com.dudewheresmyjar.web [dwmj.web]
[INFO]    task-segment: [org.ops4j:maven-pax-plugin:1.4:import-bundle]
          (aggregator-style)
[INFO] ------------------------------------------------------------------------
[INFO] [pax:import-bundle]
[INFO] Adding Spring Framework: Web MVC as dependency to
          com.dudewheresmyjar:web:bundle:1.0.0-SNAPSHOT
[INFO] ------------------------------------------------------------------------
[INFO] BUILD SUCCESSFUL
[INFO] ------------------------------------------------------------------------
[INFO] Total time: 5 seconds
[INFO] Finished at: Fri Mar 20 21:23:45 CDT 2009
[INFO] Final Memory: 8M/19M
[INFO] ------------------------------------------------------------------------
web%
```

Finally, as we learned with the spider bundle, the JarFile class brings with it a transitive dependency on Compass annotations. That means that we're going to need the Compass bundle.

```
web% pax-import-bundle -g com.dudewheresmyjar.dwmj \
?                       -a org.compass-project.compass -v 2.1.1-001-SNAPSHOT
[INFO] Scanning for projects...
[INFO] ------------------------------------------------------------------------
[INFO] Building com.dudewheresmyjar.web [dwmj.web]
[INFO]    task-segment: [org.ops4j:maven-pax-plugin:1.4:import-bundle]
          (aggregator-style)
[INFO] ------------------------------------------------------------------------
[INFO] [pax:import-bundle]
[INFO] Adding com.dudewheresmyjar.dwmj:org.compass-project.compass:
          jar:2.1.1-001-SNAPSHOT as dependency to
          com.dudewheresmyjar:web:bundle:1.0.0-SNAPSHOT
[INFO] ------------------------------------------------------------------------
[INFO] BUILD SUCCESSFUL
[INFO] ------------------------------------------------------------------------
[INFO] Total time: 5 seconds
[INFO] Finished at: Fri Mar 20 20:58:43 CDT 2009
[INFO] Final Memory: 8M/16M
[INFO] ------------------------------------------------------------------------
web%
```

And now we're ready to develop the web bundle code.

Constructing the Web Application

We could develop the web bundle using any one of the countless web frameworks that are available to Java developers, including JavaServer Faces, Struts, and Tapestry. But since we're already using Spring for dependency injection, it seems natural to use Spring-MVC.

Handling Web Requests

In Spring MVC, web requests are handled by objects called *controllers*. For our application, we need only a single controller that responds to HTTP GET requests with a search form and processes the data submitted on an HTTP POST request. The class in SearchController.java does just that.

dwmjs/web/src/main/java/dwmj/web/SearchController.java

```java
package dwmj.web;

import java.util.List;

import org.springframework.beans.factory.annotation.Autowired;
import org.springframework.stereotype.Controller;
import org.springframework.ui.ModelMap;
import org.springframework.web.bind.annotation.RequestMapping;
import org.springframework.web.bind.annotation.RequestMethod;

import dwmj.domain.JarFile;
```

```
import dwmj.index.IndexService;

@Controller
@RequestMapping("/search.htm")
public class SearchController {

    @RequestMapping(method = RequestMethod.GET)
    public String showSearchForm(String searchString, ModelMap model) {
        if(searchString != null) return doSearch(searchString, model);
            return "searchForm";
    }


    @RequestMapping(method = RequestMethod.POST)
    public String doSearch(String searchString, ModelMap model) {

        List<JarFile> matches = indexService.findJarFiles(searchString);
        model.addAttribute(matches);
      return "searchResults";
    }

    @Autowired
    IndexService indexService;
}
```

As of Spring 2.5, it's possible to write a controller by tagging an otherwise plain Java class with annotations that identify methods to handle requests. In this case, SearchController is annotated in four places with three different annotations that make it work as a Spring MVC controller:

- At the class level, SearchController is annotated with @Controller to identify the class as a controller. In a moment, we'll see how this annotation is used to automatically register SearchController as a bean in the Spring application context.

  SearchController is also annotated at the class level with @RequestMapping. As used here, @RequestMapping tells Spring MVC this controller will handle requests with a URL pattern of /search.htm.

- The showSearchForm() method is annotated with @RequestMapping. But in this case, @RequestMapping is used to indicate that the showSearchForm() method will handle HTTP GET requests to /search.htm. If the GET request carries a searchString parameter, then it calls the doSearch() method to perform a search. Otherwise, it returns the logical view name of *searchForm* to tell Spring MVC to display the search form.

- Likewise, the doSearch() method is annotated with @RequestMapping to declare that it will handle HTTP POST requests. It uses an IndexService to find matching JarFiles. It places whatever is found into the model and then returns *searchResults* as the logical name of the view to display the results.

- As for the IndexService, it is an instance variable that is annotated with @Autowired so that Spring will automatically inject it with a matching bean (which we expect will be the service published by the index bundle).

Regarding the showSearchForm() and doSearch() methods, both return a String containing the logical name of a view to display in the user's browser after the request has been handled. We'll see how that logical view name is mapped to an actual view soon. But first, let's take a look at the two JSP files that define those views.

Creating the Web Views

When an HTTP GET request arrives for SearchController, the showSearchForm() method handles the request by returning *searchForm*. This value is a logical view name that is ultimately mapped to the actual view implementation, /WEB-INF/jsp/searchForm.jsp:

```
dwmjs/web/src/main/webapp/WEB-INF/jsp/searchForm.jsp
<html>
  <head>
    <title>Dude, Where's My JAR?</title>
  </head>

  <body>
    <h2>Dude, Where's My JAR?</h2>
    <form method="POST" action="search.htm">
      <input type="text" name="searchString"/> 
      <input type="submit" value="Search"/>
    </form>
  </body>
</html>
```

This JSP file contains a simple form that asks the user to enter a search string and then submits the entry, via HTTP POST, to /search.htm.

That's where the doSearch() method steps in. After it has finished collecting matching JarFiles from the index service, it returns *searchResults*, a logical view name corresponding to /WEB-INF/jsp/searchResults.jsp.

```jsp
<%@ page info="Search results page" %>
<%@ taglib prefix="c" uri="http://java.sun.com/jsp/jstl/core" %>

<%@page import="dwmj.domain.JarFile"%>
<html>
  <head><title>Dude, Where's My JAR?</title></head>

  <body>
    <form method="POST" action="search.htm">
      <input type="text" name="searchString"/> 
          <input type="submit" value="Search"/>
    </form>

    <c:choose>
        <c:when test='${empty jarFileList}'>
          <h2>Where's your JAR, dude?</h2>
          <p>I couldn't find the JARs you were asking for.</p>
        </c:when>
        <c:otherwise>
    <h2>Here's your JAR(s), dude!</h2>
    <p>I found these JAR files:</p>

    <table border="1">
      <thead>
        <tr>
          <td><b>Repository</b></td>
          <td><b>Group</b></td>
          <td><b>Artifact</b></td>
          <td><b>Version</b></td>
          <td><b>Snapshot?</b></td>
          <td><b>Source?</b></td>
          <td><b>Javadoc?</b></td>
          <td><b>Symbolic Name</b></td>
          <td> </td>
        </tr>
      </thead>
      <tbody>

      <c:forEach items="${jarFileList}" var="jarFile">
        <tr>
          <td><c:out value="${jarFile.repository}" /></td>
          <td><c:out value="${jarFile.groupId}" /></td>
          <td><c:out value="${jarFile.artifactId}" /></td>
          <td><c:out value="${jarFile.version}" /></td>
          <td><c:out value="${jarFile.snapshot}" /></td>
          <td><c:out value="${jarFile.hasSource}" /></td>
          <td><c:out value="${jarFile.hasJavadoc}" /></td>
          <td><c:out value="${jarFile.bundleSymbolicName}" /></td>
          <td><a href="<c:out value="${jarFile.rawUrl}" />">Download</a></td>
        </tr>
      </c:forEach>
```

```
    </tbody>
  </table>
      </c:otherwise>
    </c:choose>
  </body>
</html>
```

This JSP cycles through the list of JarFiles that were found, displaying them to the user. And, it offers the user another search form so that they can search again.

One small detail about these web views still needs to be settled. Since searchResults.jsp uses JSTL, we'll also need to be sure to make that available at runtime:

```
dwmjs% pax-import-bundle -g org.springframework.osgi -a jstl.osgi \
?                        -v 1.1.2-SNAPSHOT
[INFO] Scanning for projects...
[INFO] ------------------------------------------------------------------
[INFO] Building com.dudewheresmyjar.dwmj (OSGi project)
[INFO]     task-segment: [org.ops4j:maven-pax-plugin:1.4:import-bundle]
           (aggregator-style)
[INFO] ------------------------------------------------------------------
[INFO] [pax:import-bundle]
[INFO] Importing JSTL 1.1.x (OSGi version) to
           com.dudewheresmyjar.dwmj.build:provision:pom:1.0.0-SNAPSHOT
[INFO] ------------------------------------------------------------------
[INFO] BUILD SUCCESSFUL
[INFO] ------------------------------------------------------------------
[INFO] Total time: 5 seconds
[INFO] Finished at: Fri Mar 20 21:25:11 CDT 2009
[INFO] Final Memory: 8M/17M
[INFO] ------------------------------------------------------------------
dwmjs%
```

At this point we've created our web bundle project and have stocked it with a Spring MVC controller and a couple of JSP files. But the functional contents of a web bundle are only half of the story. Before we can see our application present itself in a web browser, we need to address some configuration details.

7.4 Deploying the Web Bundle

In a conventional Java web application, the WEB-INF/web.xml file configures any servlets, filters, and/or listeners that are part of the application. And, if that web application is a Spring MVC application, there'll also be at least one Spring context definition file to declare the Spring controllers, URL handlers, and view resolvers.

An OSGi web bundle is no different. We'll still need a web.xml file, and we'll need a Spring context file. A web bundle is different from a conventional WAR file, however, in that it will also need a MANIFEST.MF file to make it an OSGi bundle. And the Spring context will also need to include a *<reference>* to the index service that it will use.

Configuring the Web Bundle

Just like any web application, we'll need to configure the web bundle by creating a web.xml file. More specifically, because we're using Spring MVC, we'll need to configure ContextLoaderListener and DispatcherServlet:

`dwmjs/web/src/main/webapp/WEB-INF/web.xml`

```xml
<web-app xmlns="http://java.sun.com/xml/ns/j2ee"
        xmlns:xsi="http://www.w3.org/2001/XMLSchema-instance"
        xsi:schemaLocation="http://java.sun.com/xml/ns/j2ee
                http://java.sun.com/xml/ns/j2ee/web-app_2_4.xsd"
        version="2.4">

  <display-name>Dude Where's My Jar? Web Application</display-name>

  <context-param>
    <param-name>contextClass</param-name>
    <param-value>
    org.springframework.osgi.web.context.support.OsgiBundleXmlWebApplicationContext
    </param-value>
  </context-param>

  <context-param>
    <param-name>contextConfigLocation</param-name>
    <param-value>/WEB-INF/dude-osgi.xml</param-value>
  </context-param>

  <listener>
    <listener-class>
        org.springframework.web.context.ContextLoaderListener
    </listener-class>
  </listener>

  <servlet>
    <servlet-name>dude</servlet-name>
    <servlet-class>
        org.springframework.web.servlet.DispatcherServlet
    </servlet-class>
    <init-param>
      <param-name>contextClass</param-name>
      <param-value>
    org.springframework.osgi.web.context.support.OsgiBundleXmlWebApplicationContext
      </param-value>
```

```
    </init-param>
    <load-on-startup>1</load-on-startup>
  </servlet>

  <servlet-mapping>
    <servlet-name>dude</servlet-name>
    <url-pattern>*.htm</url-pattern>
  </servlet-mapping>
</web-app>
```

DispatcherServlet is Spring's front controller, handling HTTP requests as they come in and directing them to the appropriate controller class for processing. Here the *<servlet-mapping>* configures it to respond to any request that ends with .htm.

When DispatcherServlet is started, it loads its Spring context from an XML file whose name is based on the servlet's name (as specified by the *<servlet-name>* element). In this case, DispatcherServlet will load its Spring context from WEB-INF/dude-servlet.xml:

```
<?xml version="1.0" encoding="UTF-8"?>
<beans xmlns="http://www.springframework.org/schema/beans"
       xmlns:xsi="http://www.w3.org/2001/XMLSchema-instance"
       xmlns:context="http://www.springframework.org/schema/context"
       xsi:schemaLocation="http://www.springframework.org/schema/beans
       http://www.springframework.org/schema/beans/spring-beans-2.5.xsd
       http://www.springframework.org/schema/context
          http://www.springframework.org/schema/context/spring-context-2.5.xsd">

<bean class=
 "org.springframework.web.servlet.mvc.annotation.DefaultAnnotationHandlerMapping

<bean id="viewResolver"
    class="org.springframework.web.servlet.view.InternalResourceViewResolver">
  <property name="prefix" value="/WEB-INF/jsp/" />
  <property name="suffix" value=".jsp" />
</bean>

<context:component-scan base-package="dwmj.web" />

</beans>
```

This Spring configuration declares two *<bean>*s. As a request is received by DispatcherServlet, the DefaultAnnotationHandlerMapping bean will map URL patterns declared with @RequestMapping to the SearchController's methods. After the controller is finished, DispatcherServlet will use InternalResourceViewResolver to map the logical view name returned by the controller to JSP view implementations in the /WEB-INF/jsp directory.

The <component-scan> element from Spring's context namespace rounds out the Spring configuration file. This near-magical element is configured to scan the dwmj.web package looking for classes that are annotated with either @Component, @Controller, @Aspect, @Repository, or @Service and to automatically register those classes as beans in the Spring context. As it turns out, SearchController is in that package and is annotated with @Controller—so a SearchController bean will be created.

What's more, <component-scan> will arrange to have the SearchController bean's indexService property automatically wired with an implementation of IndexService. That's because the indexService property is annotated with @Autowired. But where is the IndexService bean that will be injected into the indexService property?

Defining Additional Spring Configuration

In order to keep the OSGi-specific Spring configuration separate from the rest of the beans, I've placed the reference to the index service in a separate Spring configuration file. This is what the ContextLoaderListener is for. Whereas DispatcherServlet will load the Spring application context from only a single configuration file, ContextLoaderListener loads more context configuration from one or more additional files. In this case, the contextConfigLocation context parameter identifies /WEB-INF/dude-osgi.xml as the file that contains additional Spring configuration details:

```
<?xml version="1.0" encoding="UTF-8"?>
<beans:beans xmlns="http://www.springframework.org/schema/osgi"
      xmlns:xsi="http://www.w3.org/2001/XMLSchema-instance"
      xmlns:beans="http://www.springframework.org/schema/beans"
      xsi:schemaLocation="http://www.springframework.org/schema/beans
      http://www.springframework.org/schema/beans/spring-beans-2.5.xsd
      http://www.springframework.org/schema/osgi
          http://www.springframework.org/schema/osgi/spring-osgi.xsd">

  <reference id="indexService"
      interface="dwmj.index.IndexService" />

</beans:beans>
```

This Spring configuration should look a little familiar, because it's not much different from the OSGi configuration file we used for the spider bundle. In both cases, the <reference> element is used to look up the index service from the OSGi service registry and add a reference to it as a bean in Spring. Because the service being referenced implements IndexService, it is autowired into SearchController's indexService property.

Filling Out the Web Bundle's Manifest

We're almost ready to run the application again and see the web bundle in action. But there are a few loose ends to tie up with regard to the bundle's manifest:

- Unlike typical bundles, web bundles follow the WAR file convention of having their classpaths rooted in WEB-INF/classes and WEB-INF/lib. We'll need to tell the OSGi framework about this.
- We used several Spring classes (such as DispatcherServlet and DefaultAnnotationHandlerMapping) in non-Java files. BND will automatically create Import-Package: entries in the manifest for dependencies it finds in Java code. But we'll need to help it out for dependencies that are used only in web.xml or Spring configuration files.
- We also used the JSTL tag libraries in our JSP. We'll need to make those packages available to our bundle too.
- When the web bundle is installed in Jetty or Tomcat, it will be given a context path (the path in the application's URL) that is based on the bundle's symbolic name. We should probably give it a friendlier context path. Perhaps something as simple as *dude*.

The following osgi.bnd file should take care of all of the previous:

```
#----------------------------------------------------------------
# Use this file to add customized Bnd instructions for the bundle
#----------------------------------------------------------------
Bundle-Classpath: .,WEB-INF/classes
Import-Package: *,\
  org.springframework.osgi.web.context.support,\
  org.springframework.web.servlet,\
  org.springframework.web.servlet.handler,\
  org.springframework.web.servlet.mvc,\
  org.springframework.web.servlet.view,\
  dwmj.domain,\
  org.springframework.web.servlet.mvc.annotation,\
  org.springframework.web.context
Require-Bundle: org.springframework.osgi.jstl.osgi
Web-ContextPath: dude
```

The Bundle-Classpath: header specifies the path, relative to the root of the bundle's JAR file, that should be included in the bundle's classpath. By default, Bundle-Classpath: is set to . to indicate that the classpath should be the root of the bundle JAR. Here I've set it to also include WEB-INF/classes, because that's where the compiled SearchController class will be found.

Use Require-Bundle Sparingly

In the case of JSTL, Require-Bundle: is a convenient way to make the entire tag library available and to cut down on the number of explicitly imported packages. But Require-Bundle: should be used with caution.

Require-Bundle: has approximately the same effect as using Import-Package: to import all the packages within a given bundle. Import-Package: declares that a bundle needs to import certain packages but doesn't care which bundle(s) they come from. Require-Bundle:, on the other hand, mandates that all exported packages of a specific bundle must be imported, creating what is usually an undesirable coupling with a specific bundle.

Import-Package: is set to include all the Spring packages that we use outside our Java code. It also includes * to indicate that we also want to include any packages that BND will import as it scans our Java code for dependencies.

In order to make the JSTL libraries available, I've added Require-Bundle:. Although I could have used Import-Package: to import the JSTL classes, Require-Bundle: is far more convenient in this case, because it will import all of the packages from the JSTL bundle.

Finally, Web-ContextPath: specifies the context path with which the application will be deployed to the web container. By setting this to *dude*, we will be able to navigate to the application using a URL such as http://localhost:8080/dude.

In fact, I think we're ready fire up the application and see it in a web browser.

Firing It Up

First things first. Before we can start the application and kick the tires on the web bundle, we'll need to build it. But before we can build it, we need to tweak the Maven pom.xml file.

You see, when we created the web bundle project with pax-create-bundle, what we got was a pom.xml file with bundle packaging. That is, the artifact produced by Maven will be an OSGi bundle. That's exactly what we want, but we also want a little bit more. We also want the web bundle to be a WAR file and to have the internal structure of a WAR file.

So, it would seem that we're facing a dilemma. Do we tell Maven to create a bundle or to create a WAR file?

Fortunately, we can get both. The Maven WAR plugin does a great job of producing WAR files, so we'll set the packaging of our project to be *war*:

```
<packaging>war</packaging>
```

Then we'll need to add that Felix Bundle plugin so that an OSGi manifest will be created for the web bundle:

```
<plugin>
  <groupId>org.apache.felix</groupId>
  <artifactId>maven-bundle-plugin</artifactId>
  <executions>
    <execution>
      <id>bundle-manifest</id>
      <phase>process-classes</phase>
      <goals>
        <goal>manifest</goal>
      </goals>
    </execution>
  </executions>
  <configuration>
    <supportedProjectTypes>
      <supportedProjectType>jar</supportedProjectType>
      <supportedProjectType>bundle</supportedProjectType>
      <supportedProjectType>war</supportedProjectType>
    </supportedProjectTypes>
<!-- ... -->
  </configuration>
</plugin>
```

Finally, we'll need to tweak the configuration of the WAR plugin so that it will include the manifest generated by the bundle plugin:

```
<plugin>
  <groupId>org.apache.maven.plugins</groupId>
  <artifactId>maven-war-plugin</artifactId>
  <configuration>
    <archive>
      <manifestFile>
          ${project.build.outputDirectory}/META-INF/MANIFEST.MF
      </manifestFile>
    </archive>
  </configuration>
</plugin>
```

Now that we've arranged for Maven to build a bundle that is also a WAR file, let's kick off the build:

```
web% mvn install
[INFO] Scanning for projects...
...
[INFO] ------------------------------------------------------------------------
[INFO] BUILD SUCCESSFUL
[INFO] ------------------------------------------------------------------------
[INFO] Total time: 8 seconds
[INFO] Finished at: Fri Mar 20 21:30:19 CDT 2009
[INFO] Final Memory: 14M/28M
[INFO] ------------------------------------------------------------------------
web%
```

It looks like it built cleanly. Now let's kick it off with pax-provision and pull up the application in a web browser and see what happens. As you'll recall, we set the context path to *dude* and mapped SearchController to respond to /search.htm. Therefore, we will need to point our browser to http://localhost:8080/dude/search.htm. You should see the application's home page with a simple search form in your web browser.

Woo-hoo! The application is asking us to enter some search criteria. So far so good. Let's try searching for something. How about something like *spring*?

Depending on how far along the spider has gotten in indexing the repository, the application may respond with some results, as shown in Figure 7.3, on the next page. Of course, if the spider hasn't got around to indexing any JARs that would match the search criteria, you may be disappointed in what it finds (or doesn't find).

Our application seems to work. But before we move on, let's step back and think about what we've done. In this chapter, we have done the following:

- Set up a web server (either Tomcat or Jetty) within the OSGi framework
- Installed the Spring-DM web extender so that we can deploy WAR files as bundles
- Developed and deployed the web portion of our application as a WAR bundle

That last item is worth expanding on. Although we've deployed a WAR file, this isn't a conventional web application. It's an OSGi bundle that just borrows some of the characteristics of a WAR file.

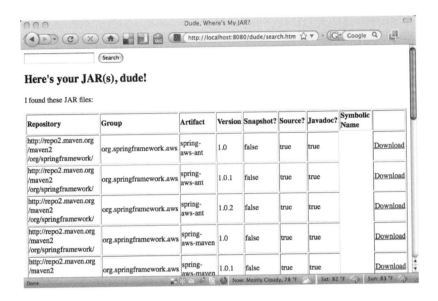

Figure 7.3: THE SEARCH RESULTS PAGE AFTER SEARCHING FOR *spring*

Unlike a conventional WAR file, this web bundle doesn't carry all of its dependencies internally. Instead, it will consume services from the OSGi runtime that it is deployed in. This not only makes the web bundle a bit skinnier than a conventional WAR file but also decouples the web portion of the application from the rest of it.

You've no doubt noticed that the look and feel leaves a lot to be desired. Unfortunately, OSGi can't help you make your application look prettier. But as you'll see in the next chapter, it can help you separate the look and feel of your application (JSPs, style sheets, and images) from the rest of the web layer code. So, go ahead and celebrate our progress with a cold beverage of your choice. Then come back, and let's see how to use something called *fragments* to package the look and feel in its own bundle.

Chapter 8

Extending Bundles

One of the most significant tenets of object-oriented programming is that software entities should be open for extension but closed for modification. The open-closed principle is often cited in reference to classes but is, in fact, applicable to modules as well.

In OSGi, the mechanism for extending bundles is to create a special kind of bundle known as a *fragment bundle* (or *fragments*, as they're typically called). Fragments provide a way to add new content to an established bundle at runtime, without rebuilding the bundle.

In this chapter, we're going to create a fragment that extends the web bundle that we created in the previous chapter, providing the look and feel of the application. This will effectively decouple the client-side presentation of our application from the server-side controllers that respond to user input.

8.1 Introducing Fragments

Fragments are much like regular bundles in that they are a unit of deployment in OSGi. They're packaged as JAR files and are described in metadata in the META-INF/MANIFEST.MF file. Unlike regular bundles, however, fragments are useless by themselves. They must be connected to another bundle.

Think of the relationship between bundles and fragments as being like the relationship between a home entertainment system and DVDs. A typical modern home entertainment system probably includes at least a television and a DVD player. Although the entertainment system is probably useful on its own for viewing broadcast programs, a DVD

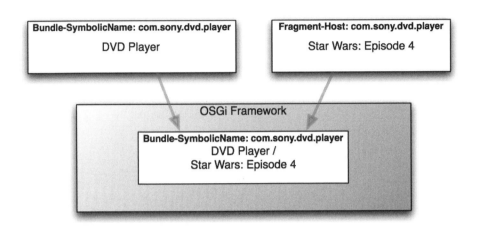

Figure 8.1: ALTHOUGH THEY'RE TWO SEPARATE PHYSICAL ENTITIES, AN OSGI FRAGMENT BECOMES ONE WITH ITS HOST BUNDLES AT RUNTIME.

has little utility beyond that of a shiny drink coaster without the DVD player. By placing the DVD into the player, you give the DVD purpose and, at the same time, extend the capability of the entertainment system.

Likewise, a fragment is nothing more than a JAR file until it is given to a bundle. Unlike a DVD that can be played in any compatible DVD player, however, a fragment specifies the bundle to which it should be associated with a Fragment-Host: entry in its manifest. For example, if we were to develop our DVD example as OSGi bundles and fragments, the DVD fragment's MANIFEST.MF might look like this:

```
Bundle-ManifestVersion: 2
Bundle-SymbolicName: com.lucasfilm.movies.starwars4
Bundle-Description: Star Wars, Episode 4: A New Hope
Bundle-Version: 1.0.0
Fragment-Host: com.sony.dvd.player
```

In this contrived example, the DVD fragment is asking to be joined to the bundle whose symbolic name is com.sony.dvd.player, as illustrated in Figure 8.1.

Specifying a Fragment-Host: is just about all there is to creating a fragment. The only thing that's left is to fill the fragment's JAR file with contents. When the OSGi framework joins a fragment to a bundle at runtime, the contents of the fragment effectively become the contents

Using Felix? Then No Fragments for You

I've mentioned this before, but it's worth repeating again. As I write this, the current version of Felix (1.4) does not support fragments. That means that this chapter doesn't apply to you if you're using Felix. (If, however, you're using Equinox, then you'll be OK—Equinox supports fragments.)

There is an item in Felix's issue-tracking system to add fragment support to Felix. You can follow the progress of the Felix fragment issue at http://issues.apache.org/jira/browse/FELIX-29.

of the hosting bundle. They become one logical runtime bundle, even though their contents are spread across two (or more) physical JAR files.

Now that you know what fragments are, let's see how we can use them to manage the look and feel of our application.

8.2 Creating a UI Fragment

Unfortunately, there's nothing in the OSGi specification that can directly impact the usability and aesthetics of our application. It will still be up to us to flex our creativity muscles to give our application a polished look and feel. But what OSGi can offer, through fragments, is a way to separate the look and feel of the application from the application itself so that each can be developed and modified independently of the other. This separation of an application's user interface from its functionality is commonly known as *skinning*.

The OSGi specification says that one of the key use cases for fragments is to provide translation files for different locales. Although localization isn't exactly the same as look and feel, they're both a type of skinning. Localization just happens to be a way to skin an application with a specific language. If fragments can be used for localization, then they can certainly also be used for skinning our application to make it look nice.

We'll start by creating the fragment project.

Setting Up the Fragment Project

Because fragments are just a special kind of bundle, we can use Pax Construct's pax-create-bundle command to set up our fragment project:

```
dwmjs% pax-create-bundle -p dwmj.web -n ui -v 1.0.0-SNAPSHOT \
?                        -- -Dinterface=false -Dinternals=false
[INFO] Scanning for projects...
...
[INFO] ------------------------------------------------------------------------
[INFO] BUILD SUCCESSFUL
[INFO] ------------------------------------------------------------------------
[INFO] Total time: 5 seconds
[INFO] Finished at: Fri Mar 20 22:15:12 CDT 2009
[INFO] Final Memory: 10M/19M
[INFO] ------------------------------------------------------------------------
dwmjs%
```

As always, the -p, -n, and -v parameters specify the bundle's base package, name, and version (respectively). But notice the double dash (--) and the two items that follow it. The double dash indicates that all parameters that follow are Maven parameters (and not for pax-create-bundle).

In this case, I am using the double dash to set two properties used by the Maven archetype that works under the covers of pax-create-bundle. By setting the interface property to false, I am telling the archetype to not create the sample OSGi service interface. Similarly, setting internals to false tells the archetype not to create the same code in the internals package. Our user interface fragment won't be needing any of that stuff.

In fact, since the fragment will contain only web artifacts like JSP, CSS, and image files, we won't need any Java content created at all. Therefore, the package name given with the -p parameter is irrelevant. But, pax-create-bundle considers it a mandatory parameter, so I had to provide it.

Now let's add some web content to the user interface (UI) fragment.

Adding Web Files

The web bundle had only three JSP files—one in the root (the index.jsp welcome file) and two in WEB-INF/jsp (a search form page and a search results page). The index.jsp file does nothing more than redirect requests for the application root to the search page and has no look and feel aspect to it. So, it is fine where it is. But we'll need to move the other two JSP files into the UI fragment.

As we move them over, let's embellish them to be more aesthetically pleasing. First, here's the new searchForm.jsp:

```
dwmjs/ui/src/main/resources/WEB-INF/jsp/searchForm.jsp
```

```html
<html>
  <head>
    <title>Dude, Where's My JAR?</title>
  </head>

  <body style="text-align:center;">
      <br/>
      <br/>
      <br/>
      <img src="images/dwmj-logo.png" />
      <br/>
      <br/>
      <form method="POST" action="search.htm">
        <input type="text" name="searchString" size="55" />
        <br/>
        <br/>
        <input type="submit" value="      Find My JAR      " />
      </form>
      <br/>
      <br/>
      <br/>
      <span style="font-family:arial;font-size:8pt;">Copyright &copy; 2009</span>
  </body>
</html>
```

The key thing that's changed here is the addition of some HTML for layout purposes as well as an *<img>* tag to display the *Dude, Where's My JAR?* logo. We'll need to remember to put the logo's image file (dwmj-logo.png) in src/main/resources/images so that it will end up in the fragment JAR file when we build the project. Don't worry if your graphic design skills are lacking—I've included a logo image file in the example download.

Next up is the searchResults.jsp file (abridged here to save space):

```
dwmjs/ui/src/main/resources/WEB-INF/jsp/searchResults.jsp
```

```jsp
<%@ page info="Search results page" %>
<%@ taglib prefix="c" uri="http://java.sun.com/jsp/jstl/core" %>
<%@ taglib prefix="fn" uri="http://java.sun.com/jsp/jstl/functions" %>

<%@page import="dwmj.domain.JarFile"%>
<html>
  <head>
      <title>Dude, Where's My JAR?</title>
      <link href="css/dude.css" rel="stylesheet" type="text/css">
```

```html
    <script src="jquery/jquery.js"></script>
    <script>
    $(document).ready(function(){

        $('.summaryRow').click(function() {
            $(this).siblings().slideToggle("slow");
        });

        $('.downloadLink').click(function() {});
    });
    </script>
</head>

<body>
  <form method="POST" action="search.htm">
    <a href="search.htm"><img src="images/dwmj-logo-50.png"
        align="middle" border="0"/></a>
    <input type="text" name="searchString" size="55"
        value="${param.searchString}" /> 
    <input type="submit" value="     Find My JAR     " />
  </form>

  <div class="resultsHeader">
    Dude, I found <c:out value="${fn:length(jarFileList)}" /> JARs
  </div>
  <c:choose>
    <c:when test='${empty jarFileList}'>
      <div style="text-align:center;">
        <h2>Where's your JAR, dude?</h2>
        <p>I couldn't find any JARs that match "<c:out
            value="${param.searchString}" />".</p>
        <p>Try searching again with new search criteria.</p>
      </div>
    </c:when>
    <c:otherwise>
      <br/>
      <div class="resultsList">
        <c:forEach items="${jarFileList}" var="jarFile">
<!-- ... -->
        </c:forEach>
      </div>
    </c:otherwise>
  </c:choose>
  </body>
</html>
```

As you can see, this JSP is significantly more advanced than the one we created before. Aside from layout changes and the addition of the logo, this JSP uses jQuery[1] to add some dynamic capabilities to the result

---

1. http://www.jquery.com

listing. It also uses an external style sheet to define the overall style of the result page. Therefore, we'll need to be sure to include the jQuery file and the CSS file in the project.

I am using version 1.2.6 of the packed jQuery JavaScript file. Place jquery-1.2.6.pack.js in src/main/resources/jquery so that it will end up in the jquery directory inside the fragment.

As for the CSS file, it should be placed in src/main/resources/css. The dude.css file looks like this:

```
dwmjs/ui/src/main/resources/css/dude.css
body {
    font-family:arial;
}

.firstEntry {
    border-top: 1px solid #999999;
}

.entry {
    border-bottom: 1px solid #999999;
    font-size:small;
}

.summaryRow {
    font-weight:bold;
    font-size:small;
    width:100%;
}

.detailsRow {
    font-size:small;
    display:none;
    background-color:#eeeeee;
    width:100%;
}

.resultsList {
    margin-left:50px;
    margin-right:50px;
}

.resultsHeader {
    width:100%;
    background-color:#eeeeff;
    border-top:1px solid #000099;
    padding:3px;
    font-size:small;
}
```

```
.label {
    text-align:right;
    font-weight:bold;
}

.pomDependency {
        font-family:monospace;
        whitespace:pre;
        border-top: 1px solid black;
        border-bottom: 1px solid black;
}
```

Now all of the web artifacts are in place, and we're almost ready to build the fragment and try using it. But first we need to make sure that we're building a fragment and not a regular bundle.

Specifying the Fragment Host

Up until now, most of the what we've done in this chapter has been typical web design work. We'd probably create CSS and HTML files, work with JavaScript, and design logo graphics for any web application we create, whether we're working with OSGi or not.

But now, before we can build the fragment, we need to finally do the one little bit of OSGi-related work that will make this bundle a fragment bundle. We need to specify the Fragment-Host: in the osgi.bnd file:

```
#------------------------------------------------------------------
# Use this file to add customized Bnd instructions for the bundle
#------------------------------------------------------------------

Fragment-Host: com.dudewheresmyjar.web
```

In this case, we've specified that the fragment will be hosted by the bundle whose symbolic name is com.dudewheresmyjar.web. That just happens to be the symbolic name of our web bundle. Consequently, when we deploy the fragment along with the web bundle (as shown in Figure 8.2, on the next page), the JSP, CSS, and image files in the bundle will be merged into the web bundle at runtime—as if they were in the web bundle all along.

Again, Fragment-Host: is all you need (aside from the obligatory Bundle-SymbolicName: header) to create a fragment bundle. Now let's build it and try it.

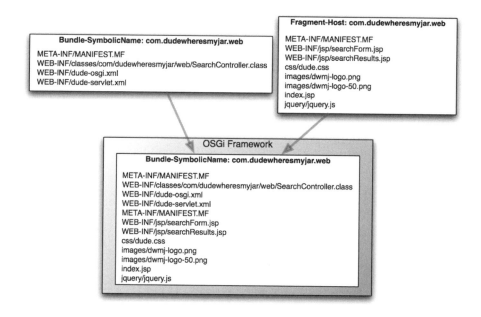

Figure 8.2: The UI fragment attaches JSP, CSS, and image files to the web bundle when deployed in the OSGi framework together.

8.3 Trying It

Before we can fire up the OSGi framework and see the UI fragment applied to the web bundle, we'll need to build it:

```
ui% mvn install
[INFO] Scanning for projects...
...
[INFO] ------------------------------------------------------------------------
[INFO] BUILD SUCCESSFUL
[INFO] ------------------------------------------------------------------------
[INFO] Total time: 7 seconds
[INFO] Finished at: Fri Mar 20 22:22:40 CDT 2009
[INFO] Final Memory: 13M/30M
[INFO] ------------------------------------------------------------------------
ui%
```

The build is successful, so we're ready to go, right? Not quite. We have a little cleanup to do first.

Cleaning Up the Web Bundle

One thing that I haven't told you about fragments yet is that they can only add new content to their hosting bundle. They cannot replace any of their host's existing content. Since our web bundle already has searchForm.jsp and searchResults.jsp in its WEB-INF/jsp directory, the UI fragment won't be able to replace them with the new JSP files. Therefore, if our UI fragment is to have any effect, we'll need to clean up the web bundle, removing the old versions of the application's JSP files:

```
ui% cd ../web
web% rm -R src/main/webapp/WEB-INF/jsp
web%
```

After the web bundle is rebuilt, we're finally ready to give our UI fragment a spin.

Starting the Application

As usual, we'll use pax-provision to kick off the OSGi framework and install and start our bundles, effectively starting our application. Once everything has started, let's issue the ss command to see the bundles in the OSGi framework, focusing specifically on the web bundle and our UI fragment:

```
osgi> ss

Framework is launched.

id      State       Bundle
0       ACTIVE      org.eclipse.osgi_3.4.2.R34x_v20080826-1230
1       ACTIVE      org.eclipse.osgi.util_3.1.300.v20080303
2       ACTIVE      org.eclipse.osgi.services_3.1.200.v20070605
...
35      ACTIVE      com.dudewheresmyjar.web_1.0.0.SNAPSHOT
                    Fragments=36
36      RESOLVED    com.dudewheresmyjar.dwmj.ui_1.0.0.SNAPSHOT
                    Master=35

osgi>
```

Notice that the web bundle (id=32) and the UI fragment (id=33) reference each other. The web bundle's entry includes *Fragments=33*, which indicates that the web bundle is augmented by the fragment whose ID is 33.[2] As for the fragment, it includes *Master=32*, indicating that this item is a fragment and that it is hosted by the bundle whose ID is 32.

---

2. Also notice that "Fragments" is plural. That's because it's possible for a bundle to host more than one fragment. On the other hand, a fragment can be hosted by a single bundle only.

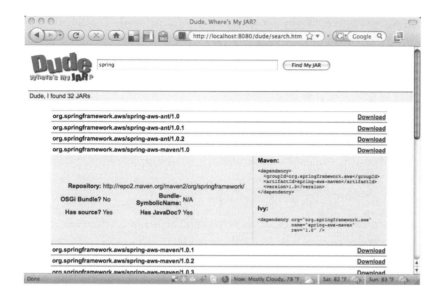

Figure 8.3: A SEARCH RESULTS PAGE AFTER APPLYING THE UI FRAGMENT

You've probably also noticed that the UI fragment seems to be stuck in the RESOLVED state and is not ACTIVE. That's because fragments do not do anything on their own and therefore are never actually started. Just as with regular bundles, the RESOLVED state indicates that the fragment's dependencies have been met, but that's as far as a fragment will go in the bundle life cycle.

Let's see the fruit of our labor. Open up your web browser, and point it at http://localhost:8080/dude. You should see the new and more visually appealing home page. Now let's try submitting a search. The results found when I tried searching for *spring* are shown in Figure 8.3.[3]

Each line of the result set includes the Maven group ID, artifact ID, and version number, along with a link to download the JAR file. Also, thanks to our use of jQuery's slide-toggle animation, you can expand a row to see more information by clicking it. Clicking it again will collapse the row.

---

3. Note that I performed this search on an index that was created by spidering only a subset of a repository. Your results may be different, depending on what repository you spider and what items are in your index when you submit the search.

Of course, there's a lot more that we could do with the presentation aspects of our application (paging the result set comes to mind), but the main topic of this chapter was how to develop fragment bundles and secondarily how to use fragments to separate the appearance of an application from its function.

In this chapter, we've seen how to use OSGi fragments to extend bundles with additional content. Specifically, we've extended our application's web bundle with visual content, decoupling the application's view from its controllers. Effectively, the fragment we created in this chapter contains the "skin" of our application.

However, there are a lot of things we could do with fragments aside from using them as vessels for JSP and CSS. What kinds of things? In the last chapter, it was a fragment that told Spring-DM that we'd rather use Jetty than Tomcat for our web container. And, before this book is done, we'll see two more fragments that solve very different problems.

Speaking of finishing this book, the application is functionally and visually complete. There's no reason that we couldn't deploy it in production —except that we don't know how to deploy OSGi applications yet. That's what we'll figure out in the next chapter.

Part III

Finishing Touches

Chapter 9

OSGi in Production

Up until now, we've been developing our bundles using Pax Construct—and it has served us well. Not only have we used it to construct our application's project structure, but we have leaned heavily on its pax-provision command to run the application.

But Pax Construct is a development tool, and it would be inappropriate, and perhaps even unreasonable, to expect Pax Construct to be available in a production setting. As our application moves beyond development and into a QA or production setting, we need a way to run the application without relying on pax-provision.

In this chapter, we're going to extract the bundles from our Pax Construct project into a ready-to-run distribution. As we do, we'll also address a few concerns that will take our application out of development and make it production-ready.

9.1 Distributing the Application

Under the covers, the pax-provision script from Pax Construct uses a different OPS4J project, called Pax Runner. Pax Runner's mission in life is to start an OSGi framework and to install and start a selection of bundles. That sounds like exactly what we need. Fortunately, Pax Runner can be used without Pax Construct, so that's what we'll use.

But first, we'll need a way to draw our application's bundles out of their Pax Construct habitat and into a distribution for Pax Runner to work with.

> ### Cutting a Release
>
> Up until now, we've been in development mode and have kept our projects versioned at 1.0.0-SNAPSHOT. But now as we create a distribution to take the project into production, it's probably a good idea to bump the version up to a final 1.0.0 and then build our distribution zip file from the 1.0.0 project.
>
> Since our project is based on Pax Construct, which is itself based on Maven, I recommend using the Maven release plugin. This plugin handles the job of bumping version numbers up and even ensures that the project is in a releasable state prior to performing the release. The details of the release plugin are outside of the scope of this book, but if you want to know more, visit the release plugin home page.*
>
> ---
> *. http://maven.apache.org/plugins/maven-release-plugin

Creating a Distribution Project

Since our project is based on Maven (thanks to Pax Construct), we are afforded the opportunity to use Maven's assembly plugin. The assembly plugin is a perfect way to collect project artifacts and dependencies in a zip file for distribution. All we need is a project that has all the bundles as dependencies for the assembly plugin to gather up.

Fortunately, the vast majority of the bundles that our application needs are already listed in a Maven POM file. Every time we have used pax-import-bundle to add a dependency bundle to our project, it added a dependency element to the pom.xml file in the provision directory. So, we'll base the distribution project's pom.xml file on the provisioning pom.xml so that it inherits its dependencies.

First, create the distribution project. Pax Construct isn't going to help us much here, so we'll resort to standard DOS/shell commands:

```
dwmjs% mkdir dist
dwmjs% cd dist
dist%
```

Then, we'll start creating the Maven pom.xml file in the dist directory.

dwmjs/dist/pom.xml

```xml
<project xmlns="http://maven.apache.org/POM/4.0.0"
    xmlns:xsi="http://www.w3.org/2001/XMLSchema-instance"
    xsi:schemaLocation="http://maven.apache.org/POM/4.0.0
        http://maven.apache.org/maven-v4_0_0.xsd">
  <modelVersion>4.0.0</modelVersion>

❶  <parent>
    <relativePath>../provision/</relativePath>
    <groupId>com.dudewheresmyjar.dude.build</groupId>
    <artifactId>provision</artifactId>
    <version>1.0.0</version>
  </parent>

  <groupId>com.dudewheresmyjar</groupId>
  <artifactId>distribution</artifactId>
  <packaging>pom</packaging>
  <name>Dude, Where's My JAR? Application Packager</name>

  <version>1.0.0</version>

  <repositories>
    <repository>
      <id>OPS4J</id>
      <url>http://repository.ops4j.org/maven2</url>
    </repository>
    <repository>
      <id>com.springsource.repository.bundles.external</id>
      <name>SpringSource Enterprise Bundle Repository (External Bundles)</name>
      <url>http://repository.springsource.com/maven/bundles/external</url>
    </repository>
  </repositories>

  <build>
    <plugins>
      <plugin>
❷      <artifactId>maven-assembly-plugin</artifactId>
        <configuration>
          <finalName>dude-${project.version}</finalName>
          <descriptors>
            <descriptor>src/main/assembly/assembly.xml</descriptor>
          </descriptors>
        </configuration>
      </plugin>
    </plugins>
  </build>

  <dependencies>
  </dependencies>
</project>
```

By basing the distribution pom.xml on the provisioning pom.xml ❶, the distribution project will inherit all the dependencies from the provisioning pom.xml. That will make them available to the assembly plugin for placement in a distribution zip file.

But that won't be enough. Although many of the project's dependencies are listed in the provisioning pom.xml file, there are some that are not. First, our own project's bundles (domain, spider, index, web, and ui) aren't in the provisioning pom.xml file. So, we'll need to add those to the distribution pom.xml ourselves:

```
dwmjs/dist/pom.xml
<dependency>
  <groupId>com.dudewheresmyjar</groupId>
  <artifactId>domain</artifactId>
  <version>${project.version}</version>
</dependency>
<dependency>
  <groupId>com.dudewheresmyjar</groupId>
  <artifactId>spider</artifactId>
  <version>${project.version}</version>
</dependency>
<dependency>
  <groupId>com.dudewheresmyjar</groupId>
  <artifactId>index</artifactId>
  <version>${project.version}</version>
</dependency>
<dependency>
  <groupId>com.dudewheresmyjar</groupId>
  <artifactId>web</artifactId>
  <version>${project.version}</version>
  <type>war</type>
</dependency>
<dependency>
  <groupId>com.dudewheresmyjar.dude</groupId>
  <artifactId>ui</artifactId>
  <version>${project.version}</version>
</dependency>
<dependency>
  <groupId>com.dudewheresmyjar.dude</groupId>
  <artifactId>org.compass-project.compass</artifactId>
  <version>2.1.1-SNAPSHOT</version>
</dependency>
```

Since we'll be using Pax Runner, we'll need to make sure it is available.

`dwmjs/dist/pom.xml`

```xml
<dependency>
  <groupId>org.ops4j.pax.runner</groupId>
  <artifactId>pax-runner</artifactId>
  <version>0.17.0</version>
</dependency>
```

Finally, we'll need to be sure to include the OSGi framework itself. If we don't include Equinox bundles, Pax Runner will try to get them itself when we start the application. But we can save it the trouble if we include those bundles in the distribution:

`dwmjs/dist/pom.xml`

```xml
<dependency>
  <groupId>org.eclipse</groupId>
  <artifactId>osgi</artifactId>
  <version>3.4.2.v20080826-1230</version>
</dependency>
<dependency>
  <groupId>org.eclipse.osgi</groupId>
  <artifactId>util</artifactId>
  <version>3.1.300.v20080303</version>
</dependency>
<dependency>
  <groupId>org.eclipse.osgi</groupId>
  <artifactId>services</artifactId>
  <version>3.1.200.v20070605</version>
</dependency>
```

Now let's turn our attention to the assembly plugin ❷. Note that it is configured to create an assembly whose base name includes "dude-" and the project version. As for what goes into that assembly, the plugin turns to the descriptor file in src/main/assembly/assembly.xml. Let's create that descriptor file next.

Defining the Distribution

Again, we'll need to turn to manual means to create the directory where the assembly descriptor will reside. Use the Unix mkdir command:

```
dist% mkdir -p src/main/assembly
dist%
```

Now, in the src/main/assembly directory, we'll create the following assembly.xml file:

```
dwmjs/dist/src/main/assembly/assembly.xml
```

```
Line 1  <assembly>
          <formats>
            <format>zip</format>
          </formats>
5
          <dependencySets>
            <dependencySet>
              <useTransitiveDependencies>false</useTransitiveDependencies>
              <outputDirectory>/lib</outputDirectory>
10            <includes>
                <include>*:*</include>
                <include>org.eclipse.osgi:org.eclipse.equinox.cm</include>
              </includes>
              <excludes>
15              <exclude>org.eclipse:*</exclude>
                <exclude>org.eclipse.osgi:org.eclipse.osgi</exclude>
                <exclude>org.eclipse.osgi:org.eclipse.osg.services</exclude>
                <exclude>org.eclipse.osgi:services</exclude>
                <exclude>org.eclipse.osgi:util</exclude>
20              <exclude>org.ops4j.pax.runner:*</exclude>
              </excludes>
            </dependencySet>
            <dependencySet>
              <outputDirectory>/bin</outputDirectory>
25            <includes>
                <include>org.ops4j.pax.runner:*</include>
              </includes>
            </dependencySet>
          </dependencySets>
30
          <repositories>
            <repository>
              <outputDirectory>equinox</outputDirectory>
              <includes>
35              <include>org.eclipse:*</include>
                <include>org.eclipse.osgi:*</include>
              </includes>
            </repository>
          </repositories>
40
          <fileSets>
            <fileSet>
              <directory>src/main/etc</directory>
              <fileMode>0755</fileMode>
45            <outputDirectory></outputDirectory>
            </fileSet>
          </fileSets>
        </assembly>
```

This assembly descriptor is sort of complicated, so let's break it down line by line.

To start, lines 2 through 4 tell the assembly plugin that we want to create a zip file. Since we configured the assembly plugin with a final name of dude-${project.version}, it means that the assembly plugin will produce a file called dude-1.0.0.zip.

Next up are two dependency sets (lines 6 through 29) that are used to pull project dependencies into the assembly. The first dependency set (lines 7 through 22) will place all the project's dependencies in the assembly's lib directory. It places all of them, that is, except for those whose group ID is org.eclipse, org.eclipse.osgi, or org.ops4j.pax.runner. We'll need those dependencies to be placed elsewhere in the assembly.

The second dependency set (lines 23 through 28) places the Pax Runner JAR file in the assembly's bin directory. In a moment, we'll create a script that executes this JAR to start the application.

But first, we continue our exploration of the assembly descriptor with the <repositories> element (lines 31 through 39). When Pax Runner starts up, it will try to install the Equinox bundles from a Maven repository. Normally, that repository would be on the Internet somewhere. But to avoid unnecessary network communication during startup, I'm creating a miniature Maven repository within the assembly itself using <repositories>. This way, Pax Runner will be able to find the Equinox bundles from the equinox directory and not have to go to the Internet.

Finally, the <fileSets> element (lines 41 through 47) picks up any and all artifacts within the src/main/etc directory and makes them available in the root of the assembly. Specifically, this will pick up the startup script. And it will set its mode to 0755, making it executable in a Unix filesystem.

Speaking of the startup script, that's the only thing we have left to add to the distribution project.

The Startup Script

Recall that one of the dependency sets in the assembly descriptor places the Pax Runner JAR file in the assembly's bin directory. Pax Runner comes as an executable JAR file, but it can't start itself. So, we'll need to create a script that runs the JAR file:

dwmjs/dist/src/main/etc/bin/start.sh

```
exec java -jar pax-runner-0.17.0.jar
```

This is a fairly simple script that simply passes the JAR file as an argument to Java's -jar parameter. From there, the JVM kicks in, loads Pax Runner, and starts running the OSGi framework.

But there's more to it than that. By default Pax Runner reads in its arguments from a file named runner.args in the same directory. So, let's fire up the editor and create the following runner.args file in dist/src/main/etc/bin:

```
--platform=equinox
--repositories=file:../equinox
scan-dir:../lib
```

The first argument, --platform=equinox, tells Pax Runner that we want to use Equinox (instead of its default, Felix). And we tell it, using --repositories=file:../equinox, to retrieve Equinox bundles from the mini-repository that we had the assembly plugin create for us. Finally, scan-dir:../lib tells Pax Runner to scan the lib directory and to install and start all of the bundles it finds there.

Assembling the Distribution

Now that we've defined what the distribution should look like, we're ready to let Maven create it. To do that, we'll need to ask Maven to run the assembly:assembly goal:

```
dist% mvn assembly:assembly
[INFO] Scanning for projects...
...
[INFO] ------------------------------------------------------------------------
[INFO] BUILD SUCCESSFUL
[INFO] ------------------------------------------------------------------------
[INFO] Total time: 36 seconds
[INFO] Finished at: Fri Mar 20 23:00:12 CDT 2009
[INFO] Final Memory: 11M/30M
[INFO] ------------------------------------------------------------------------
dist%
```

When Maven has finished, there will be a ZIP file in the target directory. You could take that ZIP file and unzip it anywhere you want to install the application. For now, though, let's just unzip it into the target directory to try it:

```
dist% cd target/
target% unzip dude-1.0.0.zip
Archive:  dude-1.0.0.zip
...
dude-1.0.0%
```

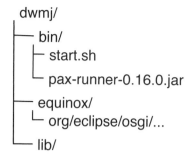

```
dwmj/
├── bin/
│   ├── start.sh
│   └── pax-runner-0.16.0.jar
├── equinox/
│   └── org/eclipse/osgi/...
└── lib/
```

Figure 9.1: THE STRUCTURE OF THE DISTRIBUTION ZIP FILE

After unzipping the distribution, you'll get a new directory called dwmj-1.0.0. The directory contents are shown in Figure 9.1.

Within the distribution directory, we find three subdirectories:

- bin: This directory contains the start.sh startup script as well as the Pax Runner JAR file

- equinox: This directory is the Maven mini-repository that contains the Equinox bundles that Pax Runner will load.

- lib: This directory contains all the other bundles that our application needs. This includes both third-party libraries and our own domain, index, spider, web, and ui bundles.

It looks like everything is in order, so let's try starting the application. At development time, we'd use pax-provision to start it up. But this is a production distribution, so we'll use the start.sh script instead:

```
dude-1.0.0% cd bin
bin% start.sh

   _____  _____   __   __
  /  _  / /  _   / / / / /
 /  __/ / /  _  / /_\ \ _/
/  /   / / / / // / /_\ \
/__/   /__/ /__/ /__/ /__/


Pax Runner (0.17.2) from OPS4J - http://www.ops4j.org
----------------------------------------------------
...

osgi>
```

As evidenced by the *osgi>* prompt, everything seems to have started OK. You could also issue the ss command to see that all our bundles are started. But the best way to check to see that our application has started successfully is to open up a web browser and point it at http://localhost:8080/dude. Go ahead and try it—I'll wait. Barring any surprises (and this is software, so there is *always* potential for surprises), you should be greeted with the *Dude, Where's My JAR?* home page.

Everything seems good to go. So, let's ship it! Right? Well, hold back your enthusiasm. I see at least one problem that we need to address.

After starting the application, we're given the familiar Equinox *osgi>* prompt. That was handy during development, but I'm not so sure that we want that exposed in a production runtime. It opens up the possibility for troublemakers to walk up to the server and indiscriminately stop or uninstall our bundles—or worse, install their own bundles to cause mischief. We need to lock down the Equinox console.

9.2 Adding an Administration Console

Fortunately, it's rather simple to shut off the Equinox console by adding the --noConsole argument to the Pax Runner arguments:

```
--noConsole
--platform=equinox
--repositories=file:../equinox
scan-dir:../lib
```

Now if we were to start the application, there'd be no way for any ne'er-do-well to access the Equinox console and wreak any havoc on our application. The only downside is that although the bad guys can't access the console, neither can we. What if we need to update a bundle or perform some other administrative tasks?

Wouldn't it be great if there were some way to provide secured access to the OSGi framework?

Installing the Felix Web Console

As you may have guessed by now, there is a way to administer the OSGi framework that is more secure than the standard Equinox console. The Felix project offers the Felix Web Console,[1] which provides a web-based administration console for OSGi.

---

1. http://felix.apache.org/site/apache-felix-web-console.html

Accessing the Equinox Console via Telnet

Another option for accessing the Equinox console is to have it listen on a Telnet port. To do that, we need to pass a port number to Equinox's -console option. But since Pax Runner hides the details of the underlying OSGi framework, it's not obvious how to set that option.

The trick is to set FRAMEWORK_OPTS to include the -console option. For example, if we want the Equinox console to be available on port 8888, our runner.args file might look like this:

▶
```
-DFRAMEWORK_OPTS="-console 8888"
--platform=equinox
--repositories=file:../equinox
scan-dir:../lib
```

Note that although this offers an alternate way to access the Equinox console, it doesn't address any form of security. Anyone with a Telnet client and knowledge of the port number can access the Equinox console.

Wait a minute. We're using Equinox, not Felix. How can we use the Felix Web Console if we're not using Felix?

As it turns out, the Felix Web Console is not specific to the Felix OSGi implementation and can be used with any OSGi framework implementation. This fact is a testament to the portability of OSGi bundles across all OSGi implementations.

All that you need to do to add the Felix Web Console is to add a handful of bundles to the OSGi runtime. For the purposes of our application distribution, this means adding those bundles as *<dependency>*s to the distribution project's pom.xml file. First, we'll need to add the web console bundle itself:

dwmjs/dist/pom.xml

```
<dependency>
  <groupId>org.apache.felix</groupId>
  <artifactId>org.apache.felix.webconsole</artifactId>
  <version>1.2.2</version>
</dependency>
```

The web console bundle depends on the Felix Service Component Runtime (SCR), the Felix Preferences Services, and the Felix Shell.

So, we'll also need to add those dependencies to pom.xml:

dwmjs/dist/pom.xml

```
<dependency>
  <groupId>org.apache.felix</groupId>
  <artifactId>org.apache.felix.prefs</artifactId>
  <version>1.0.2</version>
</dependency>
<dependency>
  <groupId>org.apache.felix</groupId>
  <artifactId>org.apache.felix.scr</artifactId>
  <version>1.0.6</version>
</dependency>
<dependency>
  <groupId>org.apache.felix</groupId>
  <artifactId>org.apache.felix.shell</artifactId>
  <version>1.0.2</version>
</dependency>
```

Finally, the web console needs a web server. We already have the Jetty bundles installed to serve the web front end for the application. But what the web console needs is an implementation of the OSGi HTTP Service, as defined in section 102 of the OSGi Service Compendium. Jetty, by itself, doesn't implement the HTTP Service and therefore is unsuitable for serving the web console.

Fortunately, our friends at OPS4J provide Pax Web, an implementation of the OSGi HTTP Service that should do the trick. We'll add it to pom.xml with the following <dependency> XML:

dwmjs/dist/pom.xml

```
<dependency>
  <groupId>org.ops4j.pax.web</groupId>
  <artifactId>pax-web-service</artifactId>
  <version>0.5.1</version>
</dependency>
```

Since Pax Web isn't available in the central Maven repository, we'll also need to add the OPS4J Maven repository to the distribution's pom.xml file:

dwmjs/dist/pom.xml

```
<repositories>
  <repository>
    <id>OPS4J</id>
    <url>http://repository.ops4j.org/maven2</url>
  </repository>
</repositories>
```

All the bundles for the web console are in place, and we're almost ready to try the web console. But first, we need to sort out a small conflict between Pax Web and Jetty.

Changing the Web Console's Default Port

After adding Pax Web to the mix, we have two web servers in play: Jetty and Pax Web. And they both default to listening on port 8080. If we were to fire up the application now, we'd certainly see a port conflict, and one of the two web servers would fail to start.

So, let's ask Pax Web to listen on port 8888 instead of 8080. The way to do that is to set the org.osgi.service.http.port system property to 8888 (or whatever port number you'd like). We'd normally do that using the -D option when we start the JVM. The gotcha here is that we need to make sure we're setting that variable on the correct JVM.

When we start Pax Runner in start.sh, we start a JVM that runs Pax Runner. But then, Pax Runner starts another JVM to run Equinox. It will do no good for us to set org.osgi.service.http.port on the Pax Runner JVM, because Pax Runner doesn't know anything about the HTTP Service. We need to set that variable on the JVM that runs Equinox. To do that, we must use Pax Runner's --vmOptions option (in runner.args):

```
--noConsole
--vmOptions=-Dorg.osgi.service.http.port=8888
--platform=equinox
--repositories=file:../equinox
scan-dir:../lib
```

As you can see, --vmOptions tells Pax Runner that we want to pass some options along to the JVM that it starts to run Equinox. More specifically, we ask it to pass along -Dorg.osgi.sevice.http.port=8888.

Using the Web Console

Now we're ready to try using the web console. First, we'll need to rebuild the distribution (using mvn assembly:assembly) and unzip the resulting ZIP file. Then, when you start the application (by running the start.sh script), you should be able to navigate to http://localhost:8888/system/console to access the web console. After entering the username and password (by default, both the username and password are "admin"), you should see a page that looks a little something like Figure 9.2, on the following page.

Figure 9.2: The Felix Web Console

From the web console, you'll be able to stop, start, uninstall, and install bundles.

To recap, in this chapter we've released our application into the wild from its development-time Pax Construct habitat. We've wrapped all of its bundles along with Pax Runner and a startup script in a ZIP file ready for distribution.

At this point, we should have a working, ready-to-install application and a web console to administer its bundles. But if you're like me, you may be a bit uneasy with the security for the web console. Sure, it's protected by a username and password—but it wouldn't take a very resourceful hacker to guess that admin/admin will get you in. We need a way to configure the web console to set its username and password.

But the truth is that the web console is just one of several things about our application that we need to be able to configure. We also need to adjust logging settings as well as configure the repositories that the spider will crawl.

As we wrap up our OSGi adventure in the final chapter, we'll see how to add configurability to our application by using the OSGi Configuration Admin Service.

Chapter 10

Configuring the Application

The OSGi specification comes paired with a compendium of standard services that could be available in an OSGi framework. We've already mentioned a few of the services described in the compendium: the Logging Service and the HTTP Service. In this chapter, we're going to focus on the Configuration Admin Service to see how it can be used to configure various aspects of our application.

The Configuration Admin Service is a service that is responsible for providing configuration information to bundles and other services that need externalized configuration. I won't bore you with the low-level details of how the Configuration Admin Service works, because we won't be coding to the low-level OSGi APIs to access the service. If, however, you are interested in the inner workings of the Configuration Admin Service, then I refer you to section 104 of the OSGi Service Compendium.[1]

Adding the Configuration Admin Service to our application is a simple matter of adding a *<dependency>* to the distribution project's pom.xml:

`dwmjs/dist/pom.xml`

```
<dependency>
  <groupId>org.eclipse.osgi</groupId>
  <artifactId>org.eclipse.equinox.cm</artifactId>
  <version>1.0.0.v20080509-1800</version>
</dependency>
```

---

1. http://www.osgi.org/Download/Release4V41

Here I've chosen the Equinox implementation of the Configuration Admin Service. However, I could have just as easily chosen another implementation of the Configuration Admin Service, such as the Felix implementation:

dwmjs/dist/pom.xml

```
<dependency>
  <groupId>org.apache.felix</groupId>
  <artifactId>org.apache.felix.configadmin</artifactId>
  <version>1.0.4</version>
</dependency>
```

The Configuration Admin Service is in place and is ready to start feeding configuration data to bundles. But where does it get that configuration data from? To answer that question, we'll turn to another one of the utility bundles proved by the Pax project: Pax ConfMan.

10.1 Installing Pax ConfMan

One of the great things about the Configuration Admin Service is that it is rather unspecific about where the configuration data comes from. Different Configuration Admin agent implementations could enable you to feed configuration data to the Configuration Admin Service from sources such as LDAP, a relational database, or a web-based console. Call me old-fashioned, but I like using a basic Java properties file for configuration my applications. Therefore, I favor Pax ConfMan, a properties-file based configuration admin agent.

To add Pax ConfMan to our application, we have to add it as a *<dependency>* in our distribution project's pom.xml:

dwmjs/dist/pom.xml

```
<dependency>
  <groupId>org.ops4j.pax.confman</groupId>
  <artifactId>pax-confman-propsloader</artifactId>
  <version>0.2.2</version>
</dependency>
```

We also need to tell ConfMan where to look for property files. By default, ConfMan looks in a directory called runner/configurations. The problem is that the runner directory is Pax Runner's working directory and doesn't exist until after the first time we start our application. That makes it a very inconvenient place for us to place configuration details.

Instead, let's have ConfMan look in a directory called conf that is a peer to the bin, lib, and equinox directories. To do that, we'll tack on an additional system property value through Pax Runner's --vmOptions:

```
--noConsole
--vmOptions=-Dorg.osgi.service.http.port=8888
        -Dbundles.configuration.location=../../conf
--platform=equinox
--repositories=file:../equinox
scan-dir:../lib
```

(Note that the --vmOptions definition is split into two lines to fit on a page and should be a single line in the real runner.args file.)

Notice that because ConfMan's base directory ends up being the Pax Runner working directory (which is in bin/runner), we must use relative paths, backing up two directories to the root of the application distribution.

10.2 Configuring the Web Console

Now that ConfMan is in place, configuring the Felix Web Console involves nothing more than creating a properties file for ConfMan to consume. Specifically, we'll need to create a file named org.apache.felix. webconsole.internal.servlet.OsgiManager.properties in a directory called services under the conf directory.

That was a mouthful. Let me explain how that properties file got its name.

When a bundle uses the Configuration Admin Service, it identifies itself to the Configuration Admin Service using a persistent identifier (PID). ConfMan looks up configuration details by looking for a properties file whose base name is the PID of the bundle it is to configure. As it turns out, the web console's PID is org.apache.felix.webconsole.internal.servlet. OsgiManager—which explains the name we'll give to the properties file. To explain the services directory, however, I must first explain a bit about how the Configuration Admin Service works.

In short, there are two types of things that the Configuration Admin Service can configure: managed services and managed service factories. A managed service is a class through which the Configuration Admin Service gives a bundle its configuration data. Typically, a configured bundle needs only a single instance of a managed service (which Conf-Man configures with a properties file in the services directory). But if, for

Property	Default	What It Does
realm	OSGi Management Console	The name of the HTTP Authentication realm when prompting the user for administrator credentials
username	admin	The administrator username
password	admin	The administrator password
manager.root	/system/console	The context root of the web console application
default.render	bundles	The name of the default page to display in the web console

Figure 10.1: THE PROPERTIES FOR CONFIGURING FELIX WEB CONSOLE

whatever reason, it needs many managed services, you'll configure the bundle through a managed service factory (which ConfMan configures with a properties file in a factories directory).

Because the web console is configured through a single managed service, its properties file will reside in the services directory.

Within the web console properties file, we can configure several things. The properties that can be configured for the Felix Web Console are shown in Figure 10.1.

Recall that we weren't too pleased with the default username and password for the web console. So, let's configure those first:

```
username=dudeadmin
password=letmein01
```

Now, just for fun, we can also tweak the authentication realm so that the login box is more suitable for our application:

```
realm=Dude, Where's My JAR? Administration
```

And, let's tweak the application path to be a bit shorter:

```
manager.root=/admin
```

That should do it. Now, when we rebuild our distribution and restart the application (using start.sh), the web console will be available at http://localhost:8888/admin, and we'll need to log in with a username of "dude-admin" and a password of "letmein01." You'll also notice that the login dialog box identifies the application as *Dude, Where's My JAR?* Administration.

The web console isn't the only thing we can configure with the Configuration Admin Service and Pax ConfMan. Let's see how we can use them to adjust the logging of our application.

10.3 Adjusting Logging

You may have noticed that after starting the application, there's an enormous amount of information written to the console. That happens for three reasons:

- We haven't asked Pax Runner to not tell us about everything it does.

- We haven't configured Pax Logging to log to a file instead of the console.

- The default logging level is TRACE.

The chattiness of Pax Runner is easy to fix. To tell Pax Runner to run a bit more silently, we need to add two lines to the Pax Runner arguments file:

```
►   --downloadFeedback=false
►   --log=NONE
    --noConsole
    --vmOptions=-Dorg.osgi.service.http.port=8888
            -Dbundles.configuration.location=../../conf
    --platform=equinox
    --repositories=file:../equinox
    scan-dir:../lib
```

(As before, the --vmOptions definition is split into two lines to fit on a page and should be a single line in the real runner.args file.)

The first argument, --downloadFeedback, tells Pax Runner to not tell us what it's doing as it downloads bundles. This includes any feedback about copying bundles from the lib directory into Pax Runner's working directory. As for --log=NONE, this will tell Pax Runner to not log anything itself.

Those two arguments will make Pax Runner run more silently, but it won't stop our bundles (or any dependency bundles) from logging their activity. To control the logging of our application and its dependency bundles, we need to configure Pax Logging. As it turns out, Pax Logging can be configured through the Configuration Admin Service.

Pax Logging's PID is "org.ops4j.pax.logging," so we'll need to create a file under conf/services called org.ops4j.pax.logging.properties. Since we're using Pax Logging through its Log4J API, we can configure Pax Logging by filling org.ops4j.pax.logging.properties with Log4J configuration. For example:

dwmjs/dist/src/main/etc/conf/services/org.ops4j.pax.logging.properties

```
log4j.rootLogger=WARN, file

log4j.appender.file=org.apache.log4j.DailyRollingFileAppender
log4j.appender.file.threshold=INFO
log4j.appender.file.File=/Users/wallsc/logs/dude.log
log4j.appender.file.MaxBackupIndex=20
log4j.appender.file.MaxFileSize=20MB
log4j.appender.file.layout=org.apache.log4j.PatternLayout
log4j.appender.file.layout.ConversionPattern=%d [%t] %-5p %c - %m%n
```

Here, I've not only tightened the log level to WARN, but I've also configured it to log to a rolling daily log file instead of the console. Once you rebuild the distribution ZIP, unzip it, and start the application, you'll notice a lot less noise going to the console. (There will still be some logging to the console that takes place before the Pax Logging bundle gets started.)

Configuring the web console and the logging framework are one thing. But what about configuring our own portion of the application? Let's see how to bring configuration closer to home by configuring the spider and index services.

10.4 Configuring Application Details

As we developed the index bundle, we cheated a little bit by hard-coding the path to the Compass index in the Spring context definition. We cheated again in the spider bundle by hard-coding the URL to the Maven repository. That's carried us through most of this book. But now as we prepare the application for deployment into a production environment, we really need to be able to externally configure those details.

Fortunately, Spring-DM can help us out in two different ways:

- By supplementing Spring's property placeholder facility with values from the OSGi Configuration Admin Service

- By autowiring Spring bean properties with values taken from the OSGi Configuration Admin Service

Let's start by seeing how to use Spring's property placeholder facility to configure the index bundle's index path. Then, we'll configure the spider bundle's Maven repository URL using Spring-DM's support for autowiring bean properties from the Configuration Admin Service.

Configuring Spring Beans with Property Placeholders

The Spring Framework supports externalization of configuration details with a utility element known as *<util:property-placeholder>*. This handy element makes it possible to replace hard-coded values in a Spring context definition with placeholder variables. Then, at runtime, Spring replaces those placeholders with values from some separate source of property values.

For example, using *<util:property-placeholder>*, we can swap out the hard-coded path to the Compass index with a placeholder variable:

```
<compass:compass name="compass" >
  <compass:connection>
    <compass:file path="${index.location}" />
  </compass:connection>
  <compass:mappings>
    <compass:class name="dwmj.domain.JarFile"/>
  </compass:mappings>
</compass:compass>
```

Instead of configuring Compass with a specific path for the index, we're giving it a placeholder variable called ${index.location}. We will use *<util:property-placeholder>* to replace that placeholder variable with a value that is configured elsewhere.

Typically, *<util:property-placeholder>* pulls property values from a properties file, as specified by its location= attribute. But we want it to pull configuration details from the OSGi Configuration Admin Service. That means we're going to pull off some special Spring magic.

As of Spring 2.5.6, *<util:property-placeholder>* has a new properties-ref= attribute to indicate that it should pull its property values from another Spring bean of type java.util.Properties.

For example, we could add the following XML to the index bundle's index-context.xml:

```
<beans xmlns="http://www.springframework.org/schema/beans"
   xmlns:xsi="http://www.w3.org/2001/XMLSchema-instance"
   xmlns:compass="http://www.compass-project.org/schema/spring-core-config"
   xmlns:ctx="http://www.springframework.org/schema/context"
   xsi:schemaLocation="http://www.springframework.org/schema/beans
      http://www.springframework.org/schema/beans/spring-beans-2.5.xsd
      http://www.compass-project.org/schema/spring-core-config
      http://www.compass-project.org/schema/spring-compass-core-config-2.0.xsd
      http://www.springframework.org/schema/context
      http://www.springframework.org/schema/context/spring-context.xsd">

  <!-- ... -->
  <ctx:property-placeholder properties-ref="cmProps" />

    <!-- ... -->
</beans>
```

In this case, the properties-ref= attribute specifies that <util:property-placeholder> should refer to another Spring bean whose ID is cmProps. Presumably, the cmProps bean is an instance of java.util.Properties.

But where does the Configuration Admin Service come into play?

As it turns out, Spring-DM provides an <osgix:cm-properties> element in a compendium Spring namespace. This element reads properties from the Configuration Admin Service and creates a bean in the Spring context that holds those property values. It just so happens that the bean created by <osgix:cm-properties> is of the type java.util.Properties—perfectly suitable for wiring into <util:property-placeholder>.

So, if we're going to use the OSGi Configuration Admin Service to provide properties for <util:property-placeholder>, then we need to add the following <osgix:cm-properties> to index-osgi.xml:

```
<beans:beans xmlns="http://www.springframework.org/schema/osgi"
     xmlns:osgix="http://www.springframework.org/schema/osgi-compendium"
     xmlns:beans="http://www.springframework.org/schema/beans"
     xmlns:xsi="http://www.w3.org/2001/XMLSchema-instance"
     xsi:schemaLocation="http://www.springframework.org/schema/osgi
         http://www.springframework.org/schema/osgi/spring-osgi.xsd
         http://www.springframework.org/schema/osgi-compendium
         http://www.springframework.org/schema/osgi-compendium/
                                 spring-osgi-compendium-1.2.xsd
         http://www.springframework.org/schema/beans
      http://www.springframework.org/schema/beans/spring-beans-2.5.xsd">
```

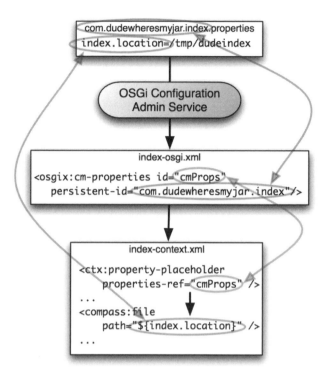

Figure 10.2: SPRING-DM's <osgix:cm-properties> PULLS CONFIGURA-TION DETAILS FROM THE OSGI CONFIGURATION ADMIN SERVICE AND MAKES IT AVAILABLE TO SPRING'S PROPERTY PLACEHOLDER FACILITY.

► `<osgix:cm-properties id="cmProps" persistent-id="dwmj.index">`
► `  <beans:prop key="index.location">/tmp/dudeindex</beans:prop>`
► `</osgix:cm-properties>`

```
<service ref="indexService"
    interface="dwmj.index.IndexService" />
```

`</beans:beans>`

As illustrated in Figure 10.2, the persistent-id= attribute specifies that <osgix:cm-properties> should consult the Configuration Admin Service using dwmj.index as its PID. Therefore, we'll need to create a new dwmj.index.properties file:

dwmjs/dist/src/main/etc/conf/services/dwmj.index.properties

```
index.location=/tmp/dudeindex
```

It Works with util:property-override Too!

Spring's *<util:property-placeholder>* isn't the only way to externalize configuration in Spring. There's also a *<util:property-override>* element that overrides a bean's property values where the key of a property is made up of a bean ID and a property name.

For instance, when using *<util:property-override>*, if a property has a key of spider.repositoryUrl, then the value of the property will be injected into the repositoryUrl property of the bean whose ID is spider.

If *<util:property-override>* looks useful to you, then you may be interested to know that it also has a properties-ref= attribute. That means you can use *<util:property-override>* with the OSGi Configuration Admin Service by wiring the java.util.Properties produced by *<osgix:cm-properties>* into the properties-ref= attribute.

And there's the value that Spring's *<util:property-placeholder>* will plug into the ${index.location} variable when configuring Compass.

Remember that we've added Pax ConfMan only to the distribution build and not to the provisioning pom.xml. That means if we run the application using pax-provision in the development environment, there won't be a Configuration Admin Service. And that means the index location won't be populated.

In other words, it won't be populated unless we provide a default value. That's why I've nested a *<beans:prop>* element within the *<osgix:cm-properties>* element. The *<beans:prop-element>* defines a default value for the index.location property in the event that the Configuration Admin Service isn't available or doesn't have a value defined for that property.

Autowiring Bean Properties from the Configuration Admin Service

An even more direct way to configure Spring beans in OSGi is to use Spring-DM's *<osgix:managed-service>* element. When nested within a Spring *<bean>* declaration, this handy element will autowire the bean's properties with values taken from the Configuration Admin Service.

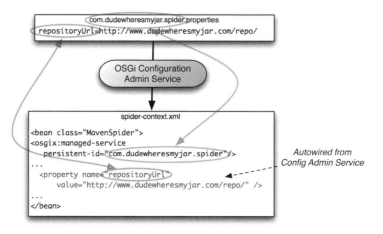

Figure 10.3: SPRING-DM'S *<osgix:managed-service>* AUTOWIRES A BEAN'S PROPERTIES WITH VALUES PULLED FROM THE OSGI CONFIGURATION ADMIN SERVICE.

For example, consider the following change to the MavenSpider bean:

```
<beans xmlns="http://www.springframework.org/schema/beans"
   xmlns:osgix="http://www.springframework.org/schema/osgi-compendium"
   xmlns:xsi="http://www.w3.org/2001/XMLSchema-instance"
   xsi:schemaLocation="http://www.springframework.org/schema/beans
     http://www.springframework.org/schema/beans/spring-beans-2.5.xsd
     http://www.springframework.org/schema/osgi-compendium
     http://www.springframework.org/schema/osgi-compendium/
                         spring-osgi-compendium-1.2.xsd">

  <bean class="dwmj.spider.internal.MavenSpider"
      init-method="run" destroy-method="stop">
      <osgix:managed-service persistent-id="dwmj.spider"
          update-strategy="container-managed" />
      <constructor-arg ref="indexService" />
      <property name="repositoryUrl" value="http://repo2.maven.org/maven2/" />
      <property name="jarFilePopulators">
        <list>
          <bean class=
            "dwmj.spider.internal.PomBasedJarFilePopulator" />
          <bean class=
            "dwmj.spider.internal.JarContentBasedJarFilePopulator" />
        </list>
      </property>
  </bean>
</beans>
```

By adding <*osgix:managed-service*> under the bean declaration, we're asking Spring-DM to automatically inject values from the Configuration Admin Service (where the PID is dwmj.spider) into the MavenSpider's properties. More specifically, we want Spring-DM to inject the repositoryUrl property. Therefore, we'll need to be sure to include a value for repositoryUrl in the dwmj.spider.properties file:

```
dwmjs/dist/src/main/etc/conf/services/dwmj.spider.properties
```

```
repositoryUrl=http://www.dudewheresmyjar.com/repo/
```

The relationship between the Spring context file and the properties file is illustrated in Figure 10.3, on the previous page.

Again, the Configuration Admin Service will be available only in the distribution build. Therefore, in the event that the values can't be auto-wired from the Configuration Admin Service (such as when running the application using pax-provision), we can provide a default value for the property by simply using the <*property*> element. Any values found by <*osgix:managed-service*> will always override those specified by <*property*>.

10.5 Configuring the Web Server

We've configured logging, the Felix Web Console, and our application's Spring beans. Before we put the topic of configuration to rest, we have one more thing that we can configure: the web server itself.

We've already configured the HTTP Service that serves the Felix Web Console. But remember that our application is served by a separate Jetty instance and not by the HTTP Service. The web server that serves our application is a full-blown Jetty (or Tomcat) server and is configured separately from the HTTP Service.

The trick to configuring the application's web server is to wrap up a configuration file in a fragment that is hosted by the web server's starter bundle. In the case of Jetty, that means creating a jetty.xml file and packaging it in a fragment that is hosted by the Jetty starter bundle.

The first thing we need to do is create a new bundle project for our fragment. Once again we turn to our old friend, the pax-create-bundle script. Since we're not going to need the sample Java files produced by pax-create-bundle, we'll be sure to set the interface and internals settings to false.

```
dwmjs% pax-create-bundle -p jetty -n jetty-config -g com.dudewheresmyjar
                          -v 1.0.0 -- -Dinterface=false
                          -Dinternals=false
[INFO] Scanning for projects...
[INFO] ------------------------------------------------------------------------
[INFO] Building com.dudewheresmyjar.dude (OSGi project)
[INFO]    task-segment: [org.ops4j:maven-pax-plugin:1.4:create-bundle]
          (aggregator-style)
[INFO] ------------------------------------------------------------------------
[INFO] Setting property: classpath.resource.loader.class => 'org.codehaus.plexus.
          velocity.ContextClassLoaderResourceLoader'.
[INFO] Setting property: velocimacro.messages.on => 'false'.
[INFO] Setting property: resource.loader => 'classpath'.
[INFO] Setting property: resource.manager.logwhenfound => 'false'.
[INFO] ****************************************************************
...
[INFO] Archetype created in dir: /Users/wallsc/Projects/bookProjects/CWOSG/Book/
          code/dwmjs/jetty-config
[INFO] ------------------------------------------------------------------------
[INFO] BUILD SUCCESSFUL
[INFO] ------------------------------------------------------------------------
[INFO] Total time: 9 seconds
[INFO] Finished at: Mon Jan 05 23:14:29 CST 2009
[INFO] Final Memory: 10M/19M
[INFO] ------------------------------------------------------------------------
dwmjs%
```

When pax-create-bundle is finished, the project will have only two files in it: the Maven pom.xml file and the osgi.bnd file. We'll leave pom.xml alone, but we need to edit osgi.bnd to include a Fragment-Host: header that will identify the bundle that hosts the fragment. So, we're going to replace the entire contents of the generated osgi.bnd file with the following one line:

dwmjs/jetty-config/osgi.bnd

```
Fragment-Host: org.springframework.osgi.jetty.start.osgi
```

Inside the Jetty starter bundle[2] is a default Jetty configuration file. But when the starter bundle hosts a fragment containing an /etc/jetty.xml file, it will favor the fragment's Jetty configuration over its own.

As for the content of the /etc/jetty.xml file, it's a standard Jetty configuration file—no different from a jetty.xml file that you may use to configure Jetty in a non-OSGi setting. That means you can configure pretty much

---

2. The Jetty starter bundle is the one whose symbolic name is org. springframework.osgi.jetty.start.osgi.

every facet of Jetty. For example, let's suppose we want to change the port that Jetty listens for HTTP requests on from 8080 (the default) to 8180. Then we'd need to change the settings on Jetty's channel connector as follows:

dwmjs/jetty-config/src/main/resources/etc/jetty.xml

```
<Call name="addConnector">
  <Arg>
      <New class="org.mortbay.jetty.nio.SelectChannelConnector">
        <Set name="host"><SystemProperty name="jetty.host" /></Set>
        <Set name="port"><SystemProperty name="jetty.port" default="8180"/></Set
        <Set name="maxIdleTime">30000</Set>
        <Set name="Acceptors">2</Set>
        <Set name="statsOn">false</Set>
        <Set name="confidentialPort">8143</Set>
        <Set name="lowResourcesConnections">5000</Set>
        <Set name="lowResourcesMaxIdleTime">5000</Set>
      </New>
  </Arg>
</Call>
```

Or suppose that we want to adjust Jetty's thread pool settings. In that case, we'd tweak the following portion of jetty.xml:

dwmjs/jetty-config/src/main/resources/etc/jetty.xml

```
<Set name="ThreadPool">
  <!-- Default bounded blocking threadpool
  -->
  <New class="org.mortbay.thread.BoundedThreadPool">
    <Set name="minThreads">10</Set>
    <Set name="maxThreads">250</Set>
    <Set name="lowThreads">25</Set>
  </New>
</Set>
```

The HTTP port and thread pool are just two examples of how you can configure Jetty, and these examples are just excerpts from a larger jetty.xml configuration. See Jetty's documentation[3] for more information on what can go into jetty.xml.

We're nearing the finish line on the Jetty configuration fragment. The only thing left to do is to build it.

---

3. http://docs.codehaus.org/display/JETTY/Jetty+Documentation

```
jetty-config% mvn clean install
[INFO] Scanning for projects...
[INFO] ------------------------------------------------------------------------
[INFO] Building jetty-config [jetty]
[INFO]    task-segment: [clean, install]
[INFO] ------------------------------------------------------------------------
...
[INFO] ------------------------------------------------------------------------
[INFO] BUILD SUCCESSFUL
[INFO] ------------------------------------------------------------------------
[INFO] Total time: 9 seconds
[INFO] Finished at: Tue Jan 06 13:21:59 CST 2009
[INFO] Final Memory: 15M/27M
[INFO] ------------------------------------------------------------------------
jetty-config%
```

With the fragment (and our settings in jetty.xml) in place, the next time we start our application (either with pax-provision or by running the start-Dude.sh script in the distribution), Jetty will serve it on port 8180 and with any other adjustments we may have made.

In this chapter we've taken advantage of the OSGi Configuration Admin Service to configure various facets of our application. This included using Spring-DM's configuration support to replace values in the Spring application context with configuration details from the Configuration Admin Service.

Now our application is complete. What's more, it is composed of several modules, each having a cohesive purpose and being loosely coupled with the other modules. Recalling the benefits of modularity, we can now develop and test each module of the application independently. We can even swap out any module for a new version or different implementation with no impact to the rest of the application.

Not only is our application complete, but so is our adventure in creating modular applications with OSGi and Spring. It was a lot of fun, and I think we learned a little something along the way. As modularity comes to the forefront in the Java platform, you'll be prepared to develop the next generation of web applications that take advantage of OSGi.

What About Tomcat?

If instead of Jetty you were to choose Tomcat as the web server, you would configure it in much the same way. You'd still need to create a fragment. But instead of being hosted by the bundle whose name is org.springframework.osgi.jetty.start.osgi, the Tomcat configuration fragment should be hosted by the bundle whose symbolic name is org.springframework.osgi.catalina.start.osgi. And instead of etc/jetty.xml, Tomcat's configuration should be in conf/server.xml (within the fragment). The conf/server.xml file should be a standard Tomcat configuration file.

Manifest Headers

A.1 OSGi R4 Headers

Bundle-ActivationPolicy
> Specifies how the framework should activate the bundle once it is started.

Bundle-Activator
> Identifies the fully qualified name of the class used to start and stop the bundle.

Bundle-Category
> A comma-separated list of category names.

Bundle-ClassPath
> A comma-separated list of one or more path specifications (either JAR files or directories) contained within the bundle. The default is "." to indicate the root of the bundle's JAR file.

Bundle-ContactAddress
> Provides the contact address for the bundle's vendor.

Bundle-Copyright
> Details the copyright specification for the bundle.

Bundle-Description
> Provides a brief description of the bundle.

Bundle-DocURL
> Specifies a URL the points to documentation for the bundle.

Bundle-Localization
> Identifies the location in the bundle where localization files can be found. The default value is OSGI-INF/l10N/bundle.

Bundle-ManifestVersion

Declares the version of the OSGi specification that this bundle adheres to. A value of 1 (the default) indicates OSGi R3, while 2 indicates OSGi R4.

Bundle-Name

Defines a brief, human-readable name for the bundle.

Bundle-NativeCode

Specifies a native code library contained within the bundle.

Bundle-RequiredExecutionEnvironment

Identifies one or more execution environments that must be available.

Bundle-SymbolicName

A unique, nonlocalizable name for the bundle. By convention, the name should be based on reverse domain name.

Bundle-UpdateLocation

Specifies a URL from which updates to this bundle can be found.

Bundle-Vendor

Identifies the vendor of the bundle.

Bundle-Version

Specifies the version of the bundle.

DynamicImport-Package

A comma-separated list of packages to be dynamically imported when needed.

Export-Package

Specifies one or more packages to be exported by the bundle.

Fragment-Host

Used to identify a bundle (by its symbolic name) that will be the host for a bundle fragment.

Import-Package

Specifies one or more packages imported for use by the bundle.

Require-Bundle

Specifies a bundle that is required by this bundle. The bundle cannot be resolved unless the required bundle is available.

Spring-DM Configuration

Spring Dynamic Modules (Spring-DM) works wonders at eliminating the hassle of publishing and consuming OSGi services, among other things. And it accomplishes much of its magic by providing a few configuration namespaces that enable declarative publication of Spring beans as OSGi services and wiring of consumed services into properties of Spring beans.

This appendix catalogs the configuration namespaces provided by Spring-DM, as of version 1.2.

B.1 Spring-DM Core Configuration Elements

Spring-DM's core namespace provides a handful of elements for publication and consumption of OSGi services in Spring. To use the Spring-DM namespace, include it in the root element as follows:

```
<beans xmlns="http://www.springframework.org/schema/beans"
▶   xmlns:beans="http://www.springframework.org/schema/osgi"
    xmlns:xsi="http://www.w3.org/2001/XMLSchema-instance"
▶   xsi:schemaLocation="http://www.springframework.org/schema/osgi
▶     http://www.springframework.org/schema/osgi/spring-osgi.xsd
      http://www.springframework.org/schema/beans
      http://www.springframework.org/schema/beans/spring-beans-2.5.xsd">
    ...
</beans>
```

In this case, it uses the *osgi* prefix. Alternatively, if all (or most) of the configuration within a given Spring context definition file is OSGi-oriented, you should consider making the Spring-DM namespace the default namespace. That way, you won't have to prefix any of the elements except for those that aren't part of the Spring-DM namespace.

```
<beans:beans xmlns:beans="http://www.springframework.org/schema/beans"
▶   xmlns="http://www.springframework.org/schema/osgi"
    xmlns:xsi="http://www.w3.org/2001/XMLSchema-instance"
▶   xsi:schemaLocation="http://www.springframework.org/schema/osgi
▶      http://www.springframework.org/schema/osgi/spring-osgi.xsd
       http://www.springframework.org/schema/beans
       http://www.springframework.org/schema/beans/spring-beans-2.5.xsd">
  ...
</beans:beans>
```

<osgi:bundle>

Defines a bean that represents a bundle. This is useful for times when you need to interact with a bundle programmatically, because you can wire the bundle bean into the bean that will interact with the bundle.

Attributes:

action

Life-cycle action to perform on the bundle. Valid values: start, stop, install, uninstall, update.

depends-on

Specifies a bean that this bundle depends on. The bundle bean should not be created until the named bean has been created.

destroy-action

Life-cycle action to perform on the bundle when the bean is removed from the Spring container. Valid values: start, stop, install, uninstall, update.

location

The location to install, update, and/or identify the bundle.

start-level

Specifies the bundle's start level. Defaults to 0.

symbolic-name

The bundle's symbolic name. Normally used to identify an already-installed bundle to interact with.

<osgi:comparator>

Defines a comparator that will be used to sort a list or set of services. The comparator either can be a nested Spring *<bean>* of type java.util.Comparator or can be a *<natural>* element to indicate natural ordering.

Included in: *<osgi:list>*, *<osgi:set>*.

May contain: *<bean>*, *<osgi:natural>*.

<osgi:interfaces>

A collection of service interface names. When nested within *<osgi:service>*, this element defines one or more interfaces that a service should be advertised as to the OSGi service registry. When used with *<osgi:reference>*, *<osgi:list>*, or *<osgi:set>*, it identifies the interface(s) of the service(s) to be consumed.

Included in: *<osgi:list>*, *<osgi:reference>*, *<osgi:service>*, *<osgi:set>*.

May contain: *<value>*.

<osgi:list>

Defines a list of services matching a given criteria. The list members are managed dynamically, because services may come and go.

Included in: *<beans>*.

May contain: *<osgi:comparator>*, *<osgi:interfaces>*, *<osgi:listener>*.

Attributes:

bean-name

Specifies a filter expression that matches on the *bean-name* property that is automatically advertised for beans that have been published using the *<osgi:service>* element.

cardinality

Defines the cardinality of the relationship to the services. Can be 1..N, meaning that at least one service must exist, or 0..N, meaning that the services are optional. If not specified, the default cardinality is used.

comparator-ref

Refers to a bean that implements the Comparator interface used to sort the matching services.

context-class-loader

Defines how the context class loader is managed when invoking methods on the referenced service. If client, the context class loader has visibility of all the classes in this bundle's classpath. If service-provider, the context class loader has visibility into the bundle classpath of the bundle that exports the service. If unmanaged, then there is no context class loader management.

Valid values: client, service-provider, unmanaged.

Default value: client.

depends-on

Specifies a bean that this list of services depends on. The named bean must be created before the service list is created.

filter

Defines an OSGi filter expression that is used to select a list of matching services in the service registry.

greedy-proxying

Indicates whether proxies will be created for all the classes exported by the service (true) and visible to the bundle or only just the classes specified (false). Default value: false.

interface

The service interface that the services obtained are required to support.

<osgi:listener>

Defines a listener that will be notified when a service is bound or unbound.

Included in: *<osgi:list>*, *<osgi:reference>*, *<osgi:set>*.

Attributes:

bind-method

The name of the method to call on the referenced *<bean>* when a service is bound.

ref

A reference to a *<bean>* that is the service listener.

unbind-method

The name of the method to call on the referenced *<bean>* when a service is unbound.

<osgi:natural>

Specifies natural ordering for a list or set of services.

Included in: <*osgi:comparator*>.

Attributes:

basis

Selects whether the natural ordering should be applied on the service itself or on the service reference.

Valid values: service, service-reference.

<*osgi:reference*>

Defines a reference to a service in the OSGi service registry.

Included in: <*beans*>.

May contain: <*osgi:interfaces*>, <*osgi:listener*>.

Attributes:

bean-name

Shortcut for specifying a filter that matches on the bean name that is advertised for the service if the service was published using Spring-DM's <*service*> element.

cardinality

Stipulates the cardinality of the service reference. The cardinality can either be 0..1, which indicates an optional reference (that is, the service doesn't have to be available), or 1..1, which indicates a required reference (the service must be available).

Valid values: 0..1, 1..1.

context-class-loader

Defines how the context class loader is managed when invoking methods on the referenced service. If client, the context class loader has visibility of all the classes in this bundle's classpath. If service-provider, the context class loader has visibility into the bundle classpath of the bundle that exports the service. If unmanaged, then there is no context class loader management.

Valid values: client, service-provider, unmanaged.

Default value: client.

depends-on

Specifies a bean that this list of services depends on.

filter

> Defines an OSGi filter expression that is used to select a list of matching services in the service registry.

greedy-proxying

> Indicates whether proxies will be created for all the classes exported by the service (true) and visible to the bundle or only just the classes specified (false). Default value: false.

timeout

> Specifies a timeout, in milliseconds, when waiting for the referenced service to become available.

<*osgi:registration-listener*>

> Defines a listener that will be notified when a service is registered or unregistered.
>
> Included in: <*osgi:service*>.
>
> Attributes:

ref

> Identifies a Spring <*bean*> that is the registration listener.

registration-method

> The name of the method to call when a service is registered.

unregistration-method

> The name of the method to call when a service is unregistered.

<*osgi:service*>

> Publishes a Spring bean as a service in the OSGi service registry.
>
> Included in: <*beans*>.
>
> May contain: <*osgi:interfaces*>, <*osgi:registration-listener*>, <*osgi:service-properties*>.
>
> Attributes:

auto-export

> Enables Spring-DM to automatically determine the set of service interfaces for which this service would be advertised. If set to interfaces, the service will be advertised under all the interfaces that it implements. If set to class-hierarchy, the service will be advertised under all of the classes in the service implementation's class hierarchy. If set to all-classes, both

interfaces and the classes in the service class's hierarchy will be used.

Valid values: all-classes, class-hierarchy, disabled, and interfaces.

Default value: disabled.

context-class-loader

Specifies how the context class loader will be managed when methods are invoked on the published service. By default, the context class loader is unmanaged. If set to service-provider, then the context class loader will be given visibility into the classpath of the bundle that publishes the service.

Valid values: service-provider, unmanaged.

Default value: unmanaged.

depends-on

Identifies a *<bean>* that must be created before publishing the service to the service registry.

interface

The interface that the service should be advertised under when published to the service registry.

ranking

Specifies the service ranking to use when advertising the service.

Default value: 0.

ref

A reference to a Spring *<bean>* that implements the service.

<osgi:service-properties>

Defines properties for a published service.

Included in: *<osgi:service>*.

May contain: *<entry>* (from the Spring beans namespace).

<osgi:set>

Defines a set of services that match given criteria. The set membership is managed dynamically, because services may come and go.

Included in: *<beans>*.

May contain: *<osgi:comparator>*, *<osgi:interfaces>*, *<osgi:listener>*.

Attributes:

bean-name
> Specifies a filter expression that matches on the *bean-name* property that is automatically advertised for beans that have been published using the *<osgi:service>* element.

cardinality
> Defines the cardinality of the relationship to the services. Can be 1..N, meaning that at least one service must exist, or 0..N, meaning that the services are optional. If not specified, the default cardinality is used.

comparator-ref
> Refers to a bean that implements the Comparator interface used to sort the matching services.

context-class-loader
> Defines how the context class loader is managed when invoking methods on the referenced service. If client, the context class loader has visibility of all of the classes in this bundle's classpath. If service-provider, the context class loader has visibility into the bundle classpath of the bundle that exports the service. If unmanaged, then there is no context class loader management.
>
> Valid values: client, service-provider, unmanaged.
>
> Default value: client.

depends-on
> Specifies a bean that this list of services depends on. The named bean must be created before the service list is created.

filter
> Defines an OSGi filter expression that is used to select a list of matching services in the service registry.

greedy-proxying
> Indicates whether proxies will be created for all the classes exported by the service (true) and visible to the bundle or only just the classes specified (false). Default value: false.

interface

> The service interface that the services obtained are required to support.

B.2   Spring-DM Compendium Configuration Elements

In addition to the core namespace, Spring-DM also provides a compendium namespace that is primarily focused on enabling *<bean>* configuration from the OSGi Configuration Admin Service. It is typically used by declaring it under the *osgix* prefix in the root element:

```
<beans:beans xmlns="http://www.springframework.org/schema/osgi"
  xmlns:osgix="http://www.springframework.org/schema/osgi-compendium"
  xmlns:beans="http://www.springframework.org/schema/beans"
  xmlns:xsi="http://www.w3.org/2001/XMLSchema-instance"
  xsi:schemaLocation="http://www.springframework.org/schema/osgi
    http://www.springframework.org/schema/osgi/spring-osgi.xsd
    http://www.springframework.org/schema/osgi-compendium
    http://www.springframework.org/schema/osgi-compendium/
                            spring-osgi-compendium-1.2.xsd
    http://www.springframework.org/schema/beans
    http://www.springframework.org/schema/beans/spring-beans-2.5.xsd">
...
</beans:beans>
```

<osgix:cm-properties>

> Exposes properties from OSGi's Configuration Admin Service as Spring bean of type java.util.Properties. Useful for wiring into Spring's property placeholder configurer

> Included in: *<beans>*.

> Attributes:

> *id*

>> The ID of the bean.

> *local-override*

>> If true, local properties will override properties from the Configuration Admin service Defaults to false.

>> Valid values: true, false.

>> Default value: false.

> *persistent-id*

>> The persistent ID to bind to when retrieving properties from the OSGi configuration admin service.

<osgix:interfaces>

The set of service interfaces to advertise in the service registry.

Included in: *<osgix:managed-service-factory>*.

<osgix:managed-service>

Defines a bean to be autowired by name using properties from the OSGi Configuration Admin Service for a given persistent ID.

Included in: *<bean>* (from the Spring beans namespace).

Attributes:

persistent-id

The persistent ID under which the configuration for the *<bean>* is stored in the Configuration Admin Service.

update-method

The method on the bean to invoke when the values in the Configuration Admin Service are updated. Used with the bean managed updated strategy.

update-strategy

The strategy to use for updating the *<bean>*'s properties when the backing configuration changes. By default no updates are applied after the bean is initially wired. The bean managed strategy means that the method identified by *update-method* will be invoked. Container managed means that the container will autowire the *<bean>* properties.

Valid values: bean-managed, container-managed, none.

Default value: none.

<osgix:managed-service-factory>

Defines a collection of one or more *<bean>*s whose properties should be autowired with values from the OSGi Configuration Admin Service for a given persistent ID. Also functions similarly to *<osgix:service>* in that it publishes the *<bean>*s as services.

May contain: *<bean>* (from Spring's bean namespace).

Attributes:

auto-export

Enables Spring-DM to automatically determine the set of service interfaces for which this service would be advertised. If set to interfaces, the service will be advertised under all of the interfaces that it implements. If set to class-hierarchy, the service will be advertised under all of the classes in the service implementation's class hierarchy. If set to all-classes, both interfaces and the classes in the service class's hierarchy will be used.

Valid values: all-classes, class-hierarchy, disabled, and interfaces.

Default value: disabled.

context-class-loader

Specifies how the context class loader will be managed when methods are invoked on the published service. By default, the context class loader is unmanaged. If set to service-provider, then the context class loader will be given visibility into the classpath of the bundle that publishes the service.

Valid values: service-provider, unmanaged.

Default value: unmanaged.

depends-on

Identifies a *<bean>* that must be created before publishing the service to the service registry.

factory-pid

The persistent ID under which the configuration for the *<bean>*s are stored in the Configuration Admin Service.

update-method

The method on the bean to invoke when the values in the Configuration Admin Service are updated. Used with the bean managed updated strategy.

update-strategy

The strategy to use for updating the *<bean>*'s properties when the backing configuration changes. By default no updates are applied after the bean is initially wired. The bean managed strategy means that the method identified by *update-method* will be invoked. Container managed means that the container will autowire the *<bean>* properties.

Valid values: bean-managed, container-managed, none.

Default value: none.

<*osgix:registration-listener*>

Defines a listener that will be notified when a service is registered or unregistered.

Included in: <*osgi:managed-service-factory*>.

Attributes:

ref

Identifies a Spring <*bean*> that is the registration listener.

registration-method

The name of the method to call when a service is registered.

unregistration-method

The name of the method to call when a service is unregistered.

The OSGi Blueprint Service

We've spent a lot of time getting to know Spring Dynamic Modules in this book. Spring-DM's declarative model has been a real benefit to us in eliminating the need to write code to the OSGi API when we need to publish and consume services.

Spring-DM is such a good idea that, in fact, it is being formalized into part of the OSGi specification as the OSGi Blueprint Service. In OSGi 4.2, the OSGi Blueprint Service will include the declarative service model of Spring-DM along with the core pieces of Spring. As for what this means to Spring-DM, Spring-DM will become the reference implementation of the Blueprint Service.

C.1 Comparing the Blueprint Service with Spring-DM

The design of the Blueprint Service borrows many of the ideas from Spring-DM. Therefore, if you know Spring-DM already, you should be able to adapt to the Blueprint Service model fairly easy. There are, however, a few subtle differences that separate it from Spring.

First, where Spring-DM's extender looks in META-INF/spring for Spring context definition files, the Blueprint Service will look in META-INF/module-context for module context definition files. Similarly, where Spring-DM allows you to override the default context loading behavior using the Spring-Context: header in the manifest, the Blueprint Service offers an analogous Module-Context: header.

The content of those context definition files will also be different. Whereas Spring-DM context definition files leveraged the Spring configuration model, Blueprint Service context definition files use a different

XML namespace altogether to take on a more neutral (that is, Spring-agnostic) feel. For example, the spider bundle's component context might look like this using the Blueprint Service schema:

```
<?xml version="1.0" encoding="UTF-8"?>
<components xmlns="http://www.osgi.org/xmlns/blueprint/v1.0.0"
  xmlns:xsi="http://www.w3.org/2001/XMLSchema-instance"
  xsi:schemaLocation="http://www.osgi.org/xmlns/blueprint/v1.0.0
    http://www.osgi.org/xmlns/blueprint/v1.0.0/blueprint.xsd">

  <component class="com.dudewheresmyjar.spider.internal.MavenSpider"
      init-method="run" destroy-method="stop">
    <constructor-arg ref="indexService" />
    <property name="repositoryUrl" value="http://repo2.maven.org/maven2/" />
    <property name="jarFilePopulators">
      <list>
        <component class=
          "com.dudewheresmyjar.spider.internal.PomBasedJarFilePopulator" />
        <component class=
          "com.dudewheresmyjar.spider.internal.JarContentBasedJarFilePopulator" />
      </list>
    </property>
  </component>
</components>
```

And the context definition that references the index service might look like this:

```
<?xml version="1.0" encoding="UTF-8"?>
<components xmlns="http://www.osgi.org/xmlns/blueprint/v1.0.0"
  xmlns:xsi="http://www.w3.org/2001/XMLSchema-instance"
  xsi:schemaLocation="http://www.osgi.org/xmlns/blueprint/v1.0.0
    http://www.osgi.org/xmlns/blueprint/v1.0.0/blueprint.xsd">

  <reference id="indexService"
      interface="com.dudewheresmyjar.index.IndexService" />

</components>
```

To help keep track of the differences between Spring-DM and the Blueprint Service and to also guide you in a smooth transition to using the Blueprint Service, the remainder of this appendix catalogs the elements in the Blueprint Service schemas.

C.2 OSGi Blueprint Services (RFC-124) Elements

The Blueprint Service's core configuration namespace offers elements for declaratively publishing and consuming services (much like Spring-DM's core namespace). In addition, it includes some elements that re-create the core elements of the Spring Framework's *beans* namespace. The key difference is in the naming of these elements. For example, the *<beans>* element becomes *<components>*, and the *<bean>* becomes *<component>* (among others).

To use the Blueprint Service's core namespace, declare it in the root element of the configuration XML as follows:

```
<components xmlns="http://www.osgi.org/xmlns/blueprint/v1.0.0"
  xmlns:xsi="http://www.w3.org/2001/XMLSchema-instance"
  xsi:schemaLocation="http://www.osgi.org/xmlns/blueprint/v1.0.0
    http://www.osgi.org/xmlns/blueprint/v1.0.0/blueprint.xsd">
...
</components>
```

Note that since the Blueprint Service replaces much of Spring and Spring-DM, you won't be using any of the Spring-specific namespaces. Instead, the *<components>* element becomes the root element.

<component>

Defines a component in the component context. Analogous to Spring's *<bean>* element.

Included in: *<components>*.

May contain: *<constructor-arg>*, *<description>*, *<property>*.

Attributes:

class

The fully qualified class name of the component.

depends-on

The ID of another component that must be created before this component is created.

destroy-method

The method to invoke when this component is removed from the context.

factory-method

A factory method to create the bean in lieu of a constructor. The factory method is either a method on the component referenced by the factory-component attribute or, if factory-component is not specified, a static method on this component's class.

factory-component
> Used with factory-method to identify another component that provides the factory-method.

id
> The ID of the component.

init-method
> An initialization method to be invoked by the container after component creation.

lazy-init
> Specifies whether the component will be created eagerly with creation of the context or lazily when it is first needed.
>
> Valid values: true, false.
>
> Default value: the value of <*components*>' default-lazy-init.

scope
> Defines the scope of the component. Singleton-scoped components have only one instance created. In contrast, a prototype-scoped component will have multiple instances created, once for each time the component is requested. For components that will be published as services, bundle scoping will ensure that one instance of the component will be created for each client that consumes the service.
>
> Valid values: bundle, prototype, singleton.
>
> Default value: singleton.

<*components*>
> The root element of a component context definition. Analogous to Spring's <*beans*> element.
>
> May contain: <*description*>, <*type-converters*>, <*component*>, <*ref-list*>, <*ref-set*>, <*reference*>, <*service*>.
>
> Attributes:

default-availability
> Defines the default availability of <*reference*>s.

default-destroy-method
> Specifies the default destroy method of <*component*>s.

default-init-method

> Specifies the default initialization method of <component>s.

default-lazy-init

> The default lazy initialization setting for <component>s.

> Valid values: true, false.

> Default value: false.

default-timeout

> Defines the default timeout for obtaining a reference to a service.

<constructor-arg>

> Provides constructor (or factory method) argument values for a <component>. Analogous to Spring's <constructor-arg> element.

> Included in: <component>.

> May contain: <description>, <component>, <ref>, <idref>, <value>, <null>, <list>, <set>, <map>, <props>, <ref-list>, <ref-set>, <reference>, <service>.

> Attributes:

> *index*

> > The index of the constructor argument. (Helpful in resolving constructor argument ambiguity.)

> *ref*

> > The ID of a <component> to wire into the constructor argument.

> *type*

> > The type of the constructor argument. (Helpful in resolving constructor argument ambiguity.)

> *value*

> > A simple value to wire into the constructor argument.

<description>

> Describes the component context, a component, a constructor argument, or a property. Analogous to Spring's <description> element.

> Included in: <component>, <components>, <constructor-arg>, <property>.

<entry>

Defines an entry of a *<map>*. Analogous to Spring's *<entry>* element.

Included in: *<map>*.

May contain: *<key>*, *<component>*, *<ref>*, *<idref>*, *<value>*, *<null>*, *<list>*, *<set>*, *<map>*, *<props>*, *<ref-list>*, *<ref-set>*, *<reference>*, *<service>*.

Attributes:

key

Specifies a key for the entry.

key-ref

Refers to a *<component>* (by its ID) as the key for the entry.

value

Specifies a value for the entry.

value-ref

Refers to a *<component>* (by its ID) as the value for the entry.

<idref>

An error-proof way to inject a reference to another *<component>* into a property or constructor argument. Analogous to Spring's *<idref>* element.

Attributes:

component

References the ID of the *<component>* to wire into a property or constructor argument's value.

<key>

Defines a key for a *<map>* or *<prop>*. Analogous to Spring's *<key>* element.

May contain: *<component>*, *<ref>*, *<idref>*, *<value>*, *<list>*, *<set>*, *<map>*, *<props>*, *<ref-list>*, *<ref-set>*, *<reference>*, *<service>*.

<list>

Defines a list component. Analogous to Spring's *<list>* element.

May contain: <component>, <ref>, <idref>, <value>, <null>, <list>, <set>, <map>, <props>, <ref-list>, <ref-set>, <reference>, <service>.

<map>

Defines a map component. Analogous to Spring's <map> element.

May contain: entry.

Attributes:

key-type

Specifies the type of the entry keys.

<null>

Defines a null value. Useful for wiring null into a <component>'s property or constructor argument. Analogous to Spring's <null> element.

<prop>

Defines an entry of a <props> element. Analogous to Spring's <prop> element.

Attributes:

key

The key of the property.

value

The value of the property.

<property>

Injects a value or component reference into a component property. Analogous to Spring's <property> element.

May contain: <description>, <component>, <ref>, <idref>, <value>, <null>, <list>, <set>, <map>, <props>, <ref-list>, <ref-set>, <reference>, <service>.

Attributes:

name

The name of the property.

ref

A reference to the ID of a <component> to inject into the property.

value

A value to inject into the property.

<props>

Defines a properties (java.util.Properties) collection. Analogous to Spring's *<props>* element.

May contain: *<prop>*

<ref>

Defines a reference to a *<component>*. Analogous to Spring's *<ref>* element.

Attributes:

component

The ID of the referenced *<component>*.

<reference>

Creates a reference to a published OSGi service. Analogous to Spring-DM's *<osgi:reference>* element.

Attributes:

availability

Specifies the expected availability of the referenced service.

Valid values: required, optional.

Default value: required.

component-name

A convenient shortcut for creating a filter to select a service using the component name that should be provided as a property if the service is published by the Blueprint Service.

filter

Defines an OSGi filter expression used to select a list of matching services in the service registry.

interface

The service interface that the services obtained are required to support.

timeout

The timeout for waiting for the referenced service to become available.

<ref-list>

> Defines a list collection of referenced services. Analogous to Spring-DM's *<osgi:list>* element.
>
> May contain: *<comparator>*.
>
> Attributes:
>
> *availability*
>
>> Specifies the expected availability of the referenced service.
>>
>> Valid values: required, optional.
>>
>> Default value: required.
>
> *comparator-ref*
>
>> A reference to a *<component>* that implements java.util. Comparator. Used for ordering the collection.
>
> *component-name*
>
>> A convenient shortcut for creating a filter to select a service using the component name that should be provided as a property if the service is published by the Blueprint Service.
>
>> Defines an OSGi filter expression used to select a list of matching services in the service registry.
>
>> The service interface that the services obtained are required to support.

<ref-set>

> Defines a list collection of referenced services. Analogous to Spring-DM's *<osgi:list>* element.
>
> May contain: *<comparator>*.
>
> Attributes:
>
> *availability*
>
>> Specifies the expected availability of the referenced service.
>>
>> Valid values: required, optional.
>>
>> Default value: required.
>
> *comparator-ref*
>
>> A reference to a *<component>* that implements java.util. Comparator. Used for ordering the collection.

component-name
> A convenient shortcut for creating a filter to select a service using the component name that should be provided as a property if the service is published by the Blueprint Service.

filter
> Defines an OSGi filter expression used to select a list of matching services in the service registry.

interface
> The service interface that the services obtained are required to support.

<service>
> Publishes a *<component>* as a service in the OSGi service registry.

> Included in: *<components>*. Analogous to Spring-DM's *<osgi:service>* element.

> Attributes:

auto-export
> Enables the container to automatically determine the set of service interfaces for which this service would be advertised. If set to interfaces, the service will be advertised under all of the interfaces that it implements. If set to class-hierarchy, the service will be advertised under all of the classes in the service implementation's class hierarchy. If set to all-classes, both interfaces and the classes in the service class's hierarchy will be used.

> Valid values: all-classes, class-hierarchy, disabled, and interfaces.

> Default value: disabled.

depends-on
> Identifies a *<component>* that must be created before publishing the service to the service registry.

interface
> The interface that the service should be advertised under when published to the service registry.

ranking

> Specifies the service ranking to use when advertising the service.

> Default value: 0.

ref

> A reference to a <*component*> that implements the service.

<*set*>

> Defines a set component. Analogous to Spring's <*set*> element.

> May contain: <*component*>, <*ref*>, <*idref*>, <*value*>, <*null*>, <*list*>, <*set*>, <*map*>, <*props*>, <*ref-list*>, <*ref-set*>, <*reference*>, <*service*>.

<*type-converters*>

> Declares one or more embedded <*component*>s as type converters. Type converters enable complex properties to be configured with simpler String representations. This is similar to how Spring supports property editors through java.beans.PropertyEditor. In OSGi's blueprint service, however, type converters must implement org.osgi.module.context.convert.Converter.

> Included in: <*components*>.

> May contain: <*component*>, <*entry*>, <*list*>, <*ref*>, <*set*>.

<*value*>

> Defines a value for injection into a property or constructor argument. Analogous to Spring's <*value*> element.

> Included in: <*constructor-arg*>, <*property*>.

> Attributes:

> *type*
>> Stipulates the type of the value.

C.3 OSGi Blueprint Services (RFC-124) Compendium Elements

Just like the Spring-DM compendium namespace, the OSGi Blueprint Service's compendium namespace offers elements for coordinating component configuration with the OSGi Configuration Admin Service.

To use the Blueprint Service compendium namespace, include it in the *<components>* element of your Blueprint Service context definition XML:

```
<components xmlns="http://www.osgi.org/xmlns/blueprint/v1.0.0"
  xmlns:xsi="http://www.w3.org/2001/XMLSchema-instance"
  xmlns:osgix="http://www.osgi.org/xmlns/blueprint/compendium/v1.0.0"
  xsi:schemaLocation="http://www.osgi.org/xmlns/blueprint/v1.0.0
    http://www.osgi.org/xmlns/blueprint/v1.0.0/blueprint.xsd
    http://www.osgi.org/xmlns/blueprint/compendium/v1.0.0
    http://www.osgi.org/xmlns/blueprint/compendium/v1.0.0/
                              blueprint-compendium.xsd">
...
</components>
```

<config-properties>

Used to configure an exported service's service-properties using values from the OSGi Configuration Admin Service.

Included in: *<service-properties>*.

Attributes:

persistent-id

The persistent ID for which the values should be pulled from the OSGi Configuration Admin Service.

update

Specifies whether the properties will be updated if they change in the Configuration Admin Service.

Valid values: true, false.

Default value: false.

<default-properties>

This is a collection of default properties to be applied in *<property-placeholder>*.

Included in: *<property-placeholder>*.

May contain: *<prop>* (from the Blueprint Service namespace).

Attributes:

persistent-id

The persistent ID under which the configuration for the *<component>* is stored in the Configuration Admin Service.

update

> Specifies whether the properties will be updated if they change in the Configuration Admin Service.

> Valid values: true, false.

> Default value: false.

<managed-component>

> A component that is managed under a <managed-component-factory>.

> Attributes:

class

> The fully qualified class name of the component.

destroy-method

> The method to invoke when this component is removed from the context.

factory-component

> Used with *factory-method* to identify another component that provides the factory method.

factory-method

> A factory method to create the bean in lieu of a constructor. The factory method is either a method on the component referenced by the *factory-component* attribute or, if *factory-component* is not specified, a static method on this component's class.

init-method

> An initialization method to be invoked by the container after component creation.

<managed-properties>

> Defines a component to be autowired by name using properties from the OSGi Configuration Admin Service for a given persistent ID.

> Included in: <component>.

> Attributes:

persistent-id

> The persistent ID under which the configuration for the <component> is stored in the Configuration Admin Service.

update-method

> The method on the component to invoke when the values in the Configuration Admin Service are updated. Used with the bean managed updated strategy.

update-strategy

> The strategy to use for updating the *<component>*'s properties when the backing configuration changes. By default no updates are applied after the component is initially wired. The bean managed strategy means that the method identified by *update-method* will be invoked. Container managed means that the container will autowire the *<component>* properties.

> Valid values: bean-managed, container-managed, none.

> Default value: none.

<managed-service-factory>

> Defines a collection of one or more *<component>*s whose properties should be autowired with values from the OSGi Configuration Admin Service for a given persistent ID. Also functions similarly to *<service>* in that it publishes the *<component>*s as services.

> May contain: *<managed-component>*.

> Attributes:

auto-export

> Enables Spring-DM to automatically determine the set of service interfaces for which this service would be advertised. If set to interfaces, the service will be advertised under all of the interfaces that it implements. If set to class-hierarchy, the service will be advertised under all of the classes in the service implementation's class hierarchy. If set to all-classes, both interfaces and the classes in the service class's hierarchy will be used.

> Valid values: all-classes, class-hierarchy, disabled, and interfaces.

> Default value: disabled.

factory-pid

> The persistent ID under which the configuration for the *<bean>*s are stored in the Configuration Admin Service.

interface

> The interface under which the service will be advertised.

ranking

>   Specifies the service ranking to be used when advertising the service.

<property-placeholder>

>   Configures a property placeholder that pulls configuration details from the OSGi Configuration Admin Service. Roughly analogous to Spring's *<util:property-placeholder>* when used with Spring-DM's *<osgi:cm-properties>*.

>   Included in: *<components>*.

>   May contain: *<default-properties>*.

>   Attributes:

persistent-id

>   The persistent ID to bind to when pulling configuration properties from the OSGi Configuration Admin Service.

placeholder-prefix

>   The prefix of the placeholder delimiter.

>   Default value: ${.

placeholder-suffix

>   The suffix of the placeholder delimiter.

>   Default value: }.

defaults-ref

>   References a *<component>* of type java.util.Properties that contains default property values for the placeholder.

Resources

Apache Felix . . . . http://felix.apache.org
Felix is one of the leading open source OSGi framework implementations from
the Apache Software Foundation. Felix was originally known as Oscar and was
contributed to Apache from ObjectWeb.

BND . . . . http://www.aqute.biz/Code/Bnd
Peter Kriens, one of the founders of OSGi, has created a tool called BND that
offers several facilities for working with bundles, including wrapping nonbundle
JARs with OSGi metadata. BND is the basis for the Felix Maven Bundle Plugin.

Compass . . . . http://www.compass-project.org
Compass is a framework for enabling keyword search on Java objects.

Eclipse Equinox . . . . http://www.eclipse.org/equinox/
Equinox is one of the leading open source OSGi framework implementations
and is the basis for the Eclipse IDE.

Maven: The Definitive Guide . . .
        . . . http://www.sonatype.com/products/maven/documentation/book-defguide
Sonatype has made its Maven book available as a free download. This is an
excellent "getting started" guide as well as a handy reference for working with
Maven.

jQuery . . . . http://www.jquery.com
jQuery is a JavaScript library that enables simple manipulation of a web page's
DOM.

OPS4J http://www.ops4j.org
The Open Participation Software for Java (OPS4J) project is a community-
oriented open source project that has developed several very useful libraries,
bundles, tools, and utilities for OSGi development.

OSGi Alliance...http://www.osgi.org
The OSGi Alliance is an open standards organization made up of significant technology players; it defines the OSGi specification.

Pax Construct .... http://wiki.ops4j.org/display/ops4j/Pax+Construct
Pax Construct is a command-line toolkit based on Maven for developing OSGi bundle-based projects.

Pax Exam .... http://wiki.ops4j.org/display/ops4j/Pax+Exam
Pax Exam is an extension to JUnit 4 for testing OSGi bundles within one or more OSGi frameworks.

Pax Runner....................... http://wiki.ops4j.org/display/ops4j/Pax+Runner
Pax Runner is a tool for launching an OSGi framework, installing a selection of bundles, and starting those bundles.

Spring Dynamic Modules (Spring-DM)...
...http://www.springframework.org/osgi
Spring Dynamic Modules offers a declarative service model for OSGi that is based on the Spring Framework.

SpringSource Enterprise Bundle Repository...
...http://www.springsource.com/repository
SpringSource, the company behind Spring and Spring Dynamic Modules, provides a repository of commonly used open source libraries in OSGi bundle form.

Appendix E

Bibliography

[Com08]   Sonatype Company. *Maven: The Definitive Guide.* O'Reilly & Associates, Inc, Sebastopol, CA, 2008.

[GP70]   Richard Gauthier and Stephen Pont. *Designing Systems Programs.* Prentice Hall, Englewood Cliffs, NJ, 1970.

[Wal07]   Craig Walls. *Spring in Action, 2nd Edition.* Manning Publications Co., Greenwich, CT, 2007.

Index

The Pragmatic Bookshelf

Available in paperback and DRM-free PDF, our titles are here to help you stay on top of your game. The following are in print as of May 2009; be sure to check our website at pragprog.com for newer titles.

Title	Year	ISBN	Pages
Advanced Rails Recipes: 84 New Ways to Build Stunning Rails Apps	2008	9780978739225	464
Agile Retrospectives: Making Good Teams Great	2006	9780977616640	200
Agile Web Development with Rails, Third Edition	2009	9781934356166	784
Augmented Reality: A Practical Guide	2008	9781934356036	328
Behind Closed Doors: Secrets of Great Management	2005	9780976694021	192
Best of Ruby Quiz	2006	9780976694076	304
Core Animation for Mac OS X and the iPhone: Creating Compelling Dynamic User Interfaces	2008	9781934356104	200
Data Crunching: Solve Everyday Problems using Java, Python, and More	2005	9780974514079	208
Deploying Rails Applications: A Step-by-Step Guide	2008	9780978739201	280
Design Accessible Web Sites: 36 Keys to Creating Content for All Audiences and Platforms	2007	9781934356029	336
Desktop GIS: Mapping the Planet with Open Source Tools	2008	9781934356067	368
Developing Facebook Platform Applications with Rails	2008	9781934356128	200
Enterprise Integration with Ruby	2006	9780976694069	360
Enterprise Recipes with Ruby and Rails	2008	9781934356234	416
Everyday Scripting with Ruby: for Teams, Testers, and You	2007	9780977616619	320
FXRuby: Create Lean and Mean GUIs with Ruby	2008	9781934356074	240
From Java To Ruby: Things Every Manager Should Know	2006	9780976694090	160
GIS for Web Developers: Adding Where to Your Web Applications	2007	9780974514093	275
Google Maps API, V2: Adding Where to Your Applications	2006	PDF-Only	83
Groovy Recipes: Greasing the Wheels of Java	2008	9780978739294	264
Hello, Android: Introducing Google's Mobile Development Platform	2008	9781934356173	200
Interface Oriented Design	2006	9780976694052	240
Learn to Program, 2nd Edition	2009	9781934356364	230

Continued on next page

Title	Year	ISBN	Pages
Manage It! Your Guide to Modern Pragmatic Project Management	2007	9780978739249	360
Mastering Dojo: JavaScript and Ajax Tools for Great Web Experiences	2008	9781934356111	568
No Fluff Just Stuff 2006 Anthology	2006	9780977616664	240
No Fluff Just Stuff 2007 Anthology	2007	9780978739287	320
Practical Programming: An Introduction to Computer Science Using Python	2009	9781934356272	350
Practices of an Agile Developer	2006	9780974514086	208
Pragmatic Project Automation: How to Build, Deploy, and Monitor Java Applications	2004	9780974514031	176
Pragmatic Thinking and Learning: Refactor Your Wetware	2008	9781934356050	288
Pragmatic Unit Testing in C# with NUnit	2007	9780977616671	176
Pragmatic Unit Testing in Java with JUnit	2003	9780974514017	160
Pragmatic Version Control Using Git	2008	9781934356159	200
Pragmatic Version Control using CVS	2003	9780974514000	176
Pragmatic Version Control using Subversion	2006	9780977616657	248
Programming Erlang: Software for a Concurrent World	2007	9781934356005	536
Programming Groovy: Dynamic Productivity for the Java Developer	2008	9781934356098	320
Programming Ruby: The Pragmatic Programmers' Guide, Second Edition	2004	9780974514055	864
Programming Ruby 1.9: The Pragmatic Programmers' Guide	2009	9781934356081	960
Prototype and script.aculo.us: You Never Knew JavaScript Could Do This!	2007	9781934356012	448
Rails Recipes	2006	9780977616602	350
Rails for .NET Developers	2008	9781934356203	300
Rails for Java Developers	2007	9780977616695	336
Rails for PHP Developers	2008	9781934356043	432
Rapid GUI Development with QtRuby	2005	PDF-Only	83
Release It! Design and Deploy Production-Ready Software	2007	9780978739218	368
Scripted GUI Testing with Ruby	2008	9781934356180	192
Ship it! A Practical Guide to Successful Software Projects	2005	9780974514048	224
Stripes ...and Java Web Development Is Fun Again	2008	9781934356210	375
TextMate: Power Editing for the Mac	2007	9780978739232	208
The Definitive ANTLR Reference: Building Domain-Specific Languages	2007	9780978739256	384

Continued on next page

Title	Year	ISBN	Pages
The Passionate Programmer: Creating a Remarkable Career in Software Development	2009	9781934356340	200
ThoughtWorks Anthology	2008	9781934356142	240
Ubuntu Kung Fu: Tips, Tricks, Hints, and Hacks	2008	9781934356227	400

More on Java

Stripes

Tired of complicated Java web frameworks that just get in your way? Stripes is a lightweight, practical framework that lets you write lean and mean code without a bunch of XML configuration files. Stripes is designed to do a lot of the common work for you, while being flexible enough to adapt to your requirements. This book will show you how to use Stripes to its full potential, so that you can easily develop professional, full-featured web applications. As a bonus, you'll also get expert advice from the creator of Stripes, Tim Fennell.

Stripes: ...And Java Web Development Is Fun Again

Frederic Daoud

(375 pages) ISBN: 978-1934356-21-0. $36.95

http://pragprog.com/titles/fdstr

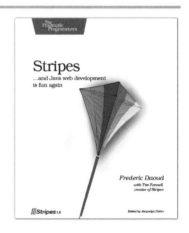

Release It!

Whether it's in Java, .NET, or Ruby on Rails, getting your application ready to ship is only half the battle. Did you design your system to survive a sudden rush of visitors from Digg or Slashdot? Or an influx of real-world customers from 100 different countries? Are you ready for a world filled with flaky networks, tangled databases, and impatient users?

If you're a developer and don't want to be on call at 3 a.m. for the rest of your life, this book will help.

Release It! Design and Deploy Production-Ready Software

Michael T. Nygard

(368 pages) ISBN: 0-9787392-1-3. $34.95

http://pragprog.com/titles/mnee

Expand Your Horizons

The Passionate Programmer

This book is about creating a remarkable career in software development. Remarkable careers don't come by chance. They require thought, intention, action, and a willingness to change course when you've made mistakes. Most of us have been stumbling around letting our careers take us where they may. It's time to take control.

This revised and updated second edition lays out a strategy for planning and creating a radically successful life in software development *(the first edition was released as My Job Went to India: 52 Ways To Save Your Job).*

The Passionate Programmer: Creating a Remarkable Career in Software Development
Chad Fowler
(200 pages) ISBN: 978-1934356-34-0. $23.95
http://pragprog.com/titles/cfcar2

Pragmatic Thinking and Learning

Software development happens in your head. Not in an editor, IDE, or design tool. In this book by Pragmatic Programmer Andy Hunt, you'll learn how our brains are wired, and how to take advantage of your brain's architecture. You'll master new tricks and tips to learn more, faster, and retain more of what you learn.

• Use the Dreyfus Model of Skill Acquisition to become more expert   • Leverage the architecture of the brain to strengthen different thinking modes
• Avoid common "known bugs" in your mind
• Learn more deliberately and more effectively
• Manage knowledge more efficiently

Pragmatic Thinking and Learning:
Refactor your Wetware
Andy Hunt
(288 pages) ISBN: 978-1-9343560-5-0. $34.95
http://pragprog.com/titles/ahptl

The Pragmatic Bookshelf

The Pragmatic Bookshelf features books written by developers for developers. The titles continue the well-known Pragmatic Programmer style and continue to garner awards and rave reviews. As development gets more and more difficult, the Pragmatic Programmers will be there with more titles and products to help you stay on top of your game.

Visit Us Online

Modular Java's Home Page
http://pragprog.com/titles/cwosg
Source code from this book, errata, and other resources. Come give us feedback, too!

Register for Updates
http://pragprog.com/updates
Be notified when updates and new books become available.

Join the Community
http://pragprog.com/community
Read our weblogs, join our online discussions, participate in our mailing list, interact with our wiki, and benefit from the experience of other Pragmatic Programmers.

New and Noteworthy
http://pragprog.com/news
Check out the latest pragmatic developments, new titles and other offerings.

Save on the eBook

Save on the eBook versions of this title. Owning the paper version of this book entitles you to purchase the electronic versions at a terrific discount.

PDFs are great for carrying around on your laptop—they are hyperlinked, have color, and are fully searchable. Most titles are also available for the iPhone and iPod touch, Amazon Kindle, and other popular e-book readers.

Buy now at pragprog.com/coupon.

Contact Us

Online Orders:	www.pragprog.com/catalog
Customer Service:	support@pragprog.com
Non-English Versions:	translations@pragprog.com
Pragmatic Teaching:	academic@pragprog.com
Author Proposals:	proposals@pragprog.com
Contact us:	1-800-699-PROG (+1 919 847 3884)